P9-AEY-447

The Days of
Duchess Anne

The Days of
Duchess Anne

Life in the Household of the
Duchess of Hamilton
1656–1716

ROSALIND K. MARSHALL

TUCKWELL PRESS

First published in Great Britain in 1973 by Collins

This new edition first published in Great Britain in 2000 by
Tuckwell Press, The Mill House
Phantassie, East Linton
East Lothian EH40 3DG
Scotland

Copyright © Rosalind K. Marshall, 1973, 2000

ISBN 1 86232 111 6

British Library Cataloguing in Publication Data
A catalogue record for this book is available
on request from the British Library

The right of Rosalind K. Marshall to be identified
as the author of this work has been asserted by her in accordance
with the Copyright, Design and Patent Act 1988

Typeset by Antony Gray
Printed and bound by
Creative Print and Design, Ebbw Vale, Wales

In memory of my parents,
Nan and Frederick Marshall

Contents

List of Illustrations   8
List of Tables   9
Acknowledgements   11

    Introduction
1   The Duchess Anne   13

PART 1: LIFE RESTORED
2   Hamilton Palace   37
3   The Servants   62
4   Clothing and Food   83
5   Entertainment, Travel, Recreation and Celebrations   104

PART 2: THE GRAND DESIGN
6   The Education of the Children   129
7   The English Influence   149
8   The Marriage of the Heir   168
9   The Great Design   189
10 The Fatal Flaw   209

Appendix: Hamilton Palace and Kinneil Castle Inventories   233
Glossary   267
Notes on Sources   269
Notes   271
Index   279

Illustrations

Colour Plates

1 Anne, 3rd Duchess of Hamilton
2 Lady Mary Feilding
3 James, 1st Duke of Hamilton
4 William, 3rd Duke of Hamilton
5 Lady Anna Cunningham
6 Margaret, Countess of Panmure
7 James, Earl of Arran and
     4th Duke of Hamilton
8 Lady Anne Spencer
9 Charles, Earl of Selkirk
10 'Queen Mary's Bed'

Plates in black and white

1 'One of My Lord's Six Children',
     possibly Duchess Anne as a child
2 'One of My Lord's Six Children',
     possibly Lady Susanna as a child
3 William, 2nd Duke of Hamilton and
     John, 1st Duke of Lauderdale
4 Hamilton Palace, drawn by Isaac Miller

5 'The Colledge of Glasgow' by Slezer

6 The south front of Hamilton Palace

7 The old north front of Hamilton Palace

8 James, 4th Duke of Hamilton

9 Lady Elizabeth Gerard

10 John, Earl of Ruglen

11 George, Earl of Orkney

12 Lord Basil Hamilton

13 Lord Archibald Hamilton

14 Monument to the 3rd Duke of Hamilton

15 Silver Communion Cups presented
by Duchess Anne to Dalserf Church

16 Duchess Anne's gold chatelaine hook

List of Tables

1   The Dukes of Hamilton   facing page 16
2   The Relatives of the Duke of Hamilton   facing page 80
3   The Family of Duchess Anne   between pages 136 and 137

Acknowledgements

More years ago now than I care to remember, Douglas, 14th Duke of Hamilton, Professor Gordon Donaldson of the Scottish History Department at Edinburgh University and Sir James Fergusson of Kilkerran, at that time Keeper of the Records of Scotland, devised an innovative arrangement whereby a research student would catalogue a section of the Duke's splendid archives and at the same time write a thesis based on the documents. I was that student, and the resulting thesis became *The Days of Duchess Anne*, commissioned by Philip Ziegler for Collins.

Time passed, I wrote other books and *Duchess Anne* went out of print, but it remained a favourite of mine and so I was delighted when John and Val Tuckwell of Tuckwell Press suggested producing a new edition. This gives me the welcome opportunity of including some additional material. 'Unfortunately, no inventory of the furnishings of the Palace in the seventeenth century has come to light', I wrote regretfully in the original edition, only to discover some years later an entire set of inventories of furnishings for both the Palace and Kinneil Castle. Transcripts of several of these form an appendix to this book, and I have rewritten the relevant part of Chapter 2.

The three gentlemen who originally arranged for the cataloguing of the Hamilton Archives are dead now, but I will always be grateful to them for giving me the opportunity of working on such a rich and rewarding collection. Letters, accounts, charters, memoranda and lists – all were carefully preserved by Duchess Anne, her husband, David Crawford their secretary and by successive generations of Hamiltons. I frequently found myself opening up bundles of papers which had been undisturbed since the day three hundred years before when the 3rd Duke labelled them, tied them up with a leather thong and put them carefully away. The correspondence and some of the other items are now in the National Archives of Scotland, but most of the financial and legal material remains at Lennoxlove.

I would like to thank the present Duke of Hamilton for allowing me to use portraits at Lennoxlove as illustrations and for permitting the inclusion of the transcripts. I am likewise grateful to the owners of the other illustrations, as well as to HarperCollins for allowing the production of this new edition of *The Days of Duchess Anne*.

R. K. M.
Edinburgh, 1 January 2000

CHAPTER 1

The Duchess Anne

On 16 January 1632 the young Marchioness of Hamilton gave birth to a second daughter, and for a second time family and friends received the news with ill-concealed disappointment. As she lay in her bedchamber in the palace of Whitehall, the Marchioness knew as well as anyone that she had been expected to present her husband with an heir. She was, after all, married to the representative of an ancient and powerful noble family. Although she herself had never visited Scotland, she was well aware that her husband's estates there stretched across the country from his island of Arran in the west to his castle of Kinneil in the east, and from his palace of Hamilton near Glasgow right down the fertile valley of the River Clyde. His family had owned many of these lands since the beginning of the fourteenth century, and great was the power and influence they wielded. Not only did they exercise this power by virtue of territorial possession. An early Lord Hamilton had married the sister of the Scottish king, and ever since then they had been very close to the throne indeed. The Hamilton of his day had been governor of the realm when Mary Queen of Scots was a child, and the Marchioness's father-in-law had been the leading Scottish favourite of James VI and I.

Brought up at the English Court and herself the niece of the great Duke of Buckingham, the Marchioness was fully conscious of the dynastic pressures of seventeenth-century society. Her husband's ancient line must continue, and the House of Hamilton must be provided with an heir. However, she could console herself with the reflection that she was only nineteen, there would no doubt be other children, and the year old

Henrietta Maria and the new baby were both pretty and endearing.

The Marquis was not present to encourage her with these cheering thoughts. Several months before, he had set off for the Continent at the head of a force which was to fight in the armies of Gustavus Adolphus. In his absence, Charles I himself took in hand all the arrangements for the baby's christening. The Marquis was his close companion and his principal adviser on Scottish affairs, the Marchioness was a Lady of the Queen's Bedchamber, and the King accordingly showed a close and protective interest in the family. When the new baby was baptised Anne, after the Marquis's mother, Charles acted as godfather.[1]

Lady Anne Hamilton was to spend her childhood on the periphery of the elegant and civilised Court of Charles I. Her father arrived back from Germany that summer, and the Marchioness decided that the lodgings at Whitehall were not really suitable for a young family. Providing alternative accommodation was something of a problem, for the Marquis owned no property in England, but the Marchioness found a solution. Her aunt, the widowed Duchess of Buckingham, owned Wallingford House. This mansion, which stood on the site now occupied by Admiralty House, had been built a generation before and had been bought by Buckingham, who lived there until he moved to the more splendid York House. Since then, Wallingford had been unoccupied, so now the Marchioness was able to rent it from her aunt. It was spacious enough to accommodate a large establishment, and it could not have been more conveniently placed, for it overlooked the Spring Gardens at Whitehall.[2]

Shortly after her own birth, Lady Anne's elder sister died, but she was not destined to be alone in the nurseries for long. A year later a third daughter, Lady Susanna, joined her, and then at last the much desired heir came along. Charles, Earl of Arran, was born in November 1634, and two other little boys followed in quick succession, James in 1635 and William in 1636.[3]

Life at Wallingford House now assumed a settled pattern, as the Marchioness created there a tranquil and stable world for her children. By temperament she was quiet and introspective.

Her portraits show her to have been something of a beauty,* and Van Dyck's painting of her in particular bears out the comment that she was tall and graceful like the rest of the Villiers family, but she never indulged in any of the idle flirtations of the Court. Her contemporaries praised her for being dignified and devout, and there is no doubt that she had a profound influence on her children in their earliest years.

They did not, in fact, see much of their father at this time, for he was constantly required to be in attendance on the King, but otherwise there was a good deal of coming and going with the Court. The Marchioness's parents were frequent visitors, and so was the Marquis's younger brother William, who had by now come to London. Ten years the Marquis's junior, he was very much the fashionable young man about town, and he was always a diverting visitor. Brief glimpses of the children themselves in these early days are afforded by a few surviving household accounts, which record the Marchioness's purchases of red baize coats, holland frocks and small petticoats for her children. They also sat for their portraits and the paintings of Lady Anne and Lady Susanna preserve to this day the likenesses of the two little girls in their dark dresses and demure caps.†

The early years were peaceful and uneventful, but they were to be all too brief. The Marchioness did not make a good recovery from the birth of her youngest son. Too many children in a short space of time had undermined her constitution, and when she developed a liver infection she had little resistance against the disease. Throughout the autumn and winter of 1637 her doctors tried to build her up with strengthening potions, but her bouts of fever became more frequent and more intense. The emulsions,

* The Marchioness was painted by Mytens about 1629 and later by Van Dyck. Both portraits are in the Collection of the Duke of Hamilton. The Mytens portrait is reproduced in François Boucher, *A History of Costume in the West* (1967), 287 – for the Van Dyck painting, see Plate 2; *c.f.* the comment on her in Gilbert Burnet, *The Memoirs of the Lives and Actions of James and William, Dukes of Hamilton* (1677), 406

† These portraits, together with another of a baby, are by an unknown Anglo-Netherlandish artist and seem to be the surviving three of a set of six described in seventeenth-century Hamilton inventories as being 'My Lord's Six Children'. They are thought to be the children of the 1st Duke, and as Duchess Anne and Lady Susanna were his only daughters to survive infancy, they are probably the little girls here represented. Although there is nothing to indicate which is which, the author suggests that the child with the pearl necklace is Duchess Anne. All three are in the Collection of the Duke of Hamilton.

the cordial boluses, the syrup of violets and the conserves of red roses had little effect and by the spring of 1638 she had resigned herself to the fact that she would not recover. She gave orders that her children were not to be brought up to her bedchamber any more, 'lest the sight of them might have kindled too much tenderness in her',[4] and on 10 May she died. She was just twenty-five.[5] 'There never lived a better nor a more religious creature', her husband wrote when he broke the news to his own mother, adding that she 'left me behind her with a sad and grieved soul.' His wife was buried at Westminster Abbey on 10 May in the vault of the Countess of Buckingham, and a few days later the Marquis took his children away with him to Hampton Court.[6]

Wallingford House had been leased to the Marchioness as a personal favour, and now her aunt wished to give it to her own daughter. Apart from that, it held too many sorrowful memories of the Marchioness's long illness. Eleven days after her death the Marquis arranged to buy the manor house of Chelsea, and on 23 June 1638 the King gave him a grant of Chelsea Place and the Manor of Chelsea.[7]

At that time, Chelsea was still a separate village outside London, and as well as being extremely fashionable, it would be a healthier place for the children, who were all reported as being 'both weak and sickly'.[8] It was not possible to move them there at once, though, for apparently there was a lack of suitable accommodation. There were two manor houses in Chelsea. The original, known as Beaufort House, had been the home of Sir Thomas More and had passed into the possession of Henry VIII, who then erected the second house there for his children. The existing houses must have been unavailable or unsuitable, for the Marquis decided to build an entirely new house for himself adjoining the New Manor.[9]

Work on the new house began almost at once, and an undated account of about that time records the purchase of 110,000 bricks, 16,000 tiles, several hundred loads of sand and quantities of brooms, ladders and nails for scaffolding. The Henry VIII manor house had been built round a courtyard, and the Marquis's adjoining building was actually a complete house, also built

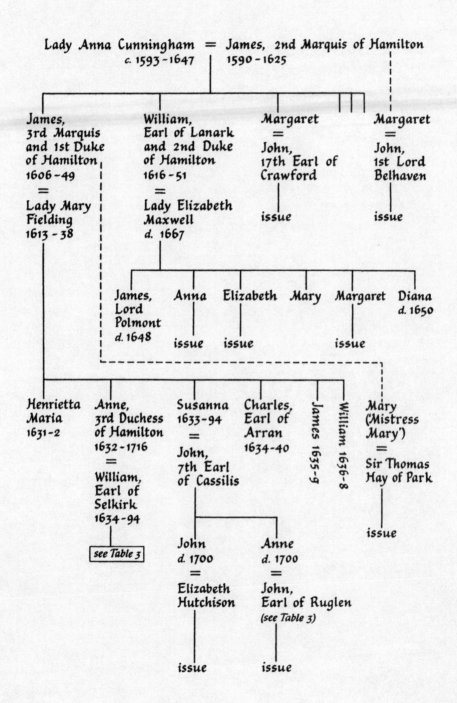

Lady Anna Cunningham = James, 2nd Marquis of Hamilton
c. 1593–1647   1590–1625

James,
3rd Marquis
and 1st Duke
of Hamilton
1606–49
=
Lady Mary
Fielding
1613–38

William,
Earl of Lanark
and 2nd Duke
of Hamilton
1616–51
=
Lady Elizabeth
Maxwell
d. 1667

Margaret
=
John,
17th Earl of
Crawford

issue

Margaret
=
John,
1st Lord
Belhaven

issue

James,
Lord
Polmont
d. 1648

Anna

issue

Elizabeth

issue

Mary

Margaret

issue

Diana
d. 1650

Henrietta
Maria
1631–2

Anne,
3rd Duchess
of Hamilton
1632–1716
=
William,
Earl of
Selkirk
1634–94

see Table 3

Susanna
1633–94
=
John,
7th Earl
of Cassilis

Charles,
Earl of
Arran
1634–40

James 1635–9

William 1636–8

Mary
('Mistress
Mary')
=
Sir Thomas
Hay of Park

issue

John
d. 1700
=
Elizabeth
Hutchison

issue

Anne
d. 1700
=
John,
Earl of Ruglen
(see Table 3)

issue

round a quadrangle. The older house had elaborate Tudor chimneys, a crenellated roof and small diamond paned windows. The Marquis's house was externally severe, and although like the Henry VIII house it was two storeys high, it was completely lacking in ornamentation.[10]

The new house was very pleasant. Ten first-floor windows looked out over a terrace to the Thames, and at the back the gardens stretched down to an orchard. The main rooms were on the ground floor, round the Fountain Court, and leading from these to the gardens was a great gallery where the Marquis hung his notable collection of Italian paintings. Upstairs were three large drawing rooms extending the entire length of the south front, and no fewer than seventeen bedchambers overlooked the gardens at the back. Above that were garrets and 'summer rooms', and the accounts also mention a banqueting house, which may well have been a separate structure.

Work on the new house, which was to be known as Chelsea Place, continued throughout 1639, a year which brought fresh tragedy to the Marquis's family. The baby, William, had fallen ill at Hampton Court in the winter of 1638, and had died there. He was buried in Westminster Abbey on 6 December. Less than six months later Lord James was taken ill and he died on 30 April. It was with all the more anxiety that the Marquis made plans to move his sadly diminished family out of London.

Lady Anne was eight when she went to Chelsea Place, old enough to retain memories of the elegant panelled rooms, the great chamber with its enormous chimney piece of Portland stone inlaid with black marble, the blue enamelled clock with its pretty gilt face. It was at this time too, that she and her sister became really acquainted with their father. The Marquis spent a good deal of time now with his children, travelling back and forth to London by water. He had installed Lady Cotterell, an old friend of his wife, as a supervisor of his household in his absence, and his steward Richard Palmer saw to the actual running of the establishment.

But the early, carefree days had gone forever. The Civil War was to disrupt the pattern of life for everyone, and a man in the Marquis's position was more involved than most. Charles I's policies in Scotland had aroused resentment on both economic and constitutional grounds, but most of all his desire for ecclesiastical change had met with fervent opposition from almost every section of the community. His efforts to introduce into the Calvinist Scottish Church a Prayer Book and the wearing of surplices were seen as dangerous innovations redolent of 'popery'. His plan to endow the Church more generously by restoring to it those church lands in lay hands brought him into conflict with the nobility, who were further infuriated by the new influence exercised by the Scottish bishops in temporal affairs. Finally, in 1638, his opponents banded together and signed the National Covenant, pledging themselves to defend the existing Church. Henceforth these opponents were known as the Covenanters, and they comprised noblemen, merchants, lawyers, ministers and country people. A few months later the Glasgow General Assembly brought about a complete breach with the King, and the Covenanters gathered together an army to send against him.

The Covenanters were particularly strong in the west of Scotland, and could count among their number the Marquis of Hamilton's mother and her family as well as many of the tenants on the Hamilton estates. The Marquis himself had been brought up as a Presbyterian, and he must have heard his mother put forward the arguments against the King's ecclesiastical policies. When he was in his early teens, however, he had gone to live with his father in London and ever since had been the King's close companion. Whatever sympathy he may have felt for the religious views of the Covenanters, he certainly could not condone their challenge to royal authority and he was a firm upholder of the King's prerogative.

In view of his family background, however, Charles I felt that he would be an acceptable mediator between himself and the Covenanters, and indeed the Marquis was a moderate man who in other circumstances might have achieved success. In his very moderation, however, lay the cause of his downfall. In vain did he try to mediate between the opposing sides. Instead of bringing about the hoped-for reconciliation, he merely incurred the odium of the Covenanting leaders and the suspicion of the King.

On a personal level too, there was new cause for grief. His

only surviving son, Charles, was now six years old. In appearance he was a miniature version of his father, and as heir to the family inheritance he was doubly precious. Like the other children he had always been delicate, and after his mother's death he had fallen seriously ill. Fears had been expressed for his life, but he had recovered. In April 1640, however, he was taken ill once more and this time the doctors could not save him. He died after a brief illness, and was buried with his mother in Westminster Abbey.[11]

Private grief apart, this was a grave blow for the Marquis. He was now a widower with only two small daughters, and for the first time he was confronted with the prospect of having no male heir to succeed him. His mother constantly urged him to remarry, but there is no hint that he ever seriously considered doing so. Instead, his thoughts turned to his only brother William, Earl of Lanark. At this time the Hamilton estates were not entailed on the male line, which meant that if his daughters survived, the elder would automatically succeed him. Certainly his mother had run his estates most efficiently for years during his absence, but with the political situation as it was, he felt that it was imperative that the family should be represented by a man. His brother had recently married and would presumably have sons. The succession would be secure in him, and the danger of a young, unprotected girl becoming head of the House of Hamilton would be averted. He therefore arranged that, in the event of his death, William should inherit everything – lands, titles, jewels, pictures, personal possessions. His daughters would be provided for in other ways, for he would marry them to Scottish noblemen.

This decision was as much an outcome of his affection for his daughters as of his concern for his inheritance. He had come to enjoy a particularly close relationship with the two girls, and his letters to them are full of tender affection. For their part, it never occurred to them to resent the plans he had made for their future, and of course they were still very young: the complicated legal arrangements for the estates had little meaning for them at that time.

Much more momentous was the decision made by the Marquis in the spring of 1642. His position at Court was becoming increasingly dangerous, and a serious illness that year brought forcible reminders of his own mortality. He therefore came to the conclusion that he could not leave his two daughters in the comparative isolation of Chelsea any longer. Lady Susanna would be sent to stay with her grandmother at Denbigh House, and when he went home to Scotland as usual in the summer he would take Lady Anne with him. Henceforth she would live with his own mother at Hamilton.

Hitherto Lady Anne had known only life in the south, in the shelter of her family circle. Now she was to be separated from her sister, and she was to live more than four hundred miles away from all she knew, in a strange country with a grandmother she had never met. The Duchess used to tell her family afterwards that she had originally been as unwilling as anyone to come to Scotland, and it must have been with no little trepidation that she took leave of Chelsea.

For the occasion, she was given a fine new silken gown made from some material left by her mother in her wardrobe at the time of her death, and she was allowed to take with her three of her English ladies, Marie Arthur, Sara Watkins and Rebecca Kimbold. The journey north took roughly a fortnight by coach, and presumably they travelled by the accustomed route through Huntingdon, Doncaster and Alnwick to Edinburgh. From there they crossed the Lowlands of Scotland to Lanarkshire and the fertile green valley of the Clyde with its gentle wooded slopes, its orchards and its fields criss-crossed with strips of wheat and barley. Beyond Dalserf the valley widens, the river meanders through flat meadows and there, a little to the west of the Clyde, stood Hamilton Palace, a rambling stone building set in gardens and parkland. Just to the left of it, surprisingly near, clustered the houses of the burgh of Hamilton, while over the north wall were the old buildings of the Nethertoun, the original part of the town.

At this point, however, Lady Anne was less concerned with the buildings themselves than with the approaching meeting with her grandmother, whose formidable reputation could not fail to be known to her. Lady Anna Cunningham had been a plain child when she married the Marquis's sophisticated father, and she had grown up into a plain woman who bore his children and, when he went to live permanently in London a few years later, ran his estates for him, managing all his Scottish business. She had continued to do so ever since, for when he died she stayed on in the Palace to look after it on behalf of her son. A daughter of the Earl of Glencairn, she shared that family's Covenanting sympathies, and with the religious troubles of the late 1630s she raised a troop of horse in support of the Covenanters and rode at its head with a pistol and a dagger at her belt.

Servants' gossip may have painted an intimidating picture of Lady Anna Cunningham, but she was not the stern, masculine character whom some historians have represented her as being. She was fond of music, and she had a weakness for diamond necklaces. She had learned to write fairly late in life, but thereafter she took a pride in keeping her own accounts, writing out each item of her expenditure in a careful, italic hand and in her highly idiosyncratic spelling. She had boundless energy, and she was continually on the move, riding round the estates, visiting her daughter in Fife, calling on friends in Ayrshire, and in fact of all her relatives it was this vigorous lady whom Lady Anne Hamilton most closely resembled, both mentally and physically.

They took to one another at once. A suite of rooms had been specially prepared for Lady Anne and her servants, new gowns were ordered for her, and a footman was hastily dispatched to Edinburgh to collect 'Lady Anna Hamilton's parrot.' By the time her father left the Palace she was settling down fast. At first the Marquis was able to pay her frequent visits, but in the spring of 1643 he was summoned to England, and the King bestowed upon him the title of Duke of Hamilton and Marquis of Clydesdale. Lady Anne's pride in these new honours was soon to be overshadowed. Her father's enemies had redoubled their efforts to discredit him, and at the beginning of the New Year came the appalling news that the King had imprisoned him in Pendennis Castle. Argyll and some of the other Covenanting leaders had persuaded the King that he was disloyal, claiming that he had been working to foment trouble between Charles and his Scottish subjects. It was an old charge and it was unjustified, but this time Charles had listened and he had been convinced.

There was nothing Lady Anne could do but stay on at Hamilton, following as best she could the progress of events in the south and trying to make the time until his release pass more quickly by filling her days with activity. There is no hint as to what education she had received in Chelsea, but now the accounts mention 'William Davidson, who teaches Lady Anna Hamilton.' What he taught her is not revealed: it may well have been writing, or she may have read theological works with him. Most ladies learned arithmetic so that they could deal with their household accounts, and Lady Anne certainly studied French at some stage. Many years later, William of Orange asked one of her grandsons if she knew the language. The young man replied that she did not, but when she came to hear of the conversation she remarked to his mother, 'You may tell him I was not angry that he told the King I had no French, which is true I have very little, but that I had once.'[12]

Lessons occupied only part of her time. It was now that she gained an intimate knowledge of the surrounding countryside and of the running of the Hamilton estates. She and her grandmother rode out together visiting tenants, inspecting livestock and supervising work in the parks. She watched the Marchioness interview the constant stream of callers at the Palace – tenants bringing in their rents, local farmers complaining that their neighbours were encroaching on their land, poor people seeking financial assistance – and she saw how her grandmother kept her accounts and supervised the work of her chamberlains. So large were the estates that there were separate chamberlains for Arran, Hamilton, Cambuslang, Machanshire, Avendale and Kinneil, each responsible for the collection of rents in his area and the estate expenditure. Managing the Hamilton estates was like running a complex business concern, and there was much to be learned.

There was time, too, for visiting Edinburgh and for getting to know Scottish relatives, especially her aunts. Lady Margaret, her father's sister, had married the Earl of Crawford and lived in the east of Scotland with her large family. Anna, one of her daughters, was only a year older than Lady Anne and became a close friend. Then there was Lady Belhaven, her father's illegitimate sister. She was accepted naturally into the family circle, and she was to be a much loved confidante of Lady Anne for many years.

For months the news from Pendennis was distressing. The Duke was kept in very close confinement, and he suffered a good deal of ill health: like many of his contemporaries he was troubled with the stone. The King refused to agree to a trial, and it was only when Pendennis Castle was captured by the parliamentary army that the Duke was released. He went at once to London, where he collected his younger daughter, and then he hastened north with her to Scotland. The happy reunion which ensued may easily be imagined.

The Duke spent the next year in Scotland, and it was as well that he returned when he did, for while she was visiting Edinburgh in the autumn of 1647 his mother was taken seriously ill. Her granddaughters begged to be allowed to go and see her, but their father advised against it. Such a journey, he told them, 'may but endanger your own healths and contribute nothing to that of our mother's. Likewise your sorrows would be increased, to be an eye-witness of her weak condition, therefore my dear children, be contented and let not grief possess your tender hearts too much.' Shortly afterwards the Marchioness died, bequeathing to Lady Anne 'the picture of her father and mother set in gold and a turquoise ring with some of her mother's hair', together with three thousand merks* 'to buy a jewel to her.' Her legacy to her granddaughter consisted in much more than jewels, however, for during the five years she had spent with the Marchioness, Lady Anne had developed the set of principles and aspirations by which she was to live for the rest of her life.

The following spring the girls said good-bye to their father for the last time. Reconciled with Charles I, he now led the fateful expedition designed to rescue the King. By this time the Covenanters had won from the King all those concessions for which they had struggled, but they had then become deeply divided within their own ranks. The more moderate among them disliked the Presbyterian extremism of their leaders and many of the nobility decided to return to their allegiance to the King. The Covenanting movement thereupon became much less broadly based, and its leaders eventually drew Scotland into the English Civil War by allying with the parliamentarians. Meanwhile the

* A merk was worth 13/4, a pound Scots being worth a twelfth of a pound sterling.

imprisonment of the King resulted in even more support for the moderate Scottish royalists and, much against his will, the Duke of Hamilton decided that he must once again play a leading role in public affairs.

On his release from Pendennis he had visited Charles and had been reconciled with him. He had hoped to spend the rest of his life in retirement, but he and his brother now evolved a plan to lead an expedition into England so that they could rescue the King. The Duke therefore took leave of his daughters and marched south at the head of a Scottish army. On 18 August 1648 he was defeated at Preston and a week later he surrendered to the Cromwellians at Uttoxeter. He was imprisoned in Windsor Castle, and it was during his stay there that he had his final sight of the King, who passed that way as he was taken to London for his execution. Shortly afterwards the Duke made an attempt to escape, but he was recaptured in Southwark and taken to St James's. His friends in Scotland were making desperate attempts to save him, and it is recorded that Lady Anne did everything in her power to persuade the Marquis of Argyll to mediate with Cromwell.[13] Argyll would do nothing, and the Duke steadfastly refused to give Cromwell the names of his English allies in exchange for his life. After a brief trial, he was executed at Whitehall on 9 March 1649.

As he was taken to his execution, he called for a pen and paper and wrote a last letter to his daughters. 'My most dear children', he began, 'It has pleased God so to dispose of me as I am immediately to part with this miserable life for a better, so as I cannot take that care of you as I both ought and would, if it had pleased my glorious Creator to have given me longer days, but His will be done.' He advised them to seek the consolation of God, and then urged them 'to follow the advice of my friends about the disposing of yourselves in marriage, and that you think not of ever coming into this kingdom where your father has ended his days in such a manner.'

When he had set out for England, he had left the girls in the care of their aunt, the Countess of Crawford, and it was at her castle in Fife that they heard the news of his death. His body was taken from the scaffold to the house of Sir John Hamilton, and from there an English skipper shipped it home to Scotland. He was buried in the parish church at Hamilton on 1 May 1649.

In accordance with his wishes, his brother now became Duke of Hamilton. He had managed to escape to Holland after Preston, and with the assumption of his new titles he underwent a complete alteration in character. Gone was the frivolous young man. His brother was dead, the King was dead, and his only son had died in childhood. He himself no longer had any desire to live. He had five little daughters of his own, but all his thoughts now turned to Lady Anne, and he frequently expressed the wish 'to employ that life is left me' in her service. He urged her to return to Hamilton Palace, for 'there is no place so fit for you to be in as that wherein you have so great interest, and probably must be preserved in your person. Take it then, dear niece, into your protection', he told her, 'join cheerfully your advice and countenance with those entrusted with managing that fortune, who will take their orders from you, and command everything as absolutely relating thereunto as I could do myself were I present there.'

He was determined that he would die for the Royalist cause, and on 21 March 1650 he made his Will at the Hague. 'Considering the extraordinary kindness my late dearest brother James, Duke of Hamilton did express to me both in his life and at his death by preferring me even to his own children', he declared, 'I conceive myself in duty and gratitude bound to prefer his to mine, and therefore I do leave and nominate my dearest niece Lady Anna Hamilton, his eldest lawful daughter, my sole executor... and freely give unto her all my jewels, silver, plate, hangings, pictures, beds and whatsoever goods else are mine.'

He returned to Scotland with Charles II. Cromwell had by then marched north and had taken possession of the southern part of the country. Charles II was crowned at Scone on the first day of 1651, and that summer he marched south with a Scottish army. The Duke of Hamilton was with him, and when they met the enemy on the disastrous field of Worcester the young King was unable to restrain the Duke from fighting in the thick of the battle until he was seriously wounded. He was carried into the town of Worcester, where it was discovered that a musket ball had shattered his leg. He lingered for almost a fortnight but on 12 September 1651 he passed peacefully away. By his death Lady Anne Hamilton became Anne, Duchess of Hamilton and Châtelherault, Marchioness of Clydesdale, Countess of Arran, Lanark and Cambridge, Lady Aven, Polmont, Machanshire and Innerdale. She was only nineteen.

Nominally Scotland's greatest heiress, Duchess Anne's actual position was very different. She was on the verge of financial ruin. Her father and uncle had contracted enormous debts in both England and Scotland as a result of the Civil War, and her tenants' crops and belongings were 'taken from them and destroyed by the armies and troubles', many of the holdings lying 'waste and untenanted.' Scotland was an occupied country, part of the Commonwealth, and all those who had been active in support of the King were severely punished. The Hamilton estates were confiscated and were handed over to various officers in Cromwell's army. General Monck was given possession of Kinneil, Colonel Alvared took Polmont, Colonel Maleverer was given Lesmahagow, Cambuslang was divided among the children of Colonel Rokeby, Bothwellmuir was given to Colonel Lilburne and Colonel Ingoldsby received the barony of Hamilton and Hamilton Palace. The Duchess and her sister were supposed to receive a small annual income from their estates, but it does not seem to have been paid regularly, if at all.[14]

She herself had gone over to the island of Arran in the summer of 1651. She had in her care her younger sister, the four surviving daughters of her uncle, and probably her half sister. (While he was imprisoned at Pendennis the Duke had become the father of a daughter, and this child, Mistress Mary, was brought up at Hamilton.) Although she suffered an illness 'which extreme grief has occasioned' after her uncle's death, she was determined to return to the mainland as soon as possible, and she was back in Hamilton by the beginning of December.[15] The Palace, of course, was in the hands of Colonel Ingoldsby, and so she moved into a small house in the woods nearby. Various traditional tales have survived, describing how she lived there with only one serving woman for company. In detail these stories are inaccurate, for she always had her sisters and cousins with her, but the house in the woods was no invention: in the summer of 1655 a barn and a byre were put up beside 'the house in the woods', and seven milk cows, a calf and a bull were brought there for the Duchess's use.

She also spent some time at Avendale Castle, a Hamilton stronghold in the high country to the south of the Palace. One day, a troop of Cromwell's men had to pass the Castle on their way to Ayr. As they rode by, they were halted in their tracks by the thundering of cannon. Somewhat nonplussed, the commander asked angrily who had the temerity to fire at the Lord Protector's soldiers. A local man supplied the answer. It was the Duchess Anne. 'She must be a bold woman indeed!' the commander exclaimed, and he rode on without taking retaliatory action.[16]

If these stories are apocryphal, they are nevertheless true to the character of the Duchess. Upheld by her firm Presbyterian faith, she had emerged from the tragic events of her girlhood as a woman of outstanding courage and resourcefulness. 'A given up battle is never won' was one of her favourite sayings, and throughout a long and eventful life she never did give up. She combined a highly intelligent mind with a completely practical outlook, and her family and friends admired her sound good sense as well as her ability to laugh at herself.

She was to need all these qualities in the years which followed. As if her situation were not unhappy enough, the Earl of Abercorn now claimed that her titles and inheritance were rightfully his. The Earl was her father's second cousin, and he argued that the Hamilton estates were entailed on the male line, and should therefore have passed back to him on the death of her uncle. In fact, the original entail had been broken by her uncle, and his settlement of the estates on the Duchess and her heirs had been legally recognised. As the Duchess's representatives said on her behalf, why the Earl should now come forward with this claim she did not know, 'her condition being so low and that family so utterly ruined by private burdens.' The lawsuit which followed dragged on for months, and to the Duchess's dismay, in 1657, Cromwell ordered that Abercorn was to be put in possession of £500 a year and the lands of Arran and Polmont until a final decision was reached. It was fortunate that by this time the

Duchess was no longer alone: the previous year she had married the Earl of Selkirk.

Lord William Douglas, Earl of Selkirk, had been born on 24 December 1634. His father, the Marquis of Douglas, was married twice. By his first wife he had three sons, and by his second wife three more, as well as a large number of daughters. The eldest of the second family was the Earl of Selkirk. On the face of it, a marriage between the Duchess of Hamilton and a younger son of the Marquis of Douglas was most unlikely. True, the Douglas lands lay to the north and to the south of the Hamilton estates, but the Marquis of Douglas was a Roman Catholic in constant trouble with the local presbytery, and his wife was 'a notorious papist'.[17]

Here, then, was the great obstacle to the match. Not only was it surprising that the Duchess, raised by her Covenanting grandmother, should contemplate marriage with a Catholic, but her uncle's entail had expressly forbidden such a union. He had laid down that, should he not be alive to choose a husband for his nieces, the heiress to the estates 'shall be bound to marry and take to husband a nobleman of the name of Hamilton, or otherwise a nobleman of any other name of the reformed Protestant religion and of an untainted loyalty and fidelity to the King . . . and if it shall happen at any time after the marriage of the said nobleman with any of our nieces . . . [he] shall fall from the true Protestant religion and change the same, or fall from his loyalty and fidelity to the King . . . in that case the nobleman so failing shall *eo ipso* omit and lose any right and title he can have to our said estate.'[18]

According to one historian, the Earl had 'gained the affection of the youthful Duchess' and 'to obtain her and her wide domains . . . consented to embrace the Protestant creed.'[19] This version of events is probably nearer the truth than any other, for the Earl was brought up in the Catholic faith, and there still exists a small piece of paper recording his conversion to Protestantism. On this he wrote, the day before his wedding, 'I do hereby declare in the presence of God and as I shall answer at the great day of judgment that I am not a papist, nor does never resolve to be (with the assistance of God), the which I do swear and subscribe with my hand at Edinburgh, the 28 of April 1656, Selkirk.'

Unfortunately no documents exist to reveal when the Duchess and the Earl first met, or who suggested the match. However, one of the witnesses to some of the settlements involved was John, Lord Bargany. Now Lord Bargany was married to the Earl's sister, and he was a first cousin of the Duchess's father, as well as having been his close friend. He was one of those whom the Duke had asked to advise his daughters 'how to dispose themselves in marriage' and it seems very probable that he was the instigator of the match.

Although the marriage did not take place until 1656, plans had already been well advanced three years before. In the earliest extant letter from the Earl to his future wife, he speaks of how his father at that time put difficulties in the way by changing his mind about the territorial settlement. The Earl deplored this delay, and drew up a paper settling an annuity on the Duchess as they had previously agreed. He sent the deed of settlement to her, with a short note declaring that 'if it were more, I would think it all too little for Your Grace, for I confess I cannot express the sense and high esteem I have of Your Grace's deservings.' In spite of this, the difficulties persisted, and many years later the Earl referred to how afraid he had been up till the very last that he would not be allowed to marry the Duchess.

There remains the question of the bride's own attitude, and perhaps the most likely explanation for an unlikely alliance is that the Earl had indeed 'gained her affection'. She herself was the first to admit that she was no beauty. Her portraits* suggest that she had a tall, graceful figure and thick brown hair, but there the legacy from the handsome family of Villiers ceased. Her wideset eyes are full of humour, but her nose and mouth are too large and her chin recedes. The general effect is of liveliness and intelligence, but she was undeniably plain.

Quite the opposite was true of the Earl of Selkirk. His saturnine good looks must have attracted more women than the Duchess

* In adult life the Duchess was painted by David Scougall and by Kneller. The Scougall portrait is in Brodick Castle and is the property of the National Trust for Scotland. The Kneller portrait is in the Collection of the Duke of Hamilton. See frontispiece

(he had an illegitimate daughter, Janet Douglas) and he was well over six feet tall and of a powerful, muscular build. Gilbert Burnet described his character in terms which were scarcely flattering. 'He was rough and sullen, but candid and sincere. His temper was boisterous, neither fit to submit nor to govern. He was mutinous when out of power and imperious in it. He wrote well but spoke ill, for his judgment when calm was better than his imagination. He made himself a great master in the knowledge of the laws, of the history and of the families of Scotland, and seemed always to have a regard to justice and the good of his country. But a narrow and selfish temper brought such an habitual meanness on him, that he was not capable of designing or undertaking great things.'[20] Of course, Burnet was prejudiced. He was a protégé of the Earl's great enemy Lauderdale, and he had quarrelled with Selkirk long before he wrote these remarks.

However much the Earl's quick temper and imperiousness of manner may have annoyed his contemporaries, the Duchess saw in him those qualities which made him the very person she needed to rescue her from her financial difficulties, and so John Nicoll was able to record in his Diary on 29 April 1656, 'The Duchess of Hamilton was married to the Earl of Selkirk . . . at the kirk of Corstorphine.'[21]* Shortly afterwards they returned together to Hamilton.

The most immediate priority was the raising of money to pay the fines demanded by the Cromwellian government, and this they set about doing by selling not only some of the lands left in their hands, but by disposing of personal belongings too – beds, a set of embroidered chairs and a furred mantle. By these expedients they managed to gather together the £7,000 necessary to reclaim the Palace. Even when this had been done, there remained the problem of the Earl of Abercorn and his pretensions. In 1658 he was still demanding to be put in possession of Arran and Polmont until such time as he was awarded the entire Hamilton estates. Luckily the Duchess seems to have found an ally in General Monck, for all that he held her barony of Kinneil. He wrote to Cromwell pointing out that, as the Duchess had paid

* Corstorphine lay just outside Edinburgh. It is now part of the city, and the church exists to this day.

the fines demanded of her, it would not be fitting to give part of her lands to Abercorn, since the Lord Protector's interest in any property technically ceased as soon as the fine was paid.

With this letter the tide began to turn. In the summer of the same year the commissioners for the administration of justice reached the conclusion that because of her uncle's Will and entail, the Duchess had the only valid claim to the dukedom, and Abercorn was finally vanquished in December when Richard Cromwell wrote a letter to the effect that as the Duchess had done all she was told to do to reclaim her estate, she should now be allowed to enjoy it and pay off the creditors as she thought fit. Then only two years later came the Restoration, bringing with it a return to normality and the possibility of planning for the future. At the Duchess's special request, Charles II created her husband Duke of Hamilton, and paid back to her more than £25,000 sterling which his father had owed hers.

Of course, this was only a beginning. There were still enormous debts to be paid, and a whole way of life to be restored, but at least the basis had been laid for the renewal of a settled existence. The Duke and Duchess now made Hamilton Palace their permanent home. Whatever the Duke's motives in marrying, he and his wife enjoyed from the start an affectionate working partnership, and early on he told her that 'when I see the ways of others and thinks on you, I cannot but acknowledge myself most happy in so virtuous a person.' The birth of a large family completed their domestic felicity. On 30 April 1657, exactly a year and a day after their wedding, their first daughter was born. She was named Mary, after both her grandmothers. Even greater was the rejoicing when, a year later, the Duchess gave birth to a son and heir, James, Earl of Arran. After that, the children followed at regular intervals: William, Anna, Katherine, Charles, John, George, Susan, Margaret, another Anna, Basil and Archibald. Mary, the eldest, died when she was nine and both little girls called Anna died in infancy, but seven sons and three daughters were to survive to adult life.[22]

As well as their own numerous children, the Duke and Duchess had various other members of the family in their household. The Duchess's sisters and cousins stayed with them until, one by one, they were found suitable husbands. Lady Margaret Kennedy, a close friend of Lady Susanna, was a permanent resident too. She was a pious Covenanting lady who for some years carried on a curious liaison with the Duke of Lauderdale and was thought to entertain hopes of becoming his second wife. The Duke of Hamilton did not share this partiality for the lady; indeed, he viewed her face across his dinner table with mounting irritation, and in the end his antipathy reached such a pitch that he made an extraordinary offer. He would, he declared, actually pay for Lady Margaret to lodge elsewhere rather than have her stay at the Palace. Here indeed was evidence of the strength of his dislike. His family were impressed, and the Duchess had to admit, 'My Lord and she did not always agree so well together', but they overruled him and Lady Margaret remained until the day when she scandalised them all by announcing that she had secretly married the young and impoverished Gilbert Burnet. She left forthwith.

The Duke also had relatives of his own staying with him. Lord James and Lady Mary Douglas, his younger brother and sister, spent part of their childhood in his care until Lord James eventually joined the army and Lady Mary died a premature death. Finally, his two nephews, the Annandale boys, were orphaned and he took them in.

The Duke and Duchess were therefore at the head of a large family, and for the Duchess in particular, the word 'family' meant more than her own children or even her immediate relatives. Throughout the Hamilton correspondence there recurs a preoccupation with 'the family' which amounts to far more than a fondness for close relations. It was, rather, a sentiment compounded of many elements: mutual affection, certainly, but also an awareness that membership of the family at the same time bestowed high social standing and demanded duty and respect: a consciousness that over the centuries the original ties of blood and the basic alliances for defence had combined into a much more complicated concept of the kinship group.

This was an attitude shared by other members of the Scottish aristocracy. There was no such thing as the clan system in the Lowlands, but the family was a highly important unit. Even quite remote connections were remembered and acknowledged, and the word 'cousin' could refer to a much more distant relation than we today would designate by such a term. The fact that many of the 'cousins' lived in the same area reinforced the natural bonds, which were further strengthened by generations of intermarriage. Then again, patronage was exercised in favour of the cadet branches of the family. Many of the appeals for assistance addressed to successive Dukes of Hamilton, for instance, came from those who shared their name. 'All the Hamiltons' were said to be troubled when the Hamilton Earl of Abercorn found himself in difficulties, even though he was regarded as being an enemy or at least a rival of the ducal line, and the Duke himself once told one of his sons, 'I know I need say little to you to do all you can for a Hamilton.' Throughout the accounts for the period the Dukes of Hamilton can be found giving money in charity 'to a boy [who] called himself Hamilton', 'to a poor man called Hamilton' and the like.

Similarly, many of the servants and retainers of a nobleman bore the same name as he himself did, and so did a large number of the tenants on his lands. As Lord Basil Hamilton was to remark, 'There is some strange thing in blood, I believe most in Scotch of any nation, non[e] knowing that of clanship [i.e. kinship] so much.' By virtue of their position at the centre of a large family group, the Dukes of Hamilton were inescapably involved with the affairs of local landowners, tenants and all the ordinary people who could claim a connection with them, and the protective attitude they had towards their dependants extended to include townspeople, servants and a host of others who had no relation to the family but who lived on their lands or worked in their service.

This situation was to last well into the seventeenth century. Certainly the local and kinship ties did lessen with the approach of union with England and the development within the Scottish Parliament of a party political system but, on the whole, the old loyalties remained an important consideration until at least 1707. In these later years, of course, it was made obvious in a rather altered form. A peer would no longer expect to impress his contemporaries by means of armed force, so he resorted to more subtle methods. This was why splendid clothes, fine coaches and liveried servants were so important, why heralds and pursuivants attended the funerals of the great, why men like Campbell of Glenorchy commissioned elaborate family trees and why the family coat of arms came into use as a decoration for domestic articles. With the new interest in the history of the family, there was a desire to maintain the honour and prestige won by earlier generations, and this explains the seventeenth century's obsession with precedence and the anxiety of the old established peerage families to preserve their status. Because they were living in a society more democratic than that of many other countries of the time, the Scottish peerage continually felt it necessary to stress their superior position and to emphasise that although they were not so very different in their way of life from the lairds and gentry, they had inherited from their forbears a definite superiority of status.

The sense of being the guardian of a noble heritage can be traced in many of the writings of the Hamiltons. The letters of the Duchess's father are singularly uninformative on this aspect of his thinking, but her uncle frequently put into words his well developed sense of family. In his last letter to his wife he exhorted her to 'prefer your duty to the preservation of the House of Hamilton to all things else in this world, and make no difference in the testimony of your kindness to it, whether the Lord shall think fit to continue the memory of that House in your own or my dear brother's issue.'

It was, however, in the next generation that the more exalted notion of the family found its fullest expression. When the Duke told his wife, 'You have been the means of preserving your family by its falling in your person, so you may still be the happy instrument of securing it to your posterity, which next livelihood is all I shall desire', he may have been expressing an attitude of mind alien to us today, but he was putting into words a way of thought which was not only explicit in much of what the Duchess said and wrote, but which was implicit in almost everything she did.

PART 1

Life Restored

CHAPTER 2

Hamilton Palace

When the Duke and Duchess began their married life, Hamilton Palace had not altered greatly since the Duchess had first seen it some ten years before. The Palace and its immediate grounds lay within a long, twisting curve of the River Clyde. From a distance, the buildings were partially concealed by trees and by the houses of the burgh of Hamilton, thatched, stone houses clustering around the outer wall of the grounds. Two turrets surmounted by weathercocks could be discerned above the treetops, and a little to the right was another weathercock on another pointed tower – the spire of the parish church.

Originally the Hamiltons had lived in Cadzow Castle, romantically situated in the High Parks, but by the early sixteenth century they had moved down to the bottom of the valley, to a stone, slated mansion known as The Orchard. In 1591 the Duchess's great-grandfather, John 1st Marquis of Hamilton, decided to build himself a fine new house, and work on Hamilton Palace began. Since his time, many additions had been made, and as the visitor rode along Castle Street to the main gates, the Palace was revealed as a substantial stone building, laid out around a courtyard.

The Palace looked northwards, over extensive gardens, over meadows and parkland, over another curve of the meandering river, towards Glasgow. The main wings of the house were three storeys high, with steeply pitched, slated roofs, and at either side of the north front was a tower, one storey higher and surmounted by a balustrade. The windows were of a fair size by contemporary standards, and in the accustomed manner they had wooden shutters on the lower half and diamond paned glass above. Over the principal doorway was a wooden balcony, decorated with round wooden balls. The north front was built in typical Scottish style of the sixteenth century, and a visitor to Culross Palace in Fife, today, will find himself looking at a house very similar in character to the Hamilton Palace which the Duchess knew in her youth.

To the left of the Palace, stables and outhouses were grouped around another, irregularly shaped courtyard. These two-storeyed, thatched buildings also housed the 'offices', those premises given over to the functions connected with the running of the household – the bakehouse, brewhouse, dairy and washhouse – and their courtyard was known as 'the Back Close'.

Returning to the Palace proper, the doorway under the balcony opened on to the Horn Hall, a spacious chamber which took its name from the antlers decorating its walls. This in turn led to the Laigh or Low Hall on one side, and to the Low Dining and Drawing Rooms on the other. Most of the principal chambers were to be found on the floor above, which was reached by the Great Stair, ascending from the corner of the Laigh Hall.

Upstairs, a Great Gallery with a round window at the end ran the entire length of the north front. The High Dining Room was round the corner in the west wing, with the High Drawing Room next to that and the Duchess's Great Bedchamber leading from there. The Duke's Bedchamber, in traditional manner, was directly above his wife's. Other members of the family and staff had chambers in the south and east wings, and further bedchambers occupied the second floor, along with the Duke's Library and a series of drawing rooms.

Throughout the building, the walls of the principal chambers were concealed by hangings. At the turn of the century, it had been the fashion to have the walls and ceilings of a room painted with elaborate designs of fruit and flowers, biblical scenes and heraldic motifs. There was at least one room in the Palace decorated in this manner, 'the Duchess's Painted Chamber', and it had been the work of a very famous craftsman. In 1627 the Duchess's grandmother had paid £266:13:4 Scots 'to Valentine Jeynkin, painter, for his work in the Palace'. This was none other than Valentine Jenkin, the Englishman who worked at the royal palaces of Holyrood and Stirling, and who was also employed by the Marchioness at her castle of Kinneil.[1]

Examples of this type of domestic art can still be seen in houses like

Culross Palace and Earlshall, but however much the colourful designs may intrigue and delight us today, by the middle of the seventeenth century they were frowned upon as being old-fashioned and tasteless. Everyone now wanted wooden panelling, and when walls were not actually made of wood they were painted to look as though they were. That was what happened at Kinneil, where Valentine Jenkin's work was overlaid with imitation wainscot, and the painter at Hamilton Palace had standing orders to do many of the chambers in 'walnut tree colour'. On top of this wood or imitation wood went hangings, fixed to the wall with battens and hooks.

Hangings were to retain their popularity for the rest of the seventeenth century. First and foremost was tapestry, usually described simply as 'arras'. Arras hangings were of two types, 'forest work' and 'imagery work'. The forest work had elaborate designs of fruit, flowers and foliage, while the imagery work depicted scenes from the Bible and from classical mythology. Each 'suite' of hangings consisted of five or six separate pieces illustrating different episodes in the same story. Originally, imagery work had been more popular, but as the century progressed the forest work tapestries came to be preferred. Seeking out hangings for the Earl of Panmure in 1696, an emissary explained that he could 'have had great bargains of second-hand hangings rich in silk and fineries of stuff' had they not been 'imagery and very large images, which I was afraid would not prove acceptable to Your Lordship after I heard you designed them for a house at Edinburgh, so I would not venture to send Your Lordship old fashion'd hangings although I found great choice that had never been used.' Instead, he forwarded 'a very fashionable suite of forest work which will fit your rooms at Edinburgh or those in the country for which they were first designed.'[2]

Before the Civil War the Duchess's father and uncle possessed many fine sets of tapestry, as a list of goods sent to her uncle in Holland reveals. There were 'five pieces of black velvet hangings embroidered with gold ... three pieces of ordinary hangings unlined ... four pieces of the history Orlando, lined, being rich wrought with silk and worset ... four pieces of the history of Orlando ... five pieces of the history of Artanasa ... five pieces of the history of Troy, very rich, all lined, wrought in silver and worset and ... three of the history of Acteon all lined ... '.*

At least some of these furnishings found their way back to Scotland, for when the Duchess was selling personal belongings to pay off her debts, among the articles she sold were 'one suite of hangings of the history of Artinisia containing seven pieces, one suite of hangings of the history of Orlando containing eight pieces, one suite of hangings of the history of Troy containing eight pieces, five pieces of black velvet hangings all wrought . . .'.

Comprehensive inventories drawn up in 1681 and again in 1690[†] show that arras hangings were to be found throughout the Palace, with figured arras in the Low Dining Room and forest work in, for example, the Duke's Bedchamber and the Low Drawing Room. A set of arras in the Great Dining Room was described as 'fine' but the arras in many of the other rooms is succinctly dismissed as 'old'. Some of the 1st Duke's hangings continued in use in the Palace during Duchess Anne's time, but tapestries have only a limited life and even at this late date they were still taken down, rolled up and moved around from one house to another. This alone caused a good deal of wear and tear, but it was the actual hanging on the walls which did most of the damage. Tapestries were hung up by their weft threads. Now the weft of a tapestry does not consist of continuous threads running right across its breadth, but of short threads making up different sections of colour. As a result, the strain placed on the weft damaged the tapestry and its design. The Duchess was continually having to tell her tailor to repair the arras[3] and indeed the 1690 inventory reveals that fourteen pieces of arras had been consigned to the Wardrobe, which was acting as a lumber room.

Of course, not all hangings were made of tapestry. The Duke had his private drawing room hung with 'green plain stuff' which had cost him over £80 Scots, and his brother-in-law the Earl of Perth possessed a large collection of hangings made of lead-coloured, snuff-coloured and clove-coloured cloth, linen and wool.[4] Perhaps the most splendid effect of all was achieved with gilt leather. As early as 1638 the Duchess's uncle, Lord Basil Feilding, had written to her father telling him about a Fleming who had been trained in Rome

* Scenes from *Orlando Furioso* made favourite subjects for tapestries. 'Artanasa' probably depicted the naval battle of Artemisium and 'Acteon' scenes from the classical legend.
† See Appendix.

and had a new method of 'making great designs and representing histories upon leather hangings in *chiara scuro*' and, as time went on, gilt leather increased in popularity. Sometimes the leather itself was dark brown, more often it was coloured – pearl colour, red or green – but the general effect was of glittering gold. The Stone Hall at Hamilton was transformed from a plain, rather gloomy chamber when its gilt hangings were in place.

The walls of seventeenth-century chambers were panelled, the ceilings were plastered, but less is known about the floors. The Palace office houses were paved with stone flags, but the main chambers had wooden floors. The trouble is that, even in the Panmure inventory of 1695 which records everything down to the brass knobs on the hearth, no mention is ever made of floor coverings as such. [5] Carpets are mentioned from time to time, but these were table coverings, the thick cloths laid on tables when they were not in use. The Duke of Hamilton's mother had four carpets in her house when she died, [6] and there was an old one in the Earl of Forth's house in Leith, [7] but these were almost certainly table carpets.

As for the Duchess's carpets, most of those mentioned in her inventories were table carpets. In 1656 Duchess Anne had sold 'a great turkey work carpet, a needlework carpet and a dozen and a half French work chairs and stools with a carpet suitable to them', and on another occasion she paid workmen 'for scouring and dressing [i.e. mending] the great carpet that was sent to Kinneil' but although the phraseology in both instances might seem to suggest floor carpets, the evidence is inconclusive. All that may be said with certainty is that when the Duchess was a girl, most of the Palace floors were covered with matting sewn together by the local tailors, and some of the rooms may have had floor carpets. By 1681, however, the Great Drawing Room did have 'a carpet for the floor', described nine years later as 'a foot carpet'.

Probably because of the elaborate nature of the rest of the chamber, window curtains seem to have been of less importance in the scheme of decoration than they are today. The Duchess once bought crimson and gold Indian curtain material, but generally she and her contemporaries were content with white serge, linen or wool, particularly in their bedchambers. The bedchamber in any noble house was dominated by the four-poster bed, which occupied most of the floor space available in all but the largest rooms. From the carved oak or fir bedstead hung sumptuous curtains of velvet or silk, heavily embroidered, trimmed with lace and lined with taffeta in a matching or contrasting colour. The velvet or silk tester had a fringed and embroidered cornice, and the whole structure was surmounted by gilded urns, balls and plumes. The quilt was made of the fabric which lined the bed curtains, and it was often embroidered too. Sir Colin Campbell of Glenorchy even had his coat of arms and his name sewn on his quilts.[8]

Very often the bed had its own accompanying furniture, made at the same time. There were usually armchairs, ordinary chairs and footstools upholstered to match the bedcurtains. Sometimes there was a long resting chair as well, and the cushions in the room and even the tablecloth were all made *en suite* with the bed. Even without its chairs and stools, the bed was the most expensive article of furniture in the house.

The colour schemes employed in these seventeenth-century bedchambers might seem excessively garish to the modern eye. The Earl of Buccleuch had a red cloth bed trimmed with green lace, Sir Colin Campbell's best bed had curtains of red Spanish taffeta faced with red and blue, while Charles II's favourite, the Duke of Lauderdale, brought his great purple damask bed with him whenever he came to Scotland.[9] The Duchess's own father possessed 'a red scarlet bed lined with blue and yellow taffeta wrought in chequer ways all fringed about with blue and yellow fringe . . . and the red bed of cloth all laced with red and yellow lace and lined with red taffeta . . . and the green taffeta bed flowered with gold.'

When the Duchess was a girl, the Palace, like many great houses, had a sumptuous bedchamber kept ready for a hoped-for visit from the King, as well as the principal bedchamber set aside for her father and then for her uncle the 2nd Duke. She herself slept in a room with a red and white flowered bed and an assortment of red, blue and green chairs and stools. After she inherited the titles and moved back into the Palace, she occupied her uncle's apartments, sleeping in 1681 in a bed with yellow mohair curtains lined with white satin which had a set of matching furniture consisting of a resting bed and eight chairs. Her table and stands were made of 'outlandish wood' and she had a cabinet containing a ewer and basin. Four paintings hung on her bedchamber walls, portraits of her husband, herself, her sister the Countess of Cassilis and her friend Mary of Modena, the young Italian Roman Catholic wife of James VII and II. Her room was also decorated with plants, for she had no fewer than ten 'flower pots', and although these had gone by the time David Crawford made the 1690 inventory, it records that she had in her dressing room 'four tea cups and five china flowerpots'. Finally, this least vain of women possessed four looking-glasses great and small, distributed between her bedchamber and her dressing-room.[10]

Upstairs, her husband had chosen red for his bedchamber. Each night he retired to his red damask bed which had been heated by a warming pan. He slept on the suffocating softness of a feather mattress, between linen sheets, beneath anything from two to four pairs of blankets and a quilt. He slept in a propped-up position on bolsters and pillows, and of course he slept with the curtains of his bed pulled tightly shut; all this in spite of the fact that he had a coal fire burning in his fireplace in winter time. Apart from his four-poster, he had a little resting bed, a fir table and stands and various chairs, and he acquired an ebony cabinet as well as a standish for pen, ink and paper.

His outer chamber also bore witness to his business and historical interests, for in it he had a new escritoire, along with two chests of drawers and two little cabinets. Hanging on the walls of the outer chamber were a portrait of his father-in-law the 1st Duke of Hamilton, no fewer than twenty other pictures, genealogies of the Royal House of Stewart, the Hamilton and the Douglas families, eleven maps and 'The Ten Commandments and the Royal Oak'. Next door to his bedchamber was the small room where his French valet-de-chambre slept, and his secretary was nearby.

Not far from the Duchess's bedchamber in the 1660s and '70s were the Palace nurseries. There were two of these, an outer nursery furnished in green, with a green bed, green coverlet and green hangings, and an inner nursery done in red. As befitted a large family, there were several cradles, including 'the rich cradle' which was probably carved, and there was special miniature furniture for children. Not only did they have their own small beds; there were little tables and chairs, scaled-down versions of their parents' furniture, and the windows had horizontal bars nailed over them to prevent any venturesome child from climbing out through the shutters.

The youngest members of the family ate in the nurseries, but the adults had two dining rooms to choose from, one on the ground floor and one upstairs. The Great High Dining Room was panelled with wainscot, which was normally concealed by a set of allegorical tapestries depicting The World. There were five pieces in the set, named Europe, Asia, Africa, America and The Ocean. All were eight feet nine inches deep, but they were of varying breadth, ranging from the seventeen-feet wide Ocean to Africa, which was a modest nine feet six inches. Thirteen portraits hung on the walls, including pictures of the Duchess's parents and the double portrait painted in Holland of her uncle the 2nd Duke and his fellow exile, the Duke of Lauderdale.

Guests sat round a long table which could be extended still further by the insertion of extra leaves, and beside the walls stood several smaller tables. 'Little tables' enjoyed great popularity, especially folding tables like the versatile one owned by the Duchess of Buccleuch. It was square, but it was capable of 'folding up in the corners, making a perfect round table.'[11] There were two dozen carpet chairs in the Palace Great High Dining Room, a fire screen, and in the evening light came from the candles in several sconces.

After the meal, the family and guests retired to the High Drawing Room. Hung with arras and more family portraits, it was furnished with two fir tables covered with embroidered velvet cloths, various gilded stands, a dozen cane chairs with rush seats and velvet cushions, and a pendulum clock. There were no bookcases, for the Duke had his own library where he spent a good deal of time. Overlooking the stables, it had 'presses' or cupboards made to his own specifications by the local carpenter.

Similarly, although paintings were hung throughout the house, most castles and palaces also had a gallery in which the family portraits and other paintings were displayed. At Hamilton, there was a particularly fine collection. The Duchess's grandfather had owned a number of Italian masterpieces, and her father assembled a magnificent collection of paintings through the good offices of his brother-in-law Lord Basil Feilding, who was ambassador to Venice. Some of the pictures he acquired in this way were for Charles I, but he kept others for himself. At the time of the Civil War his collection was confiscated and many of the finest pieces were lost to the family forever. Some, however, had already been sent to Hamilton and so they were saved. The Van Dyck portrait, *The Earl of Denbigh with a Blackamoor*, given by the sitter to the Duke, was hanging in the gallery of Hamilton Palace in the Duchess's time, along with *The Duchess of Richmond*, also once in the collection of the Duke.* Several other Van Dycks were inherited by the Duchess, and the family portraits came down to her too – the Mytens of her grandfather, father and mother, for instance.† Apart from the portraits, the Duke's Rubens of *Daniel in the Lions' Den*‡, was safely in the Palace, and so was Correggio's *Head of John the Baptist*, while over the two fireplaces in the Great Gallery hung two scriptural pieces by Raphael, presented to the Duchess's mother by Charles I.

The origin of the paintings in the Palace brings to mind the vexed question of where Scottish peers acquired the principal items of furniture for their public rooms. At one time it was believed that everything had to be imported from England, but it has since been shown that Scottish furniture makers did supply all kinds of goods themselves, and so the situation is not so simple.[12] The Duke and Duchess of Hamilton obtained their furniture from a variety of sources. Very often they employed a Hamilton carpenter by the name of Arthur Nasmith. A member of an old local family, he did all manner of work around the Palace, putting up partitions, repairing doors and altering windows. He was also called upon to make furniture. Sometimes it would be something small, like the 'making of a little square table with a drawer and covering it with black velvet' or it might be a more extensive order – for settles, or a set of turned chairs. It was he, too, who made the cradles for the Duchess's babies, the little chairs for the older children, and a school desk for the Duchess's eldest son.

Rather more of a craftsman than the burgh carpenter was James McLellan, the Edinburgh wright. He was to play a leading part in

---

* *The Earl of Denbigh*, now in the National Gallery, London, is reproduced in Boucher, *op. at.*, 256. The Duchess of Richmond is in the North Carolina Museum of Art.
† In the Collection of the Duke of Hamilton.
‡ The *is* now in the National Gallery, Washington D.C., U.S.A.

the rebuilding of Hamilton Palace, and while he was there he made furniture as well. Footstools seem to have been one of his specialities, and he provided two new leaves for the dining-room table at a modest £1 Scots each. On another occasion, he supplied 'a block to Her Grace for putting up head dresses on.

Most professional of all was William Scott, who also worked in Edinburgh and who always described himself as a cabinet-maker. (This is an early use of the term in Scotland.) At least two of the tables in the Palace were made by him, and he produced cane chairs, escritoires and looking glasses for many of the Scottish peers.[13]

Not only was it possible to engage the services of an Edinburgh cabinet-maker. The Edinburgh merchants had in their shops all manner of furniture imported from London and the continent. Mrs Edmiston sold beds complete with bedding. Robert Blackwood kept gilded leather screens and brass fenders, and John Bonar always had a fine selection of cabinets set with mother of pearl, varnished tables and leather chairs.[14]

Most types of furniture could easily be obtained at home, but some special objects were imported direct from England or the continent. The Hamiltons bought their clocks from Joseph Knibb in London, although they sent them for repair to Paul Roumieu in Edinburgh. Again, musical instruments usually came from the south. It was customary for the children of the aristocracy to learn to play an instrument, and every great house had its harpsichord or virginals. The Duchess's own daughters were taught to play the virginals, while her sons learned the flageolet, the viol and the guitar, but none of the accounts reveals where the Duchess bought these instruments. Although it has been suggested that the virginals purchased in 1680 by Sir John Foulis may have been made in Edinburgh, there is a lack of any conclusive evidence, whereas there are many examples of the importing of musical instruments: when the *Margaret* of Grangepans sailed into Bo'ness Harbour in March 1607 she was carrying five sets of virginals ordered from London by an Edinburgh merchant, and when the Earl of Panmure wanted 'a bass violin' it was to London that he wrote.[15]

Some of the more expensive furniture in the Palace originated in London, as accounts for the Duke's visits south demonstrate,[16] and occasionally he bought direct from Holland. Dutch furniture was always popular in Scotland, not least because many of the Royalist peers had established personal contacts there during the Civil War. With the coming of more peaceful times the Duke of Lauderdale went so far as to bring Dutch joiners and painters over to work for him at Lethington, and his Duchess gave Heinrich Meinner, one of the joiners, careful instructions to make for her cedar tea tables, walnut chests of drawers and cedar close stools.[17] The Duke of Hamilton did not ever send for Dutch craftsmen, but the Duchess did buy direct from Holland from time to time, particularly when she wanted long-backed chairs.

So much, then, for the furniture of the principal chambers. As well as these main rooms a considerable proportion of the Palace was given over to office houses: the kitchens, larder, bakehouse and so forth – and for these an inventory does exist. Taken up as she was with the affairs of her family and estate, the Duchess did not have a great deal of personal interest in the details of the running of her household, but she saw to it that everything was done properly, and that the offices were well equipped.

On the ground floor of the Palace was the larder. This was not merely a cupboard, but an actual room with a fireplace in it. Along the walls stood rows of barrels containing barley, herring and meal. Then there were shelves of little boxes for mustard seed and for rice. Large cheeses and sugar loaves sat alongside the boxes, together with dishes of prunes, raisins, currants and groats. A miniature chest of drawers had been specially made to hold spices, one kind in each drawer, and beside that was a pepper mill. On the floor stood four wooden chests. Two were for storing bread, and in the other two candles were kept. There were cotton candles and ordinary candles which the Duchess bought in bulk, often sending tallow to the candlemakers. Candles were the only source of artificial light in the Palace, and in winter time the household would use as many as five stones of candles a week.

Not only were food and candles kept in the larder. The dishes were stored there too. There were dozens of pewter trenchers as well as bottles of stone and glass, and the family plate reposed in a special locked cupboard.

Next door to the larder were the kitchens, three in all, each with its own huge hearth. Cooking was done over the fire, and so each hearth was equipped with metal hooks and chains from which the pots and pans were suspended. Then there were spits. Great houses always had a number of spits, anything from three or four to several dozen, and in the Palace there were usually fourteen. Gone were the days, though, when everything was cooked in great iron cauldrons. Now pots and pans were made of copper and brass as well as iron, and many varieties were available. There were broth pots with covers, sauce pans, dripping pans and frying pans. Meat was stewed in skillets, which were long-handled pans with three or four feet, or it could be done on a brander, which was the current name for a gridiron. There was an 'earthen pot for stewing pears' and venison was also cooked in earthenware pots – perhaps in something resembling a casserole.

In addition there were all kinds of utensils. Henry Harper, an Edinburgh merchant, supplied the Duchess with butter prints and 'a dry cow [or mould] for making syllabubs' and on another occasion she ordered a six foot long 'new glass square for drying of sweetmeats on.' Some of the utensils have an archaic ring about them, like the mortars and pestles which were to be found in every large kitchen of the period, or the white iron for roasting apples, but others sound distinctly familiar: there were graters, for instance, and colanders and chopping knives.

Many of these items had been bought in Edinburgh in the first place, but some were made on the premises. The smith who shod the horses in the Duke's stables also made spits, flesh forks and ladles for his kitchens. The Duchess's grandmother had always sent her pots and pans to a local tinker when they became worn, but the Duchess herself had hers taken into Edinburgh to James Miller, a coppersmith in the Canongate. He did what repairs he could, but sometimes the utensils were beyond repair and on one occasion he sent an anxious note to the steward at Hamilton explaining that he had 'tinned all your work, but the 2 colanders and the kettles which is not worthy of the tinning, and an old saucepan which ... would not tin.' Kettles in this context were simply pots.

Not far from the Palace kitchens stood the bakehouse, one of the separate, thatched buildings looking on to the Back Close. Here the principal feature was the ovens. They were large, rounded, brick ovens like those still to be seen today in Kinneil Castle. Three wooden baking tables ran the length of the main room, and large sacks of meal and flour stood against the walls. The baker had his own wheat sieves and graters, made by John Nasmith, another Hamilton wright, and he even had baking pans with false bottoms. All the bread for the Palace was baked there, and all the ale was made in the brewhouse in large wooden vats. It was then stored in the special ale cellar, next door to the wine cellar.

Another of the separate buildings in the Back Close was the washhouse. Contrary to the general assumption, the nobility in the seventeenth century did have fairly high standards of hygiene. When the Duke of Hamilton was in Edinburgh he had his washing done for him by Mrs Margaret Douglas, who lived in the Canongate, and some of the accounts she sent in still survive, revealing that at least every second day she washed muslin cravats, handkerchiefs and linen shirts and drawers all belonging to the Duke. When he was away from home the staff took the opportunity of spring cleaning his chambers in the Palace, and sheets, towels and curtains were laundered, hangings were scrubbed, and the floors were washed and sanded.

There was always a great deal of activity in the washhouse, for apart from the family's linen and nightclothes, there was napery to be kept clean too. As well as the permanent washerwoman, extra helpers were sometimes hired. One such was paid 'for scouring 2 suites of hangings and 20 pairs of blankets and helping to wash sheets and other linens'. The washing was done in large wooden tubs. Soap was kept in barrels close at hand, and there was always plenty of starch and blue. When the clothes had been washed, the women piled them into baskets and carried them out to a green in the Low Park where the wright had put up clothes poles. There they hung out the clothes to dry, taking them in finally to be finished with smoothing irons.

Apart from these traditional methods, the Duchess introduced an exciting innovation into her washhouse. There exists a letter written to her secretary from a servant of her cousin, the Countess of Rothes. This explains that 'The Countess of Rothes has caused this bearer come to Edinburgh express with the Mangle which her Ladyship promised to send to Her Grace when at Edinburgh. My Lady thought it best to send the wright with it because he would have the greatest care of it and he will teach the women how to make it go. If anything be wrong that belongs to it when it shall come to your hands he will right it. The price which My Lady did agree with him for it was 53 pounds Scots.' This was in 1696, and the first English mention of a mangle in the *Oxford English Dictionary* is in 1774. According to the same source, the word 'mangle' first appeared in Dutch in the eighteenth century, so the Countess of Rothes's mangle antedates both of these instances.

The office houses in the Back Close were completed by the porter's lodge, the stables and coachhouse, and a coalhouse. All the office houses and the chambers throughout the Palace were heated by coal fires. There were sixty-two hearths in the Palace in 1691, and a regular feature of the accounts is the payment of money 'for sweeping the lums' [chimneys]. At one time some of the Hamilton tenants had paid part of their rent in peats, but this custom had died out in the 1630s and although peat was still used sometimes for kindling fires, the normal fuel was coal. Some of it came from the Duke's coal pits up at Quarter, but much was bought in. During the first six months of 1665, for instance, the Duchess purchased no fewer than 475 loads of coal for the use of the Palace. Finally, a little way off in the park, stood the inevitable dovecot.

This complex of buildings which comprised Hamilton Palace stood in extensive grounds, and if the Duchess had little time for the minutiae of domestic life, she did take a keen interest in the gardens. There was nothing she liked better than to go for a walk in 'the yards' or to sit on her summer seat under the old fir trees in the park. The Duke was equally enthusiastic, nor was he merely content to admire the finished effect: he planned much of the work that went on in the gardens personally.

The gardens at Hamilton were already well established. Ever since the erection of the Palace a regular gardener had been employed, and Robert Hutchison, who occupied that position in the early seventeenth century, had been given £10 Scots a year to spend on seeds, travelling to East Lothian to buy them and going as far as Fife 'to see a garden'. At this period the fashion was for a series of walled gardens filled with flowers, but by the time of the Restoration tastes had changed and the new formal garden had been introduced.[18] Whether the Duke did bring in the geometrical hedges and topiary work associated with this fashion does not emerge from the accounts, but even if he did so to some extent, he retained the existing walled gardens.

There was the Statue Garden, for instance, at the front of the house. Set in its flowerbeds were the painted statues from which it took its name, and in the centre was a painted sundial. This may have been the one carved in 1648 by Ralph Rawlinson, for a payment was made to him in that year for 'the horologe stone' he made. Other small, walled gardens filled with flowers led off the Statue Garden, and many of the flowers grown for the Duchess would be perfectly familiar to us today. In the spring, there were colourful beds of crocuses and tulips. Gillyflowers were immensely popular, and there were quantities of lupins, African marigolds and hollyhocks, as well as snapdragons and scabious. Another old fashioned favourite, Sweet William, grew in the Palace flowerbeds, and so did anemones, ranunculus and peony roses.

A flight of steps led from the flower gardens to the Pond Garden, a much admired corner of the grounds where there were large fish ponds and fountains, and in 1666 the Duke employed workmen to lay out a new bowling green near the south gate. The flower gardens and the bowling green were sources of recreation, but there were other parts of the grounds which had a more practical usefulness. Every great house at this time had its herb garden for both culinary and medicinal purposes, and the Palace was no exception. Bay leaves were used for seasoning then as now, and the chervil and clary in the Palace herb garden would also be served at table: chervil resembles parsley and leaves of clary were fried in batter. The Duchess's ladies probably gathered the thyme, purslane and basil for her to drink in childbed, and anyone with a cold or a headache was given rosemary mixed in wine or fennel mixed up with vinegar. Dill was good for indigestion if drunk in white wine, or its seeds could be fried for the treatment of ulcers, while marjoram could be made into a soothing ointment.[19]

Each year the Duke stocked up with flower seeds and herbs, sending his order to Harry Ferguson, the Edinburgh seedsman whose premises were 'a little above the head of the Blackfriars Wynd'. But although flowers and herbs always featured in his order, they were very much a subsidiary part of the list. The Duke was much more concerned with the kitchen garden and with the wide selection of vegetable seeds Harry Ferguson had imported from the continent.

The very name 'kitchen garden' makes obvious its function, but one of the most common misconceptions of Scottish social history has been the belief that, as one historian states, 'vegetables were not served on table' and again, that 'turnips . . . were only in a few gardens: onions were in none.'[20] For some reason it has been assumed that, beyond a few peas and beans, vegetables never were consumed, and when accounts for the purchase of seeds suggested the contrary, they have been dismissed as recording experimental attempts at growing vegetables which remained more or less curios and never were intended for cooking and eating. This argument arises from a failure to appreciate that a mere four ounces of turnip seed can sow a fairly large area, the seeds themselves being light, so the smallness of the quantities bought is no indication of a lack of serious intent. If the household accounts do not always mention vegetables when detailing food used in the kitchens, it is because they concentrate on the expenditure of food bought in, not grown in the gardens, and again, many dishes would be cooked with vegetables in them, so that these do not appear separately in the laconic descriptions of 'boiled mutton' or 'collops'. Conclusive proof that vegetables did appear regularly on the menu can be found among the accounts of the Duke of Lauderdale: on 24 July 1670, John Broun and Grisel Bruce, the gardeners at Holyrood, were paid 15/– sterling a week by the Duke 'for furnishing the kitchen with turnips, carrots, cabbages, spinach, beets, summer savory, winter savory, rosemary, thyme, sweet marjoram, mint, balm, purslane, lettuce, sorrel, parsley, laurel and bay leaves.'[21]

Vegetables were grown in substantial quantities in Hamilton

Palace gardens from at least 1660 onwards. Each year the Duke ordered from half a pound to two pounds of Strassbourg onion seeds, and very often he supplemented this with quantities of French, Flanders and Spanish onion seed. At around seven shillings sterling a pound, onions were fairly cheap. Leeks went in each year as well, sometimes French leeks and sometimes London leeks. Very often vegetables were described by the name of a country, and the Duke regularly grew French cucumbers, Dutch parsnips and Italian celery.

Whether or not turnips really were rare, he had what amounted to a standing order for four ounces of turnip seed each year. There were other root vegetables too. Row upon row of beetroot occupied one corner of the kitchen garden and radishes were very plentiful. Then there were greens. Young cabbage plants were bought a thousand at a time, and there seems to have been a great variety available. At one time or another the accounts mention English, Scots, Dutch, Savoy and Russian cabbage. Lettuce had been put in ever since the 1620s, and spinach and endives grew nearby. Peas and beans occupied a good deal of space, and the gardener had special hotbeds for the rearing of asparagus, as well as frames for bringing on melons and gourds and for 'the upbringing of tender herbs'.

The regimented rows of peas and beans, cabbages and lettuce, had an attraction of their own, and the kitchen garden was provided with two summer houses where the Duke and Duchess could sit and admire the garden produce. Another gilded, concave sundial stood in the centre, and right across the kitchen garden stretched an avenue of alternating horse chestnut and cherry trees.

The Duke's interest in his vegetable garden was surpassed only by his enthusiasm for fruit trees, and at Hamilton he had ample scope for this particular type of planting. There have been orchards in the Clyde Valley ever since Roman times, and to this day tourists come in spring to admire the old apple and plum trees in blossom. The Palace in particular was famous for its fruit trees. In 1668 the famous Scottish judge, Lord Fountainhall, paid a visit to Hamilton, and he recorded in his journal afterwards, 'Went and saw the yards . . . Great abundance of as good

53

vines, peaches, apricots, figs, walnuts, chestnuts, philberts [nuts] etc. in it as in any part of France: excellent Bon Crestian pears . . . The walls are built of brick, which conduces much to the ripening of the fruits . . .'.[22]

At one time this description might have been dismissed as foolish hyperbole, but of course it was perfectly accurate. These fruits might seem very exotic for a country which, according to some observers, had scarcely any trees at all, but in fact fruit trees were commonplace. The Duchess's kinsman, the Earl of Crawford, had an unusual hobby: tasting fruit. One day in 1692 he sat down and made a list of 'The Earl of Crawford's Judgment of fruits in order set down as I esteem them according to their Goodness',[23] a list which reveals something of his gastronomic activities. It appears that, like many of his contemporaries, he travelled a good deal and wherever he went in Scotland, near or far, he made a point of visiting every available garden and orchard. Near home in Fife he gravely tasted the apricots growing at Craighall and Durie. He found his way into the castle orchard at Ballinbreich on the shores of the Tay, and he munched with pleasure the plums and apples from the old abbey trees at Lindores. He plucked peaches at Kilwinning in the west, licked his lips over the succulent nectarines at Durie in the east, and happily selected for himself pears from the trees beside the chapel of Wemyss. When he went to Glasgow he encountered Bailie Colquhoun and in next to no time was sampling the produce of the Bailie's town garden, and when he ran into James Clephan in Cupar he soon prevailed on him to let him taste the fruit in his yard. Needless to say, he visited Hamilton Palace, where the Duke plied him with notable Nonesuch and Malcotton pears, Duchess damsons, orange apricots, white globe gooseberries and great bright redcurrants.

The Duke seems to have been particularly fond of cherry trees, and part of the gardens was given over to a cherry yard. In the 1st Duke's time a hundred small nails had been bought 'for trees nailing to the brick walls', and the Duke extended the expanse of wall available, hiring brickmakers to come to the Palace and produce thousands of bricks for new walls. Against these, the Duke grew his peaches, apricots and cherries. His success with these fruits became well known, and in 1682 the Earl of Callander was eagerly making arrangements to find out 'at what distance My Lord Duke plants the trees on his walls.'

Some of his trees were obtained from other Scottish gardens. Two of the pear trees at Hamilton had come from Struthers, and some of the cherry trees had originated in the laird of Ormiston's East Lothian garden. Peaches and apricots were normally brought from London, and grafts, which were highly popular, were imported from the continent: on one occasion the Duke had a Bo'ness shipmaster bring over from Holland '5 peaches upon apricots, 4 peaches upon plums and 2 apricots.' At the same time, he ordered vines, mulberries and nut trees from the south.

When Lord Fountainhall paid his visit to the Palace, he was not only impressed by the fruit trees. 'Went to the wood', he confided to his journal, 'which is of a vast bounds: much wood of it is felled: there be many great oaks in it yet: rode through the length of it, it is thought to be about 5 miles about. Saw great droves of hart and hind with the young roes and fawns in companies of 100 and 60 together.' This fine deer park had been the creation of the Duchess's father, and there were few like it in Scotland. During an early visit south he had admired the deer parks of the great English mansions and had resolved to establish at Hamilton a deer park of his own. He accordingly wrote to his mother's cousin, Sir Colin Campbell of Glenorchy, early in the 1630s. He had, he explained, lately made a deer park, and he would like Sir Colin to help him stock it with red deer and roe. The roe had to be captured young, for 'we have the experience in England' that no old ones would live. He had previously given orders to his own men to capture some deer, but without success, so he was delighted when Sir Colin duly supplied red deer and young harts.

In this project, the Duke found an enthusiastic ally in his mother, who confessed to Sir Colin that she loved the deer 'extremely' and on another occasion mentioned that she kept a tame hind.[24] Thanks to their efforts, the deer park was successfully established at Hamilton, but maintaining it was not without its difficulties. The main problem was keeping the deer alive in winter time. Three of them died of starvation during the severe winter of 1691/2, and so a special allowance of oats had to be set aside for the survivors. In spite of the cold weather, they do not seem to have been kept indoors in winter, for one November the local wrights were busy putting up a little railed enclosure in the park where the deer could be fed, and the notes of the corn given to them always refer to them as being in the park rather than in any of the outhouses.

The main difficulty was caused by the climate, but there were other problems too. The sight of the herds of deer was too much of a temptation for some of the local people, and in 1689 the Duke was writing from London to tell the Duchess to bring to trial those 'who have been the hunters of our deer and punish them severely, for as you say, if such things be past, especially when you are present, what may be expected when we are both absent?' Only the previous spring John Robieson at Aven Bridge had been banished from the burgh of Hamilton during the Duke's pleasure after he had been discovered hunting the deer 'upon a Sabbath day in time of Divine Service.'

The deer were themselves liable to cause problems. A wall had to be put up for 'keeping the deer from the corn' and they were a very real menace if they were allowed near the young trees: in 1689 the Duke was writing to tell the Duchess that he was 'sorry the deer should spoil the planting in the little park, and thinks strange that the paling [fence] should be so long in putting up.' The gardeners should put stakes round every tree the deer were likely to damage until the proper fencing was put up, for it was better that the work in the gardens should be delayed than that any of the young trees should be lost.

Many of the existing trees had been planted by the Duchess's grandmother. As early as 1626 she had bought young trees from the Laird of Pollock, and Sir Colin Campbell had sent her fir seed as well as deer. 'Believe me', the Marchioness had told him when she thanked him for some packets of fir seed, 'I think more of them nor ye can imagine, for I love them more nor I do all the fruit trees in the world. I have already a four or five hundred of my own planting that is pretty trees, and . . . my son [the Duke] loves them no less nor I do and has willed me to plant a great many more.' Her son-in-law the Earl of Crawford was 'a very great planter of his age as ever I knew any', she added, 'and I am glad to cherish him to it.'[25]

There were indeed many 'great planters' in Scotland by the second half of the seventeenth century. The Duke of Lauderdale had his gardeners busy at Thirlestane putting in elms, ash, pines, chestnuts and firs: in 1671 alone they planted a thousand walnut trees and put in half as many again the following year. Sir John Foulis favoured firs and limes, and the great nurseries at Panmure in the 1680s had everything from juniper and yew to cedar and beech trees.[26] Not to be outdone, the Duke and Duchess of Hamilton put elms, ash and alders in their parks, made avenues of lime trees and elms, and edged the gravel walks in the gardens with thorns.

Apart from their palace of Hamilton, the Duke and Duchess owned various other houses throughout Scotland. Farthest west was their castle of Brodick, on the island of Arran. It exists to this day, but apart from her stay during the Civil War, the Duchess did not spend any time there, although the Duke went over for the occasional hunting trip. Similarly, Avendale Castle at Strathaven, to the south of Hamilton, was not used because damage by the English army had rendered it uninhabitable. Where Kinneil Castle was concerned, however, it was a different matter.

In addition to their extensive lands in the Clyde Valley, the Dukes of Hamilton owned the baronies of Kinneil, Carriden and Polmont on the River Forth, and their seat there was at Kinneil, just outside their port of Bo'ness. The original castle had been built as long before as 1553, but throughout its history it suffered a series of misfortunes, the first of which was that less than twenty years after its construction it was demolished by gunpowder and only the lower part of one wall survived. Shortly afterwards, the Duchess's ancestor built a new, L-shaped house nearby, and this is the part of the castle which is best preserved today.[27] The early Hamiltons stayed frequently at Kinneil but with the coming of the Civil War and the Cromwellian occupation a further disaster overtook the castle. It was captured by the Cromwellian army, the entire furniture was 'carried away by the English'[28] and the house itself together with the valuable coal and salt revenues was made over to General Monck, in whose hands it remained until after the Restoration.

On 20 July 1660 one of the Duchess's servants 'passed through the whole rooms of the said castle and, finding no manner of plenishing [furniture] therein, took real, virtual and peaceable possession of the foresaid castle and house of Kinneil by receiving the keys of the outer gate'. Once more in Hamilton hands, its fortunes took a turn for the better when the Duke and Duchess decided on an extensive programme of rebuilding. During the early 1670s they had a new block erected on the site of the original structure, adding two pavilions and linking it up with the existing house. Apparently the Duke thought of building another wing on the south side to balance the old L-shaped house, but he never did so, possibly because of the danger of subsidence, since the ditch of the Antonine Wall lay somewhere below.[29]

By the end of the seventeenth century Kinneil was generally accepted as being a very pleasant place. The castle stands on a slope above the Forth, and the windows look out on to a panoramic view of the river. Members of the family were enthusiastic when they visited the castle, and an anonymous writer of 1697 described it as 'a very fine house indeed'.

Although small, the castle was very comfortable. It had the usual dining room with two square tables and an octagonal one, and the tapestry-hung drawing room had comfortable cane chairs. The Duke and Duchess occupied a bedchamber next door to the drawing-room, sleeping in a blue taffeta bed, and as well as the other bedrooms there were well equipped kitchens and offices. To the modern eye the most notable feature of the house is the famous series of wall paintings. The exceptionally fine Good Samaritan room was painted in the sixteenth century, and then in the 1630s the Duchess's grandmother commissioned Valentine Jenkin to add a whole new series of paintings: the accounts record, 'To Valentine the painter upon his task £20:6/-' in August 1634, and 'Given to Valentine Jenkein for painting the galleys £100.' (Galleys are included in the Hamilton coat of arms.)[30]

The windows on the east front of the castle look out over a

grassy area which, three hundred years ago, was laid out in gardens. They were, of course, on a much smaller scale than at Hamilton but there was a flourishing kitchen garden which Harry Ferguson kept regularly supplied with seeds for French leeks and onions, carrot and turnip, beetroot, radish and spinach. Artichokes were tried out in the 1660s and asparagus plants were brought over from Holland.

According to the family themselves, though, the best part of the garden was the orchard. In his memorandum of the fruits he had sampled, the Earl of Crawford referred to the Murray pears and the Brethren pears which grew there, and as well as the cherry trees round the walls of the kitchen garden, there were peaches and apricots. Some of this fruit was always sent to Hamilton for the consumption of the family, but the remainder was sold and the proceeds were included in the estate revenues. An interesting note of 17 July 1696 records that Henry Anderson, gardener in Grange, and William Pinkerton, gardener in Linlithgow, 'being convened at the desire of Daniel Hamilton, chamberlain of Kinneil, to comprise and value the whole pears, apples, plums, cherries, gooseberries and currantberries of the yards of Kinneil, do find the same, (excepting those in the north yard which are reserved for Her Grace the Duchess her use) to be worth only the sum of twenty pounds Scots money.' A letter from Lord John Hamilton later that year refers to the poorness of the season, and generally the fruit from Kinneil was much appreciated by the family. Finally, mention must be made of an intriguing occupant of the castle grounds. In the 1700–2 lists of fodder for the animals, there appears a small quantity of peas fed 'to the antelope' which apparently roamed about on the hillside near the house.

Although from the very start there was always a gardener in residence at Kinneil, the castle itself was normally occupied by a very small staff because the family so rarely stayed for any length of time, and on the occasions when the Duke and Duchess did spend a few nights, they brought with them from Hamilton all the servants they needed. Carriers went constantly between the two houses when the Duke and Duchess were at Kinneil, with fresh butter, vegetables, dishes, clothing and bedding, and very often with a servant girl riding behind the carrier himself on horseback.

The Duke and Duchess spent more time in Edinburgh than they did in Kinneil, for the Duke had to go there frequently to attend the Scottish Parliament and Privy Council, and to see to the family's complicated legal business. At first when he went to the capital he took lodgings, but of course the Hamiltons had apartments in the royal palace of Holyroodhouse, for ever since the time of Charles I they had been Hereditary Keepers of the Palace. Their apartments were in the oldest part, near the famous rooms associated with Mary Queen of Scots. In the 1660s the Palace was in need of repair so they did not lodge there, but after the repairs and extensions of the 1670s they stayed frequently in their apartments, although the Palace remained a vastly uncomfortable place in which to live. Because of its low-lying position it was notoriously damp, and even after the work done in the 1670s it soon deteriorated again. A sudden thaw in the winter of 1695 caused water to pour in at the roof, flooding some of the Hamilton rooms, seeping through into the Earl of Cassilis's and ruining a fine bed and other furniture in Lord Linlithgow's chamber. The hiring of workmen to improve matters could have even more disastrous consequences as the Duke had discovered some years before when joiners working in the garrets had allowed a fire to start, endangering the entire building.

Fire was a very real danger, for the Palace was always over-crowded. Noblemen who held government office were given apartments there, and the Duke and Duchess were continually beset by problems arising from the squabbling of their fellow peers over their competing claims to rooms. When the Marquis of Tweeddale was supposed to vacate some chambers in 1694 he departed, leaving all of them locked and taking the keys with him, so that the Duke had to order the doors to be forced open, and a few months later Tweeddale's servants tried to evict the Duke's underkeeper from the latter's rightful lodgings in the Palace. Nor was it only the aristocracy who occupied rooms in Holyrood. In 1687 the Duke complained that the garrets of both the Lord Clerk Register and the Marquis of Atholl's lodgings 'are filled with the families of little tradesmen and other little people, which keeps all these stairs and that part of the house nasty and in disorder.'

Despite all the advantages of Holyrood from the point of view of convenience as a place to stay in time of Parliament, it was not surprising that the Duke and Duchess always viewed with relief their departure from Edinburgh and their return home to Hamilton Palace.

CHAPTER 3

The Servants

The household at Hamilton consisted of the Duchess, her family and a veritable fleet of servants. It was impossible to run such a complex establishment without a large staff, and one of the Duchess's most urgent problems when she inherited her estates was the organisation of her household. Her father had always employed a full complement of servants, many of whom had been with him for years, but when he was executed the future seemed so uncertain that there was no alternative but to disband the staff. On a bleak day in 1649 the Duchess reluctantly paid and dismissed Valentine Beldam, Robert Cole, Robert Nasmith and even 'Herie the sculleryman'.[1] Some of the servants followed her uncle into exile in Holland, others may have stayed on at the Palace in the employ of Colonel Ingoldsby, and a few did remain with the Duchess herself, notably her ladies.

The years of the Cromwellian occupation are poorly documented in the Hamilton Archives, but when the Duchess was able to move back to the Palace the accounts begin again. Servants are mentioned from time to time, and the old familiar names appear once more. Valentine Beldam and Robert Nasmith had returned to the Duchess's service by 1657 and so had many of those who had been with her uncle during his exile. By the time of the Restoration the household was running normally once more.

After that, there were always at least thirty servants and sometimes as many as fifty in the Palace. Some were indoor servants, some were outdoor servants, some lived in and others did not, but perhaps the most striking feature of the household staff from the modern point of view was that almost all of the servants were men.

At the top of what may be termed the servant hierarchy were four professional men, the secretary, the lawyer, the chaplain and the governor. The highest paid man in the entire household was the first of these, the Duke's secretary. The office of secretary is in itself an interesting one. The Duchess's father always had his own secretary, but after that the term seems to have disappeared from the household lists for a generation and it is not common in other family papers until the beginning of the eighteenth century: in 1703 the Earl of Seafield had a secretary, the Duchess of Buccleuch's is mentioned in 1706 and a year later the secretaries of the Duke of Atholl, the Earl of Loudoun and Lord Sinclair all became burgesses of Glasgow.[2]

At first, the Duke of Hamilton used one of his gentlemen to help him with his correspondence and accounts. In the 1670s James Smith of Smithycroft gradually took over this function, but in about 1680 a full-time secretary was appointed. This was David Crawford, who was to remain at Hamilton Palace for the next forty years and more. The son of an Ayrshire man, Duncan Crawford of Knockshinnoch, his original connection with the Hamilton family is unknown, but when he was still in his teens he was employed by the Duke and Duchess as 'the children's man'. In fact, he was a contemporary of their eldest son, and he attended Glasgow University along with their children. David studied law, but he did not undertake a legal training purely for the benefit of his employers. For a number of years he pursued his own career at the same time as acting as the Duke of Hamilton's secretary, and he had a thriving practice in Edinburgh. This conflict of interests created difficulties, of course, and he found it hard to divide his time between his own concerns and the affairs of the Duke. When the latter took him to London in 1687 he remarked testily that 'David Crawford is very pressing to be home at his business about the [Court of] Session, and truly if I could get any other, he is not worth pressing to stay.' Stay he did, however, and in 1693 the Duke was still complaining that 'David Crawfurd takes a great liberty to wait when he pleases, but servants are not to be had or he should get what time he pleased'.

Of course, in spite of all the Duke's complaints, he knew that he would have been hard put to it to find a worthy replacement. David was conscientious, he was hardworking, and anyone looking through the Hamilton Archives today soon becomes familiar with his beautifully neat writing, which survives in countless letters, memoranda and accounts. Even several of his personal account books remain, with his own notes on how to make ink and 'how to keep canary birds well'.

His legal business might take him frequently to Edinburgh, but his other interests were firmly rooted in Hamilton. He married Anne Cockburn, one of the Duchess's servants who was herself the daughter of two other servants, and he and his wife had a large family: in 1710 she presented him with a tenth son whom they named Archibald, after the Duchess's youngest child, and they also had daughters.[3] Eventually, he gave up his law business and came to live permanently at Hamilton. By that time he was a man of substance. He had been made a burgess of Hamilton and of the Canongate of Edinburgh, 'for most generous and good deeds',[4] and when he built a new house in Hamilton to accommodate himself and his family he employed the celebrated James Smith as architect. The result was so splendid that the Duchess's son Lord John wrote to tell the Earl of Arran that 'Mr Crawford has built a fine house where Mrs Nasmith's house was, but nearer to the park', adding with some asperity, 'It is after the fashion of the Laird of Livingstone's house, and as many windows in front as his, by which you may see some folks are not losers by Her Grace's service.' The Duchess obtained for him the lucrative position of clerk to the admission of notaries, and she also seems to have given him the lands of Allanton, near Hamilton. In 1711 he suffered a sad blow when his wife died, leaving him with eight surviving children, but less than a year later he married Anne Auchterlony, the widow of a wealthy Edinburgh merchant. She brought to him all her late husband's houses in the capital, along with her furniture and jewellery. He and his second wife both lived on until 1736, when they died in Edinburgh within two months of each other.[5]

David Crawford looked after the Duke's correspondence, wrote out many of the chamberlains' account books and the business documents needed in the running of the household and generally made himself indispensable. For many years he had as his colleague another lawyer, Arthur Nasmith, who is usually described simply as 'writer in Hamilton', but who was actually employed at the Palace in a legal capacity. He was a member of an old-established Hamilton family which for generations had possessed property at the Castle Wynd Port in the burgh. He eventually became town clerk of Hamilton, but in 1697, when there was 'a great mortality . . . among the young and old' in the town, he and his daughter Anna died. 'The death of Arthur Nasmith is truly a vast loss to my Lady Duchess', a friend of the family reported. 'He was an honest, faithful, intelligent person, just and serviceable to the family and to anybody who had business with them', and David Crawford described how Arthur would be sadly missed by Her Grace, since no one else understood her business so well or was so sensible and honest.

The other two professional men in the household were the chaplain and the governor. Perhaps because of the religious difficulties of the 1670s there does not seem to have been a permanent chaplain in the Palace until the following decade, when Mr Simon Gilly appears on the list of servants. From then onwards it was the Duchess's habit to employ young divinity students who had graduated but who were not yet ordained. Mr David Brodie, for instance, was educated at Aberdeen and Glasgow and was licensed by the presbytery of Hamilton in 1694. From then until 1698 he served as the Duchess's chaplain, after which he became minister of the church of Dalserf, on the Hamilton estates. Mr Gilbert Kennedy succeeded him, then followed another young minister, Mr George Peden, who was later to be minister of Kilmarnock. At £200 Scots *per annum*, the chaplains were highly paid in comparison with the other servants, and the post was obviously a useful stepping stone for an ambitious young man hoping for a charge within the sphere of Hamilton influence.[6]

The fourth professional man in the household was even more indispensable: the governor. Although the sons of the Scottish nobility were sent to school and then to university, they normally had a governor as well, to supervise their studies at home and to look after their general welfare. From at least as early as 1667

Mr John Bannantyne occupied this position in the Hamilton household. A member of the local family of Bannantyne of Corehouse, he was originally taken on as governor for the Earl of Arran, but he later extended his duties to include the younger sons. He married Margaret Hamilton, one of the Duchess's servants, and in the late 1670s they left the Palace to settle in Glasgow.

The four professional men were all selected for their positions because of their educational achievements, but other members of the household were qualified by birth rather than by training. These were the Duke's gentlemen, the Duchess's ladies and the pages who served both the Duke and Duchess.

The gentlemen were usually well born people from good local families, and they helped the Duke in a number of ways, looking after his private expenditure, supervising his wardrobe and accompanying him on his travels around the country. Some of the gentlemen had been servants in the Palace long before the Duke ever came there. Robert Kennedy was one of these. He had originally been the servant of the Duchess's uncle. He accompanied him into exile, returned to Scotland with him, fought beside him at Worcester and was present at his death. Somehow he managed to return to Hamilton afterwards, and entered the Duchess's service. He married Rebecca Kimbold, one of the ladies brought to Scotland by the Duchess when she was a girl. He remained loyal to the Duchess throughout the Cromwellian occupation, and in 1658 it is recorded that he was owed his wages for the previous six and a half years. When the Duchess married, he became officially one of her husband's gentlemen, at a salary of £120 a year.

Eventually, when he was old enough to retire from his post, the Duchess made him her under-keeper of the palace of Holyroodhouse. After that, he had permanent apartments at Holyrood. His first wife had died by then, and in 1675 he married for a second time. His choice of a second wife is interesting because it both indicates his social status and reveals something of the web of intermarriage which connected so many families. His new wife was Rachel Wilbraham, the widow of John Dalmahoy. Dalmahoy's father and uncle had both been gentlemen of the second Duke of Hamilton, and when the Duke died after the battle of Worcester, his widow married Thomas Dalmahoy, her late husband's gentleman. Robert Kennedy was therefore taking as his second wife a woman of some social standing, whom he had probably known for many years as a result of their mutual connection with the Hamilton family. He lived on into the 1680s, but he was probably dead by 1689 when Rachel is recorded as being in London, but no mention is made of Robert Kennedy.

Like the gentlemen, the pages were selected because of their birth, for the medieval notion of taking a promising young gentleman and bringing him up in a noble household still lingered on. Both the Duke and Duchess had their pages, and for several generations members of the Porterfield family served them in this capacity. They were a younger branch of the Porterfields of that Ilk, a well known western family connected with various branches of the Hamiltons. The Duchess's page John Porterfield married Mary Gray, one of her servants, and a Bethia Porterfield who also served in the Palace was probably a sister. John served as the Duchess's page for many years, despite the Duke's criticism that 'no woman here [in London] has so old or big a one'. Both he and his wife died fairly young, leaving a family of three children, Anna, James and John. All three were then brought up by the Duchess in her household, and all three eventually became servants there, John following in his father's footsteps as the Duchess's page.

The pages and the gentlemen might be termed personal servants, and within this category may also be included the Duke's valets-de-chambre. It had become the fashion for young gentlemen returning from the Grand Tour to bring back with them a French valet, and the Duke hastened to employ a valet as everyone else did. The valet looked after his clothes, shaved him, combed out his wigs and bought small toilet articles for him. On one occasion the Duke even secured the services of a French Huguenot refugee who had been a surgeon in his own country. Gaspard Chambon no doubt gave him medical advice as well as carrying out his more normal duties before he finally left to practise medicine in Glasgow.

Not all the Duke's valets were Frenchmen. One of his first, Pierre Lacoste, had been succeeded by Thomas Laing, obviously a Scot, and he in his turn had been replaced by Charles Balfour. Charles remained with the Duke longer than any of the others, and his services were much appreciated, but on 6 July 1686 he and one of the other servants were drowned when they went swimming in the Clyde.

The personal servants and the professional servants in the Palace formed a separate and identifiable group of their own, a group which was socially superior to the other principal servants. The actual running of the household was carried on by a host of lesser men and women with varying degrees of responsibility. In charge of all the catering and the domestic running of the establishment was the servant known variously as the master household, the provisor, the steward or the caterer – all four terms seem to have been used interchangeably at Hamilton. The master household was responsible for all the food which came into the household, both those provisions which were bought in and those which came in the form of rents. He kept account books of the provisions used, and he was directly responsible to the Duchess for this side of the household expenditure. He was also in charge of all the utensils, the carriage of household goods and luggage between Hamilton and Edinburgh, and the expenses of the lesser servants for clothing and travelling. The Duchess in her turn placed a good deal of reliance on him. In 1686, for instance, she told her daughter Katherine that she had taken on James Tweedie to be her master household for a second time. 'I had rather have had a sharp young man to have bred [trained] than him who I found was not honest', she declared, adding 'I know not if he will do better, but we mean to trust him less; but that place must have trust whether one will or not, and more, of such an ill housewife than I am.'[7]

When the provisions had been collected in and noted down, they were passed on to the master cook. James Greenlees presided over the Palace kitchens for more than forty years. He had two undercooks in his charge, one of whom was his son James, several kitchen boys and a number of pantry boys. The master baker was likewise in full charge of the bakehouse, and the brewer of the brewhouse. The ale and wine were kept by the butler, whose sole function at this period was to supervise the cellars. Not every household had a separate butler, and although the Marquis of Tweeddale and Sir William Bruce had their own butlers,[8] in many households the master household and the brewer saw to the wine cellars along with their other duties.

The indoor staff was completed by a small number of female servants. Chief among these were the Duchess's ladies, the equivalent of her husband's gentlemen. The ladies are usually distinguished in the household lists by the prefix 'mistress', an indication of social rather than of marital status: the mysterious 'Mrs Noah' who features in the lists was actually the Duchess's lady Miss Anne Naw. Originally the ladies were the three who had come with her from England in 1646, but gradually they married, had families and left her service. Their successors were often already the wives of Hamilton servants or, like Margaret Hamilton, married colleagues later.

One of the ladies, Mrs Mary Darlo, was placed in charge of the nurseries. Various permanent women helped her, for each of the new babies had first of all a wet nurse, then an ordinary nurse and finally one woman who was in charge of two or three of the children. Apart from that, the other women on the Palace staff consisted of one chambermaid, the washerwoman, the dairymaid and the 'henwife' or poultrywoman, and that was all. The Duchess was making a radical alteration in her household arrangements when, towards the end of her life, she appointed a female housekeeper.

The preponderance of male staff in any household was explained by the large number of men employed out of doors. Many of these were required in the stables. In charge was the master of the horse, who supervised one and later two coachmen, two postillions, several grooms, three or four footmen and a number of stable boys. The coachmen were well-paid servants, often English, and there was a fairly rapid turnover within their ranks. Grooms were more often Scottish, but one of the best known figures in the Palace stables was the English groom Valentine Beldam. Born in the south in September 1619, he was the son of John and Rebecca Beldam, who may have been of Huguenot stock. He entered the service of the Duchess's father as a young man, came to Scotland with him and married Bessie Cole, a Hamilton girl. In the winter of 1648 his wife was taken seriously ill and she made her Testament, an interesting document which reveals something of their way of life.

Bessie could not write, but one of the burgh lawyers drew up the document for her. She made her husband her sole executor, stipulating that he was to receive most of her belongings, but she also made special bequests to her own brothers and sisters. One brother, John, was to have her 'muckle [large] brass pot', a brass candlestick and a tin stoup. Her other brother, Robert, was to have some of her kitchen equipment – 'an iron chimney with raxes thereof and spit, a pair [of] iron tongs and cruiks, a meat aumbry with long settle thereof joined thereto' and to her three sisters she left a selection of clothing and furniture. Margaret was to be given the big meal chest, a little clothes chest, a bed with bedding and several waistcoats, Isabel was to have the black stuff gown, some other clothing and an oak chest, and Marie received her best gown, the best pair of plaids, two pans and a lint wheel.

Bessie died shortly afterwards, apparently leaving no children, and when the 1st Duke was executed Valentine was among various servants who were dismissed. In spite of this, it was not long before he was back in the Palace and on 12 May 1655 he signed a marriage contract with Sara Watkins, the Duchess's English servant. Marriage contracts of servants are not often extant, and so this one is particularly valuable. It is a simple document, whereby the two parties promise to marry, and it is mainly taken up with the financial provisions. Valentine was to settle on his wife a jointure of 3000 merks Scots, and she would bring him a dowry of 1000 merks. The contract was witnessed by two of the other servants, John Touch and James Cruiks. Valentine could scarcely write, but he managed a signature at the foot of the page, and Sara signed her name neatly below his.

By this time Valentine was prosperous enough to own a house and land in the Nethertoun of Hamilton. He was made a burgess of Glasgow in 1657 and of Ayr in 1664, and he lived for six or seven years after that. When he died, still a groom at the Palace, he left all his property to his wife. Sara survived him for some years, occupying the Nethertoun house with her niece Mary Watkins, and when she died in the winter of 1673 Mary sold off her goods – a bed and bedding, pewter plates, earthenware dishes, a frying pan, candlesticks, chairs, chests and a spit – and Valentine's brother William came up from Royston in Cambridgeshire to sell the land and the houses to the Duchess. All in all, one may conclude that although a groom was not necessarily an educated man in a prominent social position, he could nevertheless be well enough off to own property, live in a comfortably furnished house and take the trouble to have a lawyer draw up his more important documents.

Apart from the stables, there were the gardens and the orchards to be looked after, and for many years Hew Wood was the head gardener at Hamilton, with six men working for him. He was responsible for all the work done there, for the buying of seeds and for the upkeep of the fruit houses, the glass frames and all the implements. He played a leading part in the maintenance of the Palace grounds, but he was also a significant figure for quite another reason. He was a substantial member of the Quaker community of the west, and he provides an interesting link between the Duchess of Hamilton and the Society of Friends. Quakerism had come to Scotland during the Cromwellian period, but ever since then it had been condemned by both Church and Parliament. Quakers along with Roman Catholics were regarded as being dangerous enemies of both Church and state, and the Privy Council of Scotland took vigorous action against them.[9] They had to endure a good deal of persecution, particularly at the hands of the Covenanters, yet in spite of her Covenanting sympathies, and in contradiction to the belief of later historians that Quakers were 'unprotected by families of distinction',[10] the Duchess employed Hew at Hamilton for more than twenty-five years.

He had entered her service some time before the Restoration, and he remained with her throughout all the religious troubles of the following decades. Nor was it simply that he kept his religious beliefs secret. Quite the opposite was true. In the accounts he sent in to the Duke and Duchess he always employed the Quaker phraseology of 'thee' and 'thou' and their individual method of dating the months of the year. He held numerous Quaker meetings quite openly in his house in Hamilton, but even the Duchess's protection could not spare him the consequences of the popular prejudice against the Friends. On several occasions he and his family were threatened and assaulted, and in 1688 a meeting in his house was broken up by armed men. Four years later, there was an even more unpleasant incident when some of the local people set on him as he was walking through the town with a few companions. He was abused and knocked about, 'which was the more inhuman, he being an ancient man and had not said anything to provoke them unless to persuade them to moderation.'[11]

These were fairly isolated incidents, though, and on the whole he was left in peace to pursue his duties at the Palace. He remained in charge of the grounds there until his death on 25 March 1701, when he was buried in his own garden. His two surviving sons were both Quakers and they were both gardeners. The elder, James, began his career at Stonehill and married the daughter of a Quaker gardener in Kelso, before moving on to serve the Duke of Queensberry at Drumlanrig. The younger son, Alexander, succeeded his father as gardener at Hamilton Palace.[12]

Quakerism and gardening often seem to have been linked, and on 27 June 1680 a Quaker marriage had taken place in Hew Wood's house when a young friend William Miller became the husband of Margaret Cassie. The young man was soon employed as a gardener at Newark, and ten years later he had become famous throughout Scotland as 'The Patriarch', the leading figure in the Scottish Quaker movement. By that time he was employed by the Duke and Duchess of Hamilton as their gardener at Holyroodhouse. It has been suggested that he owed this position to the intervention of Hew Wood, but he may already have had a connection with the Hamilton family. The Duchess's chamberlain at Kinneil in the 1680s was a Quaker, and her gardener there was a James Miller. He may conceivably have been a father or brother of 'The Patriarch', whose own son George became gardener at Kinneil some years later. Whatever his origins, William Miller was very active in the Edinburgh Society of

Friends throughout his tenure of office at Holyrood. He became clerk of the meetings in the city, and his wife was apparently a vigorous preacher too: tradition has it that during the persecution of the 1690s 'Margaret Miller preached in the open air with her husband on one side and her son on the other as bodyguard.'[13]

The Duchess's own attitude to the Quakers in her employ is not expressed anywhere, but her general feeling was that any good, honest man, sincere in his beliefs and upright in his way of life, should be respected regardless of what form of religion he practised. There was no such problem with the other outside workers in the Palace grounds. Robert Darlo saw to the purely agricultural work of the estate, and the sheep and livestock were under the care of the warrender, Abraham Holywell. As his title suggests, his original function had been to look after the rabbits which abounded in 'the Wham', a large meadow to the south east of the Palace, rabbits being a valuable source of food supply. The sheep were also grazed in the Wham, and so they too came under his care. Finally, there was always a keeper of the Parks, whose task it was to see to the deer.

These men were all performing functions easily recognisable today, but there was also a group of servants who have no modern equivalent. From as early as 1546 the Hamiltons employed a trumpeter for ceremonial occasions, as did other seventeenth-century peers.[14] The Duchess's grandmother had in her household a musician named John Gray, who played the lute and who may have been responsible for teaching her daughters to play the virginals. On special occasions, such as marriages or Parliaments, the Duke and Duchess hired violers, and for some years they employed a resident harper, Jago McFlahertie. He seems to have been in charge of the other musical instruments too, for in 1682 he was sent to Edinburgh to buy strings for the virginals. There was also a permanent piper at Brodick Castle.

It is interesting to note in passing that although several Scottish peers – notably the Earls of Annandale – continued the ancient practice of keeping a fool, the Hamiltons did not do so. Probably such an addition to the household was frowned upon by the more puritanical noblemen, and indeed one can hardly imagine either the Duke or the Duchess having any time for an

73

extravagance of this sort. The Duke was not averse to other forms of entertainment, however, and he regularly employed falconers, fowlers and huntsmen.

The foregoing procession of servants – David Crawford, Robert Kennedy, John Porterfield and the others – suggests that the staff of any household was far from being a nebulous group of underprivileged men whose lives barely impinged on those of their employers. It has often been supposed that the servants formed a depressed and exploited sector of society, living a spartan existence, barefoot, poorly clad and subsisting on a diet of oatmeal, their high rate of mobility being attributed to poor conditions which forced them to make constant changes of employment in an attempt to find better conditions.[15] If this description fitted any household in Scotland, it did not apply at Hamilton.

The wage structure at the Palace reveals that the servants there were well paid. David Crawford with £530 Scots a year was the most highly paid servant there, the other professional men had £200 a year, and the personal servants had £120. The master household had £120, and the butler and the cook had between £60 and £90, as did the falconers and the fowlers. At the bottom of the scale, the footmen and the lower women servants earned £24 or so each. By comparison, the Earl of Crawford paid his staff none too well. His gentlemen had only £48 a year, his master household £30 and his cook a mere £20.[16] Lord Yester's gentlemen were allowed £36 and his postillions £24, while his father the Marquis of Tweeddale must have had a very good cook indeed since he paid him a handsome £180.[17] Lady Grisell Baillie and the Earl of Panmure paid their servants fairly average wages, and most generous of all was the Duchess of Buccleuch, whose postillions were given £72 a year as were her footmen.[18]

One can conclude from these figures that the Hamilton servants had little cause for complaint as far as wages were concerned. It is noticeable, of course, that their wages remained very much fixed throughout the period. From 1659 until 1710 the gentlewomen received £120 a year, and during all the years of his long service James Greenlees the cook had £66:13:4 annually. When wages did change, it was usually because someone had left and his successor was either better or less well qualified, so that his salary varied accordingly. When the reliable gardener Alexander Wood died, his relatively inexperienced successor received £60 less for himself and his men, and when Anthony Murray succeeded John Peacock as butler, he found he was receiving £15 less than his predecessor. Only occasionally was a real increase paid, as when Patrick Young the postillion had his fee increased from £33 to £48 in 1708. Otherwise wages were static, which was reasonable enough in a century when the value of money remained constant.

The above payments were all made in money, and were fixed when each servant was hired, but there were additional sums to be obtained in the form of drink money. Whenever any guest stayed overnight at the Palace, he was expected to leave a tip for certain servants on his departure. This money was collected by the master household, and was divided up at the end of a variable period under the supervision of the Duchess. The master household kept for himself the largest sum, about thirty pounds over a period of eighteen months. The cook and his undercooks collected sums ranging from £10 to £14 for the same period, and even the cookboys were not forgotten. They could expect £5 each, which was a very handsome sum for them. The butler, the baker and their helpers were given from £10 to £15, nor were the women of the household omitted. The housemaid and the dairymaid could count on £12 or so, and washers were paid roughly the same as the cookboys. These sums were valuable additions to their annual wages, and although the drink money was paid irregularly the recipients could always be sure that no one would be forgotten: when the Duchess's eldest son visited the Palace in adult life and gave money to all the usual servants except the under-butler, the latter was given an extra payment in compensation.

The drink money was always paid in actual cash, but as well as that, certain of the outside servants were given quantities of meal. The gardener regularly had thirty or forty bolls* of victual for himself and his men, the keeper of the Great Park had eight bolls each year, and the carters and porters received quantities of meal.

* One boll of meal represented 140 lbs.

Then the pages, the footmen and the servants in the stables received their livery, or an allowance for clothing agreed upon when they first entered the Duchess's service. On 1 April 1669, for instance, 'Henry Glen was hired . . . and is to be His Grace's fowler, to go with the setting dog and gun, and he is to have yearly £24 Scots and a suit of clothes'. Nine months later 'Finlay Robertson was hired to be footman to His Grace my Lord Duke of Hamilton. He is to serve as a footman and observe all things that are requisite to one in his station, and also when he is not employed in running he is to attend the stables and horses. He is to have £24 sterling *per annum* with his livery, shoes and stockings . . .'. The Duke was always concerned with the effect he made in public, and he liked to travel the country with an impressive entourage. He accordingly expected his servants to be well turned out. The coachman, postillions, footmen, grooms and pages had smart red livery trimmed with lace, the postillions wearing leather capes faced with red over their red suits.

Not only did the Duke provide liveries for his outdoor servants. He equipped his secretary, cooks and butlers with their everyday suits of clothes. These were not the handed-down clothes which were the rule in some households: the Earl of Forfar's servants were usually clad in clothes originally the Earl's own, but this was one economy which the Duke did not practise. On the contrary, the tailor who made the garments for the Duke's own family also supplied the clothing for the staff, and in the accounts he sent in, gowns for the Duchess and petticoats for her daughters appear alongside new suits for James Greenlees and John Porterfield. The servants all received complete new outfits several times a year, not merely the occasional coat or cap. One July, Alexander Frizel the footman was fitted out with drawers, running breeches and serge breeches, and this was a perfectly normal occurrence. In the same way, the Duke's own shoemaker supplied the servants with boots and shoes.

Many of the household staff were also provided with accommodation. Some actually owned property in the burgh, and others rented houses from the Duke and Duchess. The master cook, the keeper, the warrender and the washer did this, and the Duchess always paid for any repairs which were needed – when the roof required new thatch, the windows new glass and so on. Sometimes the Duke would arrange to board out those servants who had recently arrived at the Palace. In 1664 he was paying for his French cook's lodgings in Michael Nasmith's house in town, and a few years later he leased from John Lang a house to be occupied by his trumpeter.

Other servants were accommodated in the Palace itself, mainly on the first floor. There is little indication of how their rooms were furnished, except for a mention of a payment to the local tailor to make 'two feather beds [i.e. mattresses] and a bolster to the servants.' Normally servants' quarters were furnished with a bedstead, some tables and chairs, and perhaps a chest or two. This they supplemented with their own belongings, just as anyone living in furnished lodgings would do today.

Those servants who lived in, and indeed some of those who did not, ate together downstairs in the Lattermeat Hall. A note made by David Crawford in the spring of 1703 records that at that time a group of twenty-six servants were eating in the Palace, including the chaplain, the gentlewomen and pages, the butler, the kitchen staff and the gardener, and twenty years before, when the household was much larger, the Lattermeat Hall must have been even more crowded. The tables there were decently laid out with a linen cloth and wooden trenchers, from which the servants ate with horn spoons. Recording the arrangements for eating in the household, the master household once noted that 'The inferior servants use to get sometimes a sheep or a veal head, or a lamb's head and pluck to each of them. The ordinary allowance of the servants who did not sit at the second table was a quarter of mutton among 4 of them, and a quarter of lamb betwixt two when little, and when the aforesaid quarters of mutton, lamb or veal happened to fall out larger, they were proportionally divided amongst more. The inferior servants who received their meat separately, such as William Neilson, Christian Watson and the kitchen boys, were serv'd with the coarsest of the meat such as might be boiled in broth or fragments of the second table.' The meat was supplemented with eggs, oatmeal and herrings, and each person was given one pint of ale a day. The principal servants were allowed to have extra ale sent up to their rooms or served at table. If the diet was monotonous, at least it was sustaining.

As well as ordering the physical requirements of the servants, the Duke and Duchess saw to their education and to their spiritual welfare. Pages were educated along with their own children, and many of the other servants had attended the local school and could read and write. The Duchess paid for medical treatment when any of the staff fell ill, and she often contributed to the cost of the expenses when her servants married. (Indeed, the Scottish nobility in the seventeenth century frequently attended the weddings of their servants and the baptisms of the children.) When the servants retired they were supported as Hamilton pensioners, and when they died their funerals were financed by the Duke, any arrears of wages being punctiliously paid to the surviving relatives. The funeral account for Charles Balfour the young valet and his colleague John Murdoch still survives, recording that the Duke paid 'To the men that carried down the boat and helped them forth of the water £2:16/–; for their 2 coffins to Arthur Nasmith, wright, £18; to the grave makers £2:16/–; for the mortcloths £8:8/–; to the bellman of the tolbooth steeple 7/–; to the poor of the hospital £1:7/–; to the rest of the poor £1:8/–; an account of linen to Elizabeth Hamilton and for ribbons and pins £15:1/–'.

Of course, relations between the Hamiltons and their household staff were not idyllic, and on the part of the Duke there were the usual complaints about the servant problem. As well as condemning David Crawford and his divided interests, the Duke in 1693 declared of his caterer, 'Lamb is but a useless servant to me here, as he was on the road up [to London]', and he later went so far as to tell the Duchess 'John Lamb's a beast and Harkness [the footman] I have turned away.' The Duchess had her problems too, and she replied to the Duke's complaints by retailing her own worries about the butler, who had made off with fifty dozen bottles of wine.

For their part, the servants had definite ideas about what they should be asked to do, and about the wages they should receive. With members of the nobility all keeping up large households, there was plenty of opportunity to move around if existing employment was unsuitable. John Bailie, whose 'chief talent lies in baking', was willing to work for five pounds, 'which is the least wages he will take', and John Spens, who was the Duchess's personal servant at one time, had definite ideas of his own. When she offered to send him to help her daughter Katherine after the latter had married, she warned her, 'John desires not to be put to set meat on the table, which he says will take him much from his writing and other business. When your father was Commissioner [to Parliament] he was then with your brother Arran and would not do it though he should have been turned away on that account, which [I] think was an unreasonable humour which is still in his head. I [think] fit to let you know this so that you might rather not put him to it than that he should refuse it or do it grumbling: otherwise I believe he will serve you both diligently and humbly.'

The Duchess obviously found it politic to humour her servants to a certain extent, and they were not slow to voice their opinions of anything which did not please them. All this, however, was outweighed by the genuine good feeling which existed between the Hamiltons and most of their household. The Duke's sorrow when Charles Balfour died had been entirely genuine, and in the summer of 1698 the Duchess was reported to be very upset because news had reached her in Edinburgh that one of her grooms had just been drowned while swimming in the Clyde with some of the other servants: although an excellent swimmer, he had become entangled in the weeds and rushes.

There may, in fact, have been a particular bond between the Duchess and some of her staff as a result of the privations they had suffered together during the 1650s. Whatever the reason, although many of the staff came and went within a relatively short period, there was a permanent nucleus of longstanding servants. Some were men who spent their entire adult lives in the Palace. James Greenlees the master cook was there for over forty years and his son stayed for at least twenty. John Mitchell the groom came before 1661 and he was still there when he died in the spring of 1702. Abraham Holywell the warrender, John Peacock the butler and William Fleming the footman each stayed for more than thirty years and George Simpson and Gilbert Leith the falconers were there for almost as long. Of course, not all the servants were as settled or as devoted, but many of the names recur again and again in the household lists and at least a fifth of all the servants ever employed by the Duchess remained with her for more than ten years.

Those who left did so for a number of reasons. A tenth of the servants are known to have died in the Palace, and in that age of high mortality this number should probably be higher. Women servants left when they married, although many of them continued their work in between having their children. Men departed to other positions. Alexander Sutherland 'went home to be cook to my Lord Strathallan', Nicol Neilson the cookboy found employment with Lord Murray, John Malcolm became footman to Lord Belhaven and William Alexander went to serve Lord Ross. Others left domestic service altogether. Andrew Tofts, the master household, became steward of the college of Glasgow, no doubt through the Duke's good offices, Patrick Fleming the underbutler 'took on to be a soldier', and William Murdoch the baker settled down to be one of the bakers in the burgh of Hamilton.

In general, it would seem that there was the highest turnover among coachmen and butlers, and it can have been no coincidence that these positions were frequently occupied by Englishmen who presumably decided that they preferred the south. There were French servants in the Palace, and there was one of the fashionable Negro footmen, known to his colleagues as John Timothy the Black, but the English and foreign servants were in the minority. Most of the household staff came from local families, and not unexpectedly a proportion of them bore the surname of Hamilton. However, the long established custom of a peer being surrounded by retainers who bore his name or who had adopted it seems to have been declining throughout the seventeenth century. In 1629 when the Earl of Wigtown's son was made a burgess of Glasgow four of the Earl's servants bearing the same surname received the same honour. In 1642 two of the Earl of Findlater's servants named Ogilvie, like himself, became burgesses, and in 1645 the Marquis of Argyll had at least three Campbells with him on a similar occasion, but

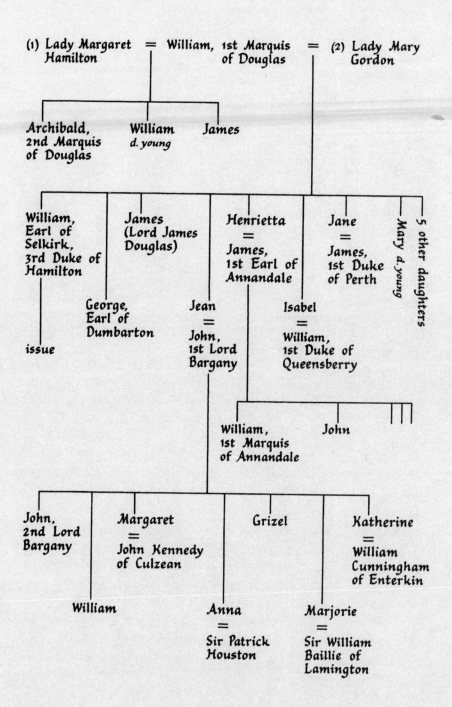

after that those servants on the burgess roll rarely shared their master's name.[19]

As evidence, this is very incomplete, but there are other indications of this movement away from employing servants linked by the bond of kinship. A list of those at Panmure in 1678/9 does not include one Maule, the Earl of Crawford did not have a single Lindsay in his Edinburgh house when the poll tax returns were made, nor were there any Hays in the Marquis of Tweeddale's town house in 1682.[20] Similarly, at Hamilton, although out of a random thirty servants of the Duchess's grandmother seven had the surname Hamilton, in the Duchess's own time only eighteen out of three hundred and ten did so. The majority of those did hold responsible positions, though: two were master households, two were head porters and three had been taken on as pages. The tendency to keep fewer servants of the family name but to employ them in positions of trust is reflected in other households too: Lord Elphinstone in 1654 had as master household an Elphinstone, one of the Duke of Queensberry's gentlemen in 1691 was a Douglas and in 1709 the Duchess of Argyll's secretary was a Campbell.[21]

The number of Hamiltons employed in the Palace may have decreased over the years, but the number of servants drawn from local families did not. The burgh of Hamilton was, after all, just over the Palace wall, and families like the Jacks, the Lambies, the Golders and the Barrs who had been living in the town for generations had a long tradition of service in the Palace itself. Incoming servants from elsewhere married local girls and made their homes in Hamilton, old servants retired and settled there, and it is noticeable how many of the townspeople and the servants named their daughters after Duchess Anne. One may speculate that this was not merely an attempt to gain favour but a token of the real goodwill which existed between the Duchess and her employees.

Perhaps all this is best epitomised in the career of Janet Dobie, the Palace washerwoman. Janet entered the 1st Duke's service in the 1640s, married a fellow-servant James Paterson, and lived with him in a house in the burgh. They had two sons and two daughters, the elder of whom was named Anne. James Paterson died in 1659, leaving his best cauldron and a black cow to Anne, his black horse to his elder son, his other cauldron to his daughter Margaret and all his other belongings to his wife. Janet continued as a washer at the Palace until at least 1664, during which time the Duchess paid for the thatching and other repairs to her house. When she retired, she was paid a substantial pension, and when she eventually died, the Duchess paid for her funeral. Her career was unexceptional, but her way of life was typical of that of the servants in Hamilton Palace.

CHAPTER 4

Clothing and Food

Along with her Palace, her gardens and her estates, Duchess
Anne had inherited a certain way of life. Her inheritance had
brought with it many obligations, not the least of these being the
duty to live in a manner which befitted the representative of a
great noble family. The Dukes of Hamilton had always lived at
the centre of a large household, with magnificence and ostentation,
and it was important that they maintain this tradition. A
peer spent much of his time in the public gaze and he was a
member of a highly competitive group. His fellow peers were
ever watchful and critical. A certain shabbiness of dress, a hint
of economy in housekeeping, and they would immediately draw
their own conclusions. Clothing is not only a means of keeping
warm, food is not simply a source of energy, and if these are self-
evident truths to the status-conscious twenty-first century they were
equally relevant in the seventeenth, all the more so for a member
of the aristocracy. A nobleman was expected to dress in luxurious
garments and to eat lavish meals so that both his rivals and his
subordinates would interpret correctly these symbols of his
wealth and power.

These considerations were important to the Duke of Hamilton
not merely because he was the representative of an ancient family
and therefore anxious to maintain their existing status. He was
an ambitious man who had no intention of living in retirement on
his estates in the reflected glory of his predecessors. He wanted
political power, and he was soon leading the opposition in
Scotland to the Duke of Lauderdale. With the Restoration,
Scotland once more had her own parliament, privy council, law
courts, customs and administrative machinery, just as any

independent country did. Her King was in London, however, and he ruled his northern subjects largely through his secretary of state, the Duke of Lauderdale.

Before long, Lauderdale made himself highly unpopular. There were, for example, his repressive measures against the Covenanters. Various Scottish ministers could not accept the ecclesiastical settlement of 1660 because, in their opinion, it was not Presbyterian enough. As a result, they were deprived, and the Covenanters who supported them held open air services or conventicles in defiance of the government. Troops were often used to break up these services, and the Covenanters rose in rebellion in 1666, when they were defeated at Rullion Green, and in 1679 when they were crushed at Bothwell Brig. Various Presbyterian noblemen shared the Covenanters' detestation of Lauderdale as a result.

Lauderdale also encountered the usual jealousy from his fellow peers who were excluded from office but felt that they were the King's traditional advisers, and then again Lauderdale's administration was notoriously corrupt. The outcome was that by 1672 his opponents were asking the Duke of Hamilton to lead a parliamentary opposition against the favourite and his policies. The Duke did so, and was for many years out of office as a result, but when Lauderdale at last fell, preferment came his way. He became a Knight of the Garter in place of his old enemy, sat on the English as well as the Scottish Privy Council and was made a Commissioner of the Scottish Treasury and an Extraordinary Lord of Session. At one time Scottish noblemen had governed the country for the King simply because they were noblemen, the monarch's traditional advisers. This system remained unchanged throughout the seventeenth century in so far as a Duke of Hamilton was appointed to high office because he was Duke of Hamilton, but since the union of the crowns in 1603 the situation had become more complicated and it was not merely a case of powerful noble families struggling directly against one another for political influence. Now the magnates had to vie with each other for the favour of the English Court, and so they had lost something of their former automatic prestige. The very name 'Duke of Hamilton' or 'Marquis of Atholl' immediately conveyed to the Scottish listener the traditional status and the territorial grandeur of the peer in question, but it could mean very little to one of the King's English advisers at Whitehall. The Scottish nobility had therefore to strive all the harder to outdo their rivals in new ways, and there was an altogether greater preoccupation with the symbols of wealth and power, with the need to keep up appearances. They now spent a good deal of energy underlining their own prestige by the magnificence of their way of life, and if financial considerations prevented them from living in quite the style of their southern counterparts, they nevertheless adopted English fashions wherever they could afford to do so.

The trouble was, of course, that there was by this time an additional complication. Those noblemen who were of the Presbyterian persuasion found themselves in something of a dilemma. Their consciences might prompt them to shun worldly pomp and vanity but as members of the aristocracy they could not afford to live in an austere manner. There was, for instance, the problem of how to dress. At first there had been no difficulty. The Duchess's grandmother, Covenanter that she was, continued throughout her life to appear in public splendidly clad and glistening with jewels, and in this she was no different from her contemporaries.[1] As time went on, though, the supporters of the Covenanting movement felt an obligation to express a desire for a more puritanical style of dress, while those who sympathised with Charles II's Episcopalian policies favoured the lavish fashions popular at Court.

Now there was no doubt where the Hamiltons' religious sympathies lay. As the years went by, the Duchess became known as a leading supporter of Presbyterianism, and although she always refused to play any direct part in politics, leaders of both church and state consulted her and valued her opinion, especially where ecclesiastical matters were concerned. Her convictions were well known, and after the Battle of Bothwell Brig the defeated Covenanters sought refuge in the grounds of Hamilton Palace. They did not hope in vain for the Duchess's protection, for she sent a message to Monmouth, who was in command of the victorious army, asking him not to enter her parks, 'lest he disturb the game.'[2] He complied, and many lives were spared. As for the Duke of Hamilton, his previous Catholicism was so much forgotten that it has been overlooked by historians ever since. In his opposition to Lauderdale he was representing the Presbyterian interest, and if his own policies were not without self-interest, he was nevertheless regarded as being a leader of the Presbyterian party. The Duke and Duchess both had to attempt to reconcile the need to dress ostentatiously with their commitment to a religion which frowned on outward show.

The Duke made up his mind early on. Status was all-important, and other considerations would have to be ignored. At first, he had most of his clothes made in Edinburgh – the long coats, the breeches, the waistcoats and the cloaks – and when he was on the point of marrying the Duchess in the spring of 1656 he equipped himself with a series of new outfits. His purchases from John Cockburn the tailor are not detailed in the surviving accounts, but they totalled £237 Scots. William Carmichael made for him dogskin gloves for hawking, white kid gloves and purple gloves, and he bought black Spanish leather shoes and an expensive pair of strong, waxed boots from James Turnbull. A fine beaver hat cost him no less than £60 Scots, and James Brown the hatter charged a further £202:16/– 'for setting your lordship's hat with silver and gold edging about the hat and gold button and looping.'

He continued to patronise James Brown throughout the 1660s and '70s, by which time his regular Edinburgh tailor was William Douglas. Douglas made a variety of outer garments for him, all of which were fairly serviceable: there were striped stuff coats and breeches trimmed with silver looping, grey stuff suits and cloth waistcoats. As time went on, however, he began increasingly to have his clothes made in London. He was going south much more often towards the end of the 1670s, and it was imperative that he should appear there in luxurious garments of the latest fashion. To come to Court in anything less splendid would give a great deal of satisfaction to his enemies, and it might well be construed as an insult to the King. In 1689, when he attended a great ball to celebrate William of Orange's birthday, he was therefore careful to wear 'a new suit with gold buttons and brocade waistcoat to compliment his majesty with.'

Clothing of the kind worn at Court was highly expensive, so

elaborate were the materials used. Early on, the Duke bought 'a
fine large long buff coat with silver and gold looplace and silver
tags with silver loops' and a 'rich vest [waistcoat] of striped stuff
with silver and gold, laced with a silver and gold lace.' A fine
cinnamon coloured coat and breeches bought in 1685 had seven
dozen gold and black buttons as well as six dozen breast buttons,
and they were sewn all over with gold and black loops. Even a
sombre dark suit could look magnificent when it had a rich gold
and silver brocade vest, gold vellum buttons, gold shoulder loops
and was worn under a purple cloak lined with scarlet.

Black velvet suits, gold brocade waistcoats, purple cloaks and
Indian gowns – the Duke of Hamilton possessed all the garments
necessary for a nobleman of his day, and he certainly spent a
good deal of money on clothing. His London tailor charged
between £10 and £20 sterling on average for making a suit, but
this price is exclusive of the materials used: it includes only the
cost of the tailor's work, the thread, and some of the trimming.
The actual cloth was bought by the Duke himself from a merchant
before ever he went to the tailor: Nathaniel Cooper and Partners
in 1693 supplied him with four and a half yards of rich, sad
coloured and gold brocade at £10:12:6 sterling, sixteen and a
half yards of richest crimson velvet at £21:9/– and six yards of
fine ratteen at £6.

Of course, the Duke was far from being an extravagant man,
and he did economise to a certain extent where his clothes were
concerned. On one occasion he instructed his son Charles to buy
a cloak for him in London, but he warned him that the finished
garment must be 'for winter as well as summer, but I will have
no velvet coat as Mr Marshall [the tailor] advises now summer's
coming on, so let it be of fine cloth my clothes is to be of.'[3]
Occasionally he had garments altered, though he does not seem
to have done this as often as many of his contemporaries did:
some had garments remade practically every season to keep up
with the latest fashion. Once he had worn his new clothes at
Court, he had them packed up and sent home to Scotland, where
he could dazzle the people of Edinburgh with his finery. In 1693
a large 'hair trunk in the dark closet at Edinburgh' contained a
variety of garments including 'a fine scarlet embroidered coat

with gold, with a gold stuff waistcoat fringed with gold, a fine scarlet cloak embroidered with gold and lin'd with blue velvet' and 'a gold stuff nightgown [i.e. dressing-gown] quilted'.

As well as these splendid outfits which would grace any formal event, the Duke required a series of garments for specific occasions. He always needed sets of mourning clothes, for this was an era when deep mourning was worn for quite remote relatives. Then, of course, there were his Garter robes, 'i.e. 1 pair of silk trousers, 1 pair of trunk breeches and doublet of silver tabby with silver lace, silver and white satin ribbon and three knots of the same ribbon and a pair of shoes: a surtout of crimson velvet lined with white taffeta with hood, sword, scabbard and belt of the same . . .'. The Duke always left these with James Marshall, the London tailor, who listed them all dutifully and promised 'the which . . . to keep as safe as my own goods by me.' In Edinburgh, it was his gown as Lord of the Session which was required, 'a rich black flowered velvet gown lin'd with black taffeta, garnished with rich gold loops and buttons and edged with a rich gold and black lace.'

Most of this clothing hung in closets in Hamilton Palace and was repaired when need be by the local tailor. He it was, too, who supplied the Duke with most of his undergarments and night clothing. He made the Duke's drawers, charging four shillings for a taffeta or linen pair and six shillings for a cotton pair. Cuffs were the same price as linen drawers, but linen waistcoats were rather more expensive at ten shillings each. The tailor sometimes made 'trews' for him too, and on one occasion he even supplied 'haffet pieces beneath his wigs', the 'haffet' being the side of the head. As for shirts and nightshirts, they were sewn up for the Duke by his wife and daughters.

Most of the Duke's hats came from Edinburgh and London, but his shoes were always made in Hamilton by James Brown. Brown was the man who supplied shoes for the entire household, family and servants alike, and he charged £2:14/– when he made an ordinary pair of shoes for the Duke, £12 for a pair of boots. He sewed up slippers at £2 a pair and he did repairs, making new heels for the Duke's shoes, and regularly waxing his great boots for him.

The Duke always took great care of his clothing, and one winter when he set off on a trip to Edinburgh he gave his daughter Katherine special instructions to look after his garments, most of which were hanging in the small room known as his closet. Not long afterwards, there was a heavy rainstorm, and to Katherine's horror she noticed from the outside that the closet window had been left open so that the rain was blowing in. Worse was to follow. Hurrying indoors, she discovered that the closet door was locked, and there was no sign of the key. A frantic search revealed nothing, and poor Katherine had hideous visions of her father's wrath when he returned home to find his expensive suits hanging in sodden rows. She could not think what to do, and finally in desperation wrote to her mother entreating her to look in Edinburgh for the missing key. Fortunately the Duchess knew all about it. She herself had deliberately brought the key to town with her for safe-keeping. She was therefore able to send it back at once to Hamilton with a soothing message to the effect that the Duke would certainly not hold his daughter responsible for any accidental damage. All ended happily when Katherine opened the closet and found everything in order.

The Duke's care of his garments arose not solely from concern for economy, for he was always fastidious about his appearance. His expenditure regularly included soap and sponges, 'an instrument for cleaning the teeth', and boxes of powder. He used almond hand powder, jasmine water and orange flower water, and like many other Scottish noblemen he kept a supply of the famous Queen of Hungary water, a concoction of rosemary, rosewater and spirits of wine, for use after bathing.[4]

In public, then, the Duke always presented a magnificent figure without apparently giving a second thought to any of the Presbyterian strictures on worldly vanity. The Duchess's attitude was rather different. Left to herself, she would always have worn plain, black gowns. Remembering the deaths of her beloved father and uncle, she felt that 'mourning . . . is most suitable for me', but she was perfectly well aware of considerations of status, and in the end she managed to effect a compromise between her own inclinations and the demands of public life.

For the most part, she was content to dress in locally made

gowns of sober colour and plain cut, provided they were always of 'good rich stuff'. Very often her dress material was selected in Edinburgh. The local shops in Hamilton did sell dimity, serge and lace, but they could not offer a very wide choice. Glasgow was the nearest town – in fact from the Palace grounds one could see the steeple of the High Church there – but although it was a busy port it was still a very small place. The days of trade with America had not yet arrived, and the town's great expansion lay in the future. In Edinburgh, though, there were plenty of merchants who imported through London grograms of silks from the Far East and calico and muslin from the East Indies. Whenever the Duchess was staying at Holyrood she laid in a supply of dress materials. In winter her gowns were made of serge, stuff, curl cloth and mohair, and for the summer there were silk mixtures – padasoy, prunella and tabby, as well as pure silk and satin. James Row in Edinburgh was the merchant she usually went to for material, and sometimes as she selected her black velvet and taffeta and her muslin and lace she would purchase a few of his other goods as well: 'four timber combs for the Duchess £3:12/– Scots . . . 1 fine fan for Her Grace £2:4/– . . . 1 rich sable tippet £36 . . . 1 ermine muff £21 . . .'.

Occasionally an Edinburgh tailor made up the garments, but more often the Duchess took the cloth home with her and called in John Muirhead. He was permanently employed at the Palace, where a ground floor room was set aside for him to work in. Not only did he repair the Duke's London clothes and make his underwear, he produced garments for the entire household, mended bed curtains, made cushions and provided the Duke with money bags and hawking bags.

The gowns which he made for the Duchess cost £1:10/– Scots, and unfortunately there is no indication of what style they were made in, of how long he took to produce a garment, or of what results he achieved. When the Duchess asked him to make a gown for her she gave him the material and presumably instructed him on what style she wished. Immediately after the Restoration bodices were tight, with a round neck, skirts were full and sleeves were elaborate. The Duchess wore this type of gown when she sat for her portrait to David Scougall.[5] In the following decades the line of the gown became much simpler and more natural, until by the 1680s it had become a very loose garment with no well-defined bodice and waist, and with the frilly edges of the shift underneath showing at the neckline and cuffs. This is the type of gown worn by the Duchess in her portrait by Kneller.[6]

Having received his instructions, John Muirhead then went over to Gilbert Hamilton's shop in the burgh and bought paper for making patterns, London pins, thread, buttons and trimmings. Sometimes he made up petticoats to match a particular gown. They would then be of the same silk or satin, and there were even petticoats of cloth of silver, but for everyday wear they were made up in the more mundane flannel, dimity and linen. The waistcoat was also a feminine undergarment, a type of bodice worn above the petticoat, and it was made of similar materials. With the tighter style of gown, the bodice of the dress itself was stiffened with whalebone, but when the line became looser the stays evolved as a separate garment made of buckram. The Duchess's undergarments were completed by silk and worsted stockings, provided by James Loudon the burgh dyer. These were held up by ribbon garters. (Like their English contemporaries, Scottish ladies did not wear drawers, which were at that time frowned upon as being not quite nice.)[7]

Shoes, of course, came from James Brown. Ladies' shoes had leather soles and cloth uppers, often trimmed with lace,[8] and it is generally said that ladies put goloshes on top of these when they went out of doors. The Duchess certainly had goloshes, but leading an active life as she did, she also required something more serviceable and so the accounts regularly record the making of walking shoes for her and her daughters. When she was in her seventies she was particularly delighted with a pair of black leather shoes lined with lambskin which Lady Katherine sent to her as a gift from Dunkeld, a town famous for its shoemakers.

Actually, the Duchess seems to have been more economical with her shoes than other members of the family. During a period of eighteen months from 1671–2 when her eldest son had twenty-two pairs of shoes and slippers made, her eldest daughter had fourteen new pairs and her page had seven pairs, she purchased only one pair of white shoes, one pair of black shoes, one pair of laced shoes and a pair of slippers. She also made a habit of having new heels put on her existing shoes. All her shoes, walking or indoors, cost £1:16/– a pair, and a pair of goloshes cost the same amount.

When she went out of doors, the Duchess wore a thick cloak over her gown, and very often a separate hood. Hats were not in fashion for ladies during the second half of the seventeenth century, because of the type of hairstyle worn. At first, ladies copied Queen Catherine of Braganza's mass of ringlets, and by the 1680s they were piling their hair high on their heads, leaving one or two long ringlets to hang down over their shoulders.[9] Neither style was suitable for a hat, and so a variety of velvet and gauze hoods was popular. In winter time the Duchess had muffs, fur scarves and gloves, and well on into middle age she always bought material for velvet riding skirts and coats.

For the most part, the Duchess was content to wear the gowns made for her by John Muirhead, but there were occasions which demanded something much more splendid, and then a London outfit was what was required. This presented something of a problem, for the Duchess went south but rarely. On those occasions when she did accompany the Duke to Court she took the opportunity of making a round of all the dressmakers, but such chances for personal shopping were infrequent and to a large extent she had to rely on the services of an intermediary. At first she employed Andrew Cole, a faithful servant of her father's, to make her purchases for her: he even bought her petticoats and stays, but once the Duke himself was going to London regularly she relied on him to do her shopping.

This method of purchase was not without its difficulties. With a heavy heart and bearing a note of his wife's measurements, the Duke would set off for the dressmaker's. There he was presented with a dazzling display of materials: great bales of scarlet satin, yard upon yard of purple silk, lengths of crimson mohair and emerald green wool, not to mention quantities of gold and silver lace, ribbons of every imaginable colour, rosettes, bows, flounces – and an interminable list of queries. Would the Duchess wish her gown to be made of this style or of that? Of what colour should

Anne, 3rd Duchess of Hamilton, by G. Kneller (The Hamilton Collection, Lennoxlove)

Lady Mary Feilding, 3rd Marchioness of Hamilton, Duchess Anne's mother, by A. Van Dyck (The Hamilton Collection, Lennoxlove)

James, 1st Duke of Hamilton, Duchess Anne's father, by D. Mytens (Scottish National Portrait Gallery)

William, 3rd Duke of Hamilton, Duchess Anne's husband, by G. Kneller (The Hamilton Collection, Lennoxlove)

Lady Anna Cunningham, 2nd Marchioness of Hamilton, Duchess Anne's grandmother, attributed to Adam de Colone (The Hamilton Collection, Lennoxlove)

Margaret, Countess of Panmure, Duchess Anne's fifth daughter, by J.B. de Medina (In a Private Collection)

James, Earl of Arran and 4th Duke of Hamilton, Duchess Anne's eldest son, by G. Kneller (The Hamilton Collection, Lennoxlove)

Lady Anne Spencer, the 4th Duke's wife, by G. Kneller (The Hamilton
Collection, Lennoxlove)

Charles, Earl of Selkirk, Duchess Anne's third son, by G. Kneller (The
Hamilton Collection, Lennoxlove)

'Queen Mary's Bed', one of the beds purchased by Duchess Anne's husband
in London and placed in their apartments in the Palace of Holyroodhouse
(The Royal Collection © 2000 Her Majesty Queen Elizabeth II)
(Photograph: John Freeman)

the dress be made? What type of trimming would she prefer? Should the petticoat be of a matching or of a contrasting colour? Fumbling his way through a maze of feminine terminology, the Duke knew despair. Sometimes he was not even certain what sort of garment he was ordering. There was the regrettable occasion when he asked the dressmaker to make up a 'sallantine' and the fellow did not seem to know what he meant. David Crawford did not know, the assistants did not know and the other customers did not know. He had to retire defeated to his lodgings, where further questioning of the landlady and the maids met with as little success. At last he wrote home in a rage to the Duchess, declaring that 'your "sallantine" I neither know what it is you mean by it nor can I find anybody that knows what it is, so explain yourself by the next [letter].' The Duchess replied at once, pointing out somewhat tartly that he had misread her writing. As everyone knew, the word was 'palatine', that highly fashionable accessory, a furred scarf. None too pleased, the Duke placed the desired order but he was soon embroiled in further difficulties. 'I wish you had let me know the price of the yard of the stuff you desire I should get to be a petticoat and mantle to Miss [their ward, Mary Dunbar] and what I should bestow on a palantine for her, and the price of the yard of the silk galloon and colour, and what of the beads and ribbons to wear on the head is for her and what for you.'

Sometimes the Duke was able to enlist the help of a female relative, and sometimes the Duchess tried to give him fairly explicit instructions. In 1678, for instance, she told her husband to go to Mr Renne the tailor and order for her a mantle of 'very grave colours', a black gown and a dark coloured petticoat. She emphasised most particularly that the garments must be of sober hue, and no doubt felt that she had been sufficiently specific in her requests. This time the Duke should have no trouble.

On receiving her letter, her husband duly set off for Mr Renne's, and as usual was shown a glittering selection of all kinds of cloth. He inspected material, looked at trimmings, fingered lace and made his choice. He returned home well satisfied. Unfortunately, history does not record the reaction of the Duchess when, some months later, the precious trunk arrived

93

from London. Opening it up, no doubt with a feeling of pleasurable anticipation, she lifted out the flannel bundles inside, unrolled them carefully, and was confronted with a scarlet satin petticoat trimmed with silver and gold lace, a coloured and flowered silk gown and a flowered gown trimmed with lace! She had reckoned without the Duke's personal tastes.

Despite the Duke's efforts to persuade his wife to dress in a more flamboyant manner she remained faithful to her black, white and sad coloured gowns. In this way she achieved a compromise between the promptings of conscience and the demands of society, and if the Duke did complain about the sombreness of her attire, she could always point out that her clothes were made of rich materials, and that by wearing some of her splendid jewellery she could achieve as impressive an effect as anyone else.

Middle class Puritans may have worn no jewellery,[10] but aristocratic Scottish Presbyterians never did give up their diamond necklaces and bracelets, and the Duchess had a fine collection of jewels. Many of these must have been inherited, and if she received most of those left by her mother they alone had a high value. Among the Duchess's papers is a list marked by her as being the 'things . . . in my mother's cabinet when she died, Lady Marie Feilding and Lady Marquess of Hamilton.' There then follows an inventory of all manner of jewels. There were diamond, emerald, sapphire and ruby rings as well as '1 great rose diamond ring enamel'd with blue . . . 1 diamond ring with 5 stones . . . 1 yellow table diamond in a plain gold ring . . .'. There was a diamond chain and a ruby and diamond pendant, there were diamond and ruby necklaces a sapphire cross and an emerald cross and there were bracelets of emeralds, turquoises and rubies. In addition to all this, there were several hundred loose diamonds: '80 small thick table diamonds, 94 thin diamonds, 50 thin diamonds of the biggest . . . 42 triangle diamonds . . .'. (Ladies of the period always kept a number of loose stones which they could have set as fashion dictated.[11]) The Marchioness had also owned a large number of semi-precious stones, like her eleven cornelian rings, her coral chains and the 'agate cut like a coney.' Some of these jewels were sold by the Duchess's father to pay for the building work at Chelsea, but before she came to Scotland the Duchess had already been given the emerald crucifix, a sapphire ring and twenty cornelian rings which had belonged to her mother, and it is reasonable to suppose that she may have inherited a proportion of the other jewels in the collection: the great pearl necklace and earrings she is wearing in the Kneller portrait are very similar to those worn by the Marchioness when she was painted by Van Dyck.

Pearl necklaces and earrings were *de rigeur* for ladies of the seventeenth century,[12] but the manner of setting and of wearing other jewels changed. When the Duchess's mother was a child, jewels were sewn directly on to gowns, but by the time she grew up they were no longer part of the garment: instead they were worn as clasps on the sleeves, and of course, as necklaces and bracelets. The manner of setting changed too, as jewellers began to surround a large stone with smaller ones. The Duchess quite often made alterations to the individual items in her collection in order to accord with the current fashion. As early as 1659 she sent to Conrad Etinger in Edinburgh a fine selection of jewels and gold which he made up into three emerald rings, five rings set with diamonds, mainly table-cut, a diamond 'in the heart fashion' in another ring, a ring with five sapphires and twelve diamonds and a ring encircled with diamonds and rubies. Etinger later made for the Duchess 'a hanger with twenty five diamonds' and she possessed diamond clasps, sapphire and gold lockets and a pair of diamond pendants.

Before leaving the subject of costume, there remains the question of children's clothing. The Duchess's sons and daughters spent the first weeks of their lives wrapped in swaddling bands which had cost £1:2/– Scots each, then as they grew older, they progressed to 'carrying' frocks and coats and 'going' [i.e. walking] frocks and coats. The little boys were dressed in petticoats for their first years and when he was five the Duchess's eldest son was still having petticoats made for him, although he also had linen trews. To a certain extent the local tailor provided the children's clothing, but very often the Duchess sent to Edinburgh. Henry Harper, one of the merchants there, sold her kitchen utensils from time to time, but he also specialised in garments for children and it is particularly interesting to note that although ready-to-wear clothes for adults did not come into vogue until long afterwards, by the early 1660s Henry Harper was selling a variety of children's ready-made clothes. In 1661, for instance, he sent the Duchess a bill for 'a boy's rose colour coat for 3 and 4 years old, 17/6; a boy's lemon colour coat for 3 and 4 years old 16/–; one large boy's and 2 large girls' white caps 7/–; 3 boys' white laced caps 6/–', and in the years which followed he supplied a long series of lemon, rose, sky blue and white carrying coats and going coats for boys and girls alike, white worsted stockings, and on one occasion 'a large carnation taffeta bonnet with a white feather' at eight and sixpence. This must surely be one of the earliest examples of 'mail order shopping': the Duchess's lady Mrs Inglis usually wrote to Henry Harper, specifying what was needed, and he sent out the required sizes of garment. One of his letters still exists, in which he inquires anxiously as to what Mrs Inglis meant by a 'douce coloured coat'. He imagined that she had misspelt 'dove coloured', but she was in fact using an old Scots word which in this context signified a quiet colour as opposed to anything gaudy.

It was not long before the children had discarded their baby clothes and were wearing garments which were miniature versions of their parents' clothing. When he was eleven the Earl of Arran went to Edinburgh with the family, and his father's tailor made for him a complete outfit of cloak, coat, justicoat and breeches, while John Muirhead was soon sewing up gowns for the girls along with the Duchess's own. Although she preferred sober colours for herself, she placed no such restraint on her children's clothes. Katherine, Susan and Margaret had gowns of red, blue, yellow and green, flowered gowns and laced gowns, and they had fashionable accessories too: sable muffs, 'vizor masks' for balls, painted fans and gauze hoods.

Clothing always had to be bought in. Food was very often the produce of the Hamilton estates. For the most part the provisions used in the Palace were relatively plain, although the seventeenth-century diet was not so unvaried as has sometimes been imagined. Unfortunately the letters and accounts for the period give no indication of the exact time at which meals were eaten, but they do make it clear that there were three main meals a day: breakfast, dinner and supper.

Breakfast was a fairly simple meal. Basically, milk, rolls, bread and eggs were served, along with one or two meat dishes. Needless to say, the milk and butter came from the Palace dairy, and rolls and bread had been made in the bakehouse. Each week an average of thirty dozen loaves made from oatmeal, twenty wheat loaves and two to three hundred wheaten rolls were used in the Palace. Perhaps it was at breakfast-time that the Duchess ate the marmalade of which she was so fond, marmalade of the original kind, made from quinces. As for the cooked dishes, mutton collops frequently appeared on the breakfast table, fried chicken was a favourite, and there were sometimes roast pigeons as well.

The main meal of the day was dinner, which was probably served quite late, at perhaps two or three in the afternoon. The first course almost invariably consisted of barley broth made with mutton or chicken, and with turnip, carrot, celery and onions from the garden. This was followed by a selection of meat dishes, both hot and cold. On 5 April 1693 the Duke was able to choose from salt beef, leg of veal, chicken fricassé, side of lamb and a dish of capons. On the following day the remains of the lamb were served cold, there were veal and chicken dishes, fried trout and a dish of pike and trout. Rather surprisingly, fish did not appear very frequently on the table. During the first ten weeks of 1702 it was served on only a dozen occasions, and it appeared even more infrequently during the rest of that year: haddock is mentioned once, pike once, an eel once and various unspecified 'fish dishes' on about a dozen other days. Meat remained the main part of the meal throughout the year. Veal was served almost every day, sometimes roasted, sometimes as a ragout, sometimes in a fricassé. Mutton and lamb were eaten in the spring, and the mutton was particularly versatile. It came roasted, boiled, baked and stewed, in cutlets and in collops. Beef featured less frequently, but it was eaten, salted, for about three months in winter, with an occasional piece of pork for the sake of variety. This fare was supplemented with game and poultry – pheasant, partridge, chicken, pigeon and venison, and shellfish were regarded as being something of a delicacy. Vegetables usually accompanied the meat dishes, and although the Duchess never did serve potatoes at the Palace her children certainly ate them when they grew up and visited England.

At one time it was believed that there were no cooked sweets at meal-times in the seventeenth century, and certainly those items designated simply as 'puddings' were usually savoury. However, the main course at dinner in Hamilton Palace was always followed by a sweet course, and as well as having the fresh fruit which was popular throughout the year, the Duke and Duchess regularly sat down to baked apple pie served with a custard, apple tart, baked apples and stewed gooseberries. There was also a great variety of biscuits to be had at this time, and to take a somewhat macabre example, when Viscount Stair died in 1695 his 'funeral biscuit' included 'plum cakes ... marchpanes ... squirts ... garnished shapes ... strawberry cakes ... almond squirts ... cinnamon biscuit ... and plum almond biscuit.'[13]

Dinner was a substantial meal: supper was more similar in nature to breakfast. Soup was not served in the evening. Instead, there was a dish of 'sowens', an oatmeal and water mixture, or of porridge, but best of all the Duke and Duchess liked bread and milk. The bread was broken up and cooked lightly in milk and sugar to form a kind of bread pudding. They had that almost every evening. Eggs were always available too, and there would be one or two other dishes. Chicken was very often served at supper, or perhaps a pigeon, with a shoulder of mutton as well from time to time.

Generally speaking, most of the food consumed in the Palace came from the Hamilton estates. Some meat was bought in from the town butchers, but in any one year the Great Parks would provide over a hundred and fifty sheep, about twenty lambs, several cows and a dozen or so stirks, while additional cattle were shipped over alive from Arran, driven to the parks and killed and salted in the Palace slaughterhouse. The game and the poultry were obtained locally as well. Several hundred rabbits and hares for the pot were caught in the Wham each year, the falconers and fowlers could be relied upon to bring in partridges, plovers and wild duck, while the dovecot supplied anything from seven to eight hundred pigeons a year. Poultry was equally plentiful. The henwife sent into the kitchen several hundred hens and a few turkeys. Then again, many of the Duchess's tenants still paid a proportion of their rent in kind. In the 1690s she was receiving from the baronies of Hamilton and Cambuslang an annual total of over nine hundred hens, a hundred capons and a small number of chickens.

Butter was another commodity used in the paying of rents. The Palace dairy produced twenty or thirty stones of butter a year, as well as cream cheese and skimmed milk cheese, but a further eighty to a hundred and thirty stones came in the form of 'kain' butter paid by the tenants as part of their rent. John Yuill in Cornhills had to supply forty stones a year in rent, William Fleming and Thomas Steven paid nine stones for their lands in Airybog, and another thirty-one stones came from James Sharp and his subtenants in Boghead. Even this amount was not sufficient for a large household, and the Duchess always made regular purchases of Clydesdale butter, even when the family was in Edinburgh. Eggs also came in as payments of rent, and nearly four hundred a week were used in the Palace, a number which is not really as excessive as it seems when it is remembered that it includes the eggs eaten by the servants and those used in baking.

There were, of course, some goods which could not be supplied from the estates. The Duchess ordered groceries regularly from the Hamilton merchants, and if necessary sent to Glasgow and Edinburgh. Sugar was usually bought in loaves of anything up to thirty pounds, either from Alexander Cunison in Hamilton or from a Glasgow merchant, so that although there were still beeskips in the Palace gardens there was no need for the medieval reliance on honey as a sweetener. Spanish salt came from Glasgow, as did vinegar and the occasional barrel of herring. Spices and dried fruits were bought in both Hamilton and Glasgow – cinnamon, mace, nutmeg, cloves, ginger and pepper. Almonds, oranges and lemons came from Edinburgh, and so did hams. As early as 1621 the Marchioness had sent to Edinburgh for hams, and her granddaughter regularly purchased Westphalian hams there.

Besides patronising well-known merchants in Glasgow and Edinburgh, the Duchess often had luxury goods imported

specially to Bo'ness. Cheeses and coffee beans came over from
Holland, and so did drinking chocolate. Then there was tea. In
1700 the Duchess had brought over specially for her a pound of
Bloom tea, a pound of green tea and a pound of Kaiser's tea. Tea
drinking was in 1702 enough of a novelty for her to remark that
her daughter-in-law, who was then staying with her, though
bored, found in the taking of tea 'some divertisement from my
old company', and in the autumn of the following year the
Duchess was herself taking 'some tea . . . with sugar candy,
without milk' as a cure for a cold.[14] By the end of that decade,
tea drinking had become an established habit among the aristocracy and the Earl of Lauderdale was able to purchase both
black 'bohae tea' and 'green tea' in Edinburgh.[15]

On the whole, though, tea remained very much a novelty and
other beverages predominated. There was always milk to drink,
and ale was taken in large quantities by the servants, but the
family themselves, including the children, always drank wine at
meal-times and the Palace cellar was kept well stocked. In the
1690s over five hundred bottles of claret, about two hundred
bottles of canary, and several dozen of Rhenish and Madeira
wine were consumed by the household each year. The Marchioness
of Hamilton had actually sent abroad for wine. Her accounts for
1638 include an entry of £133:7/– 'To Spain for wine', but her
successors were content to deal with Scottish merchants. Usually
the Duke supervised the buying of the wine himself, making an
enjoyable expedition to Glasgow to see William Anderson the
Provost or John Spreull so that he could select the hogsheads he
wanted.[16] These were then removed to the Palace cellars, where
the contents were bottled. After the Duke's death this personal
supervision was not always possible, but there were other methods
of ensuring that the wine ordered was to the liking of the buyer.
On at least one occasion the Hamilton postmaster took over to
the Palace three pints of canary 'for a taste' before the Duchess
committed herself to buying the entire consignment. Normally,
two or three hogsheads were bought at one time, costing in the
region of £60 each for French wine, although the Duke paid
only £12 for a hogshead in 1673 and another cost his wife as
much as £120 in 1711. From time to time a small quantity was

purchased for a special purpose, as in 1702 when eight pints of Rhenish wine were sent from Glasgow for Lord Basil's wife 'when lying in childbed.'

Wine was one of the most expensive items on the list of provisions, but when the family was at home the cost of catering was relatively low. Even when there were guests to be entertained, expenditure rose only slightly, unless there happened to be some large gathering for a marriage or a funeral. During the last ten weeks of 1691, when the Duke was in residence at the Palace, the total weekly cost of food bought in was only £20 or so, but the first ten weeks of that year had been spent in Edinburgh, and there the weekly bill had come to over £100. Even higher was the cost when the Duke and Duchess visited England. In Tunbridge Wells in 1685 they were paying roughly £96 Scots a week for the meals of their household, a figure which rose to nearer £275 when they moved to London. Similarly, although during the period 1683–1704 (when the accounts are most complete) an annual average of £3,200 was spent on provisions, this figure excludes the year 1688–9 when much of the time was spent in the south and a total of £7,650 Scots was paid for food.

Various reasons explain this increased expenditure when the family was away from home. Hamilton was cheaper because so much of the food came in from the estates. When the family moved elsewhere they had all the additional worry of buying in meat, bread, milk and eggs, and prices were always higher in town. A chicken which would come from the stock of kain fowl paid in rent at home would cost 2/9 Scots in Edinburgh and as much as 10/– Scots in London. In Edinburgh the butchers would charge 1/6 for a pigeon whereas their London colleagues would ask as much as 10/–, and where an Edinburgh merchant would take 2/– for a pound of barley, a London grocer would expect four times as much.[17] Then again, whenever the Duke and Duchess were in Edinburgh or London they found it necessary to do a good deal of public entertaining, and so the food served at meal-times had to be more varied and more elaborate than at home. This was particularly true when the Duke was occupying an important public position, as in 1693 when he was in residence at Holyrood as the King's Commissioner to Parliament. Throughout May and June of that year he and the Duchess gave a series of glittering banquets.

Normally the Duchess's table was covered with a fine linen cloth and set with pewter dishes. There were all sorts of plates – cracknel plates, pasty plates, large ashets for meat – and there were ivory hafted knives and a wide variety of drinking glasses. For public banquets the family plate was brought through to Edinburgh. In common with other Scottish peers of the period, the Duchess had family plate of silver, and it was engraved with the Hamilton coat of arms.[18] The constituent items varied throughout the years as the Duke and Duchess bought replacements and had the engraving done over again, but basically there were always at least three dozen individual silver plates and a number of larger dishes which were set on round silver stands. Great and little salts were made of silver, there was a silver pepper and a silver mustard box, and then there was cutlery: eighteen ivory hafted knives, eighteen forks and two dozen silver spoons. For evening meals, half a dozen pairs of silver candlesticks were set on the table.

For one of the state banquets, all this was laid out carefully on damask tablecloths, along with the drinking glasses of all kinds. Even with her own supply of dishes, the Duchess did not have enough and when the Duke was commissioner in 1693 she had to buy four dozen new ale glasses, three and a half dozen wine glasses, three dozen sack glasses and two and a half dozen coarse glasses. Several hundred bottles were purchased from Leith glassworks, and two dozen pewter dishes were added to the existing stock. The Duke and Duchess also followed the contemporary habit of borrowing utensils for a great occasion. That spring they hired nine dozen extra pewter dishes for the duration of Parliament, along with two dozen extra salts.

It was trouble enough providing the dishes and the glasses, but the food itself was an even greater problem and during the first month that Parliament sat the Duke was spending over £1,000 a week on provisions. Meat, butter and vegetables were brought in from Hamilton but even so beef had to be purchased from the Edinburgh markets, and there were all manner of other expenses. The guests at Holyrood were sitting down to meals which in-

cluded such delicacies as lobster and oysters, and as the season
advanced they enjoyed oranges, gooseberries and strawberries
with cream, accompanied by a choice of canary, claret, sherry,
brandy and white wine. The sweetmeats alone were highly
expensive. At any formal meal the guests expected an interesting
selection of confectionery, and throughout the century Scottish
peers continued to spend a good deal of money on sweetmeats.
The Duchess's grandmother had thought nothing of spending
£186 at a time 'for sugar plumdames and raisins' and when the
great Duke of Lauderdale visited Holyrood he always laid in a
supply of 'long plums, large apricots, raspberry paste, quince
paste . . . walnuts, cherry paste . . . confits . . . confections' and
quantities of sugar for preserving gillyflowers.[19] Lord Murray
spent £120 sterling on importing sweetmeats direct from
Rotterdam,[20] and those peers who could afford to do so employed
their own confectioner, like the Duke's Mr Archibald Thurman
who laboured over the sweetmeats at Holyrood and departed as
soon as Parliament was over. The contemporary enthusiasm for
sweetmeats is perhaps best reflected in a laconic entry in Lord
Fountainhall's *Historical Observes*. 'Sir John Cochrane's house of
Ochiltree was burned', he notes in 1684, 'by the negligence of
on[e] that was making confections to his Lady in it . . .'.[21]

Fortunately the Duke and Duchess of Hamilton's catering
passed off without any such disaster, and when they were in
residence at Holyrood the lavish and altogether correct scale of
their entertaining could not have failed to impress their contemporaries. Each successful banquet was a triumphant assertion
of their social and political prestige.

CHAPTER 5

Entertainment, Travel, Recreation and Celebrations

Entertaining at Holyrood on the grand scale was a necessity, even a duty. It was expensive, it was harassing, and the choice of guests was dictated by political considerations. At home in Hamilton Palace, entertaining assumed a different pattern, and personal preferences could be taken into consideration. It is perhaps surprising to find that the Hamiltons did not entertain at home on a lavish scale. Hospitality had always played an important part in the life of the peerage, partly because the exigencies of travel dictated that a guest must spend a night or two with friends before returning home. From this had grown up the tradition that a great house must be able to offer generous hospitality, and the peers of sixteenth-century England at least had spent huge sums on entertainment.[1] This outlook had altered in the south as the nobleman had begun to live more and more in London and less and less on his estates. In Scotland in the seventeenth century, life at home was regarded as being the natural state of affairs, but whether the manner of entertaining at Hamilton was typical or not remains uncertain.

In the Duchess's time a definite pattern was established. Guests would arrive in time for supper, and would spend the next two or three days in the Palace. They would not call uninvited, even if they were near relations, and they would come in small groups of two or three at a time. In this way, about half a dozen people were entertained each week, and the guest rooms were rarely without an occupant.

In the past, Hamilton Palace had accommodated many an eminent visitor. Mary Queen of Scots had stayed there briefly after her escape from Lochleven Castle, and there was still a room in the Palace known as the King's Chamber, recalling the state visit of James VI. Now, though, the guests were very different. It is often difficult to discover just who was entertained in any household at this period, but during the 1670s the Hamilton master household noted in the margin of his account book the comings and goings of all the visitors, and lists of drink money left for the servants provide supplementary information.

Predictably, about a third of all the visitors were relatives. Each summer the Duchess's sister Lady Susanna came up from Cassilis to spend a few weeks in the Palace, and their half-sister Mary Hay of Park would come several times a year, sometimes bringing her son with her. Relationships with other close connections were complicated by family quarrels and political undertones. A series of violent disagreements marred the relationship between the Duchess and her cousins, the four surviving daughters of the 2nd Duke. Anne, the eldest, was a full-blown beauty who soon won for herself an embarrassing degree of popularity at the Court of Charles II. The Duke and Duchess had married her off to the wealthy and respectable Earl of Southesk, but it was not long before she left him and went back to London.[2] There she not only carried on a scandalous friendship with a young Frenchman, but was rumoured to be one of the Duke of York's mistresses. Eventually, she went off to France, where she remained until the last few months of her life.[3]

Her sisters Elizabeth and Mary had equally colourful careers. Elizabeth's eminently respectable first husband died young, whereupon she married Sir David Cunningham of Robertland, who was her own second cousin. His aristocratic connections were no guarantee of integrity, however, and after an unsuccessful attempt to murder his father he embarked upon a long career of fraud, which culminated in his being imprisoned in the tolbooth of Ayr. It was scarcely surprising that Elizabeth and her husband were ostracised by many of their relatives.

Mary's matrimonial adventures likewise brought her a good deal of unpopularity. She too lost her first husband early, and immediately became involved in a furious territorial argument with the Duke of Hamilton. The Duke thereupon declared her to be 'the strangest unworthy person in the world', and went about telling his friends how she had fallen completely under the influence of Livingstone of Westquarter and had probably married him secretly. Mary did eventually become Livingstone's wife. By the time he died she was in her sixties, but it was not long before she eloped with the Earl of Findlater, confessing to her bridegroom with engaging candour that she was fitter for her grave than for a wedding ceremony.

Only the youngest sister, Margaret, remained on visiting terms with the Duchess, although on one occasion she declined to call at the Palace, explaining that she had Elizabeth staying with her. Had Elizabeth been in correspondence with the Duchess, they could have come together, 'but she never getting an invitation from Your Grace to come to Hamilton, it was not fit for me to desire her.'

As for the Duke's own brothers and sisters and their families, all were Catholics, so it was not always politic to receive them. Most of them remained on personally good terms with both the Duke and Duchess despite their differing convictions and Lord James Douglas, the Duke of Perth and the Earl of Annandale came as guests if they were in the area. Lord James, indeed, professed a particular respect for his sister-in-law, writing to urge the Duke to give 'my most humble service to My Lady Duchess whom I respect and esteem extremely, and I beg you will take her counsel for what concerns your soul more than I believe you do', an interesting tribute from one who remained a Catholic throughout his life.

Always welcome in the Palace without any reservations were members of the Bargany family, the children of the man instrumental in arranging the marriage of the Duke and Duchess. As well as being related to both, the Hamiltons of Bargany were enthusiastic Covenanters, and their whole outlook accorded well with that of their hosts. Consequently, the younger Lord Bargany came sometimes as often as three times a year, and his sisters almost as often. The youngest, Katherine, who married Cunningham of Enterkin, was a particularly close friend of the Duchess.

It was only to be expected that a sizeable proportion of the visitors to the Palace should be relations. What is surprising is that, apart from relatives, only a small percentage of the visitors were members of the peerage. It might have been expected that the Hamiltons would entertain only those of an elevated social standing, fellow peers and statesmen but, instead, by far the greatest number were members of the local gentry, younger sons and professional men.

The Duke and Duchess preferred the company of those with similar tastes and interests to their own. The most frequent visitor of all to the Palace was Sir Daniel Carmichael, who was invited to dinner or supper no fewer than sixteen times in the space of twelve months, sometimes with his wife, sometimes with his nephew Lord Carmichael, but often alone. Sir Daniel had been Chamberlain of Scotland and Master of Works in 1641. During the Civil War he fought on the Parliamentary side, and he later became a commissioner of the peace for Lanarkshire. His opposition to Charles I was forgotten, and with his Covenanting and local background he epitomised the men and women who were friends of the Duke and Duchess; men like Major General William Drummond, who had seen service in the Engagement campaign, had fought in Russia and had long opposed Lauderdale,[4] Sir William Hamilton of Preston with his impassioned Covenanting convictions[5] and Sir James Turner, the famous old soldier now living in retirement in the Gorbals, that pleasant little village outside Glasgow.[6] All these people shared the Duchess's religious sympathies and could talk knowledgeably about local affairs.

Not only did soldiers and local government officials sit round the great dining-room table in Hamilton Palace reminiscing, arguing and laughing over local affairs. Sometimes professional men joined them. Mr William Hamilton and Mr George Bannerman the advocates were occasionally summoned to give legal advice to the Duke and they would stay on for supper, discoursing solemnly about court cases but also keeping the company entertained with the latest gossip from the Edinburgh legal circles. Provost Anderson of Glasgow, a merchant, was often there in person to share the wine supplied by his firm, and then there were local ministers. William Vilant of nearby Cambusnethan, John Hutchison of Dundonald and John Osborne were all known for their support of the conventiclers and the Duchess enjoyed a theological discussion with them over dinner.[7]

To sum up, the selection of house guests received in the Palace was varied and remarkably democratic, for although any leading nobleman would have his own political cronies and satellites and might be expected to mix only with fellow peers, other considerations weighed more strongly with the Duke and Duchess of Hamilton. They still relied on the old local and kinship connections, and they entertained these traditional friends in modest style.

It might, of course, be argued that the difficulties of travel dictated this reliance on local society, and although this is an over-simplification, it remains true that travel had its problems. The coach was the principal method of transport other than simply going on horseback, and it was at the same time an important status symbol. As he travelled about the country a nobleman appeared before a wide public. Whenever the Duke of Hamilton entered or left a sizeable town, he did so 'with a great convoy'. In 1674, for example, it was reported that he was expected to pass through Berwick on his way home from London, and 'a very noble reception is preparing for him, and many noblemen and gentlemen of quality resolve to attend him and bring him through Berwick in great honour'. When he finally arrived in Edinburgh, 'he was accompanied with about twenty coaches besides most whereof had six horses . . . The abbey close [at Holyrood] was so filled with coaches and horses that one could not get stirred his foot, many of the windows of the abbey and the housetop beside many other windows and housetops adjacent thereto were filled with spectators'.

As early as 1604 the Duchess's great-grandfather had owned a chariot, and in 1611 her grandfather shipped home a 'carriage' from London. In that same year he was building a coach house at Kinneil, and from then onwards the Hamiltons always had at least one coach. The Duke himself owned several. In the 1690s he had with him in Edinburgh his travelling coach, a new coach, another coach and a chariot, and on another occasion he complained that 'I find all my travelling coaches quite gone [in need of repair].'

These coaches had all been made in England,[8] and the best of them were kept for travel in town, for it was all too easy for a coach to suffer serious damage. The difficulties were occasioned mainly by bad roads and inclement weather.[9] Travellers of the period were singularly intrepid, and would congratulate themselves on an uneventful journey if their coach overturned only once on the way. There was, for instance, the unfortunate accident suffered by the Duchess and her daughter Katherine in 1684. Katherine was seven months pregnant at the time but, undeterred by her condition, she decided to visit Kinneil with her mother. Everything went well until they had almost reached their destination. The coachman had never been that way before, and as they approached a sizeable stream he shouted out that he did not know how to cross it. Seeing his hesitation, the footmen, postillions and the servants riding along with the party all felt it necessary to offer advice. 'Cross by the bridge!' shouted some. 'Ford the river!' shouted others, and in Lady Katherine's own words, 'they confounded him [so much] that he knew not where to go and made him go up and down I know not how often.'

To make matters worse, there was a strong wind blowing, and a few minutes later the inevitable happened. With an ominous rumbling and amid a crescendo of screams and shouts, the coach lurched, swayed and fell over on its side. Down went Lady Katherine, hurled on to the floor; down went the Duchess, plunging on top of her; and down came their trunk, toppling off the rack to land on both of them. Total confusion reigned, but by little short of a miracle no one was seriously hurt. Certainly the Duchess's face was badly bruised, and she arrived at Kinneil with two black eyes, but she 'did not so much as keep her chamber the next day, but went up and down and saw the rooms ordered, which we were all much against, but there was no hindering of her.' She and Katherine congratulated themselves on their fortunate escape, and were able to 'laugh heartily' whenever they thought of it.[10]

Some years later they had an equally alarming experience. Katherine had been taken seriously ill on the way to London, and had to stay behind at the small village of Belford. Her mother and her sister Susan hurried there to nurse her, and after a dangerous illness she began to recover. By the time she was convalescent, however, it was the end of December, and most unsuitable weather for travelling. All three ladies were heartily tired of their enforced stay, and the Duchess and Susan were particularly anxious to get back to Edinburgh. The Duchess had a thousand things awaiting her attention, while Susan declared that she was pining for news of the latest fashions. Their impatience was turned to alarm when there were several falls of snow, and they began to fear that if they did not get away at once they might be stranded for weeks.

Eventually, they agreed to set out in their coach to see if they could get through. They had not gone far, though, when a coach wheel stuck in a deep, icy pothole. The horses were too weak to pull them out, and as Katherine put it, 'there we stuck, and could neither get back nor forward, tho' all was done that men could do, for they waded in to their middle and beat the poor horses, but could not make them stir.'

At last, someone suggested that if the coach could be made lighter it might be possible to pull it out. This seemed an excellent idea and, nothing loath, the Duchess ordered two of the grooms to lift her out through the coach window. After some manoeuvring this was accomplished, whereupon Susan was brought out, followed by her maid. Katherine was still very weak, so it was agreed that she would remain inside, 'and there I sat', she told her husband afterwards, 'not a little frightened I'll assure you, but all would not do.' The coach remained firmly stuck.

There was nothing else for it. Katherine had to be lifted out as well, 'a difficult task with my weakness'. Nevertheless, she had the good sense to hand out the coach seats before she emerged. These they laid on the snow, then they settled Katherine on top, snugly wrapped in their coats and cloaks. Poor Susan was by this time feeling sick with the cold, but at long last there came a shout of triumph. The men had put the horses behind the coach, and it had begun to move. They managed to draw it back out of the hole, the ladies piled thankfully in and they were soon on their way back to Belford.[11]

At least they had comfortable lodgings waiting for them. The Duchess was not always so fortunate. A seemingly innocuous trip to Ayrshire to see her sister brought its own perils, for she and her servants lost their way and found themselves travelling through strange countryside as darkness fell with nowhere to spend the night. The Duchess was nothing if not resourceful, and she managed to find shelter, warning her companions to keep secret the place where they eventually lodged. Servants' tongues were not so easily silenced, however, and it was not long before she received an irate letter from the Duke, then in London. 'You did not tell me', he wrote to her accusingly, 'you was necessitate to lie in a coalhouse all night betwixt Cassilis and Ayr as you went, as is reported here. I am sure I forewarned you to have a care of being in the night . . . I confess I feared some such accident and never desires you should make journeys when I am not with you.'

Local journeys were bad enough, but they could always be postponed if conditions were too unfavourable. Much worse was travel between London and Edinburgh. Scottish noblemen were constantly travelling up and down the well-worn route through Berwick, Alnwick, Durham, Newark and Royston to London, and there were established inns and post houses all along the way: the 'Eel Piehouse' at Newark was a favourite, and it actually did serve eel pies. Nothing could be done about the elements, however, and in 1674 the Duke, returning home from a trip to London, had to pay ten shillings 'to those that helped the coach out of the snow.' Even in the early autumn there could be difficulties. One September he found that the great rains had so raised the level of all the rivers that he could scarcely cross them. Added to this, he complained to his wife, 'I had 1 very ill [poor] coachman, weak horses and the postillion's horse fell and injured his leg so had to have the footman ride postillion.' He beseeched the Duchess never to cross deep water in a coach, as he had seen how dangerous it was, feared that the journey might take a fortnight (which was in fact the usual time) and declared that had he realised the conditions he would have ridden all the way to London.

This was no idle threat, but a perfectly practicable alternative, at least for a younger man. When the Earl of Arran came back from the continent he and his companions went on horseback and took just over a week to reach Edinburgh from London. The pace was rather too much for David Crawford, the secretary. He had to fall behind more than once, and he recorded in his accounts for 11 and 12 November, 'For myself and horse that night having been jaded 4 miles short of Durham 2/6d. At Durham where my Lord Arran lay, supper, wine, breakfast 10/4d. To the guides who were sent to look for me 1/–.'

Heavy rains made riding on horseback hazardous because of the need to ford rivers *en route*, as the Earl's brother John was to discover in 1687. Dispatched to take Arran's marriage contract north to the Duchess, he had to set out at the very worst time of the year, the end of November. So high were the waters that the horses had to swim across, and at one place he himself had to wade over, up to his waist in water. The horse of one of his companions fell and was almost swept away, and at Newark so great were the storms that they had to make a considerable diversion. Two hours were wasted waiting for a ferry boat to cross the Trent, and farther north horses were in such short supply that they had to ride two stages on the same horse. Needless to say, when he arrived home he was not in the best of tempers. As the Duchess said afterwards, 'He had an ill enough journey of it, but its diversion now to laugh at, but was not so in the time.'

Fatigue and storms were not the only enemies of the traveller on horseback, as Sir David Dalrymple found out. He was travelling through Bedfordshire on his way home to Scotland in 1704 when, not far from Woburn, 'he was set upon, assaulted and robbed by one highwayman on horseback being disguised with a vizor mask upon his face.' The robber had 'a pistol in his hand' and 'feloniously took from him seven guineas, five carolus pieces, and a five guinea piece, two silk gowns and three petticoats, 2 holland shirts and several sorts of muslin apparel' to the value of £80.[12]

It was not surprising that longer journeys were undertaken with reluctance. Short journeys at home were frequently made on horseback by women as well as men. The Hamilton ladies were quite accustomed to riding sidesaddle, and when she was snowed up at Belford the Duchess, then aged sixty-four, declared that she 'would ride on horseback' to Edinburgh, and was prevented from doing so only because Katherine could not travel that way. Of course, it was not always possible for ladies to use this mode of travel, and when they were pregnant, in poor health, or older they would make short journeys in town by sedan chair.

Coaches and sedans were privately owned, but it was also possible to make use of public transport. Although the Duke occasionally used his own travelling coach when he went south, he and his family often sent their own coach home at York and went on from there in the hackney coach. This was all the more sensible when a group of friends planned to go to London. They could travel together, thereby sharing the cost of the coach hire and they were assured of congenial travelling companions on the way, an important consideration on such a long journey. In 1695 Lord Basil, arranging to accompany his sister Susan and her child to Bath, decided that it was best to book the whole coach, 'to avoid being wearied with other company.'

On one trip south in 1685, the Duke and Duchess decided not to go by coach at all but to travel by sea. Yachting had become fashionable in the reign of Charles II, and they sailed from Leith on board *The Mary*, arrived at Greenwich and went by barge to London. Why they decided to travel this way remains unexplained, but it was an experiment which was not repeated.

When the Duke and Duchess travelled in Scotland other than to go to Edinburgh or Kinneil they usually stayed with relatives. The Duchess did not make social expeditions of this sort very often, but she did like to call on her aunt, Lady Belhaven, at The Biel, and when the Duke was on his way to and from London he would spend a night or two there. At other times, he and the Duchess called on her cousins at Struthers and Tyninghame and on her sister at Cassilis, but this was the extent of their visiting.

Of course, when they were in Edinburgh it was a different matter. The opportunity of meeting friends was greatly increased but, even so, social contacts came second to business considerations, and in day to day affairs there was little time for frivolity. Most of the Duke's energies were devoted to his own business matters and to affairs of state when he was in town, and even when he went for a meal out at Masterton's Inn or the Green Dragon he was to be found in the company of men with whom he could discuss such matters. Once again, many of these were people to whom he was related, and apart from these connections he was seen about with political associates like the Marquis of Atholl and the Earl of Home, or with friends like Sir William Bruce the architect, with whom he no doubt discussed the building work at Holyrood and his own plans for Hamilton.

Life was not all politics and business, however: there was time for recreation, and in these intervals for enjoyment the Scottish aristocracy continued to indulge in their favourite sports of hunting and hawking. The Duke did make an occasional trip to Leslie to enjoy the hunting available in Fife, but on the whole he preferred hare coursing, and he always kept greyhounds for rabbit hunting. He was pleased to secure 'two little greyhounds that they call lurchers for killing rabbits' when he was on a visit to London, and he sent them home to the Duchess with the instruction that the mouse coloured dog was to be called 'Mouse' and the black one 'Jennie'. Less satisfactory were two dogs presented to him by a friend of his son. He wrote to tell the Earl of Arran in the spring of 1688 that 'I was a-hunting on Saturday with Bonnington hounds, which are very good ones but to[o] fleet. We had very good sport and killed three hares. The two little bitches your Lieutenant Colonel gave me are but foul hounds . . .'.

Perhaps increasing years caused his complaint about the speed of the hounds, but if age slowed down his own swiftness at the chase it does not seem to have interfered with his pleasure in hawking, which he enjoyed with enthusiasm throughout his life. Each year he went on hawking expeditions in the Clyde valley, and if Bellshill is now a built up area on the edge of Glasgow, it was in his day a favourite hillside for a day's sport. In summer he would go as far afield as Musselburgh and Arran, and George Simpson his falconer made regular purchases of such items as 'a credence for luring His Grace's young hawks . . . two hawk-gloves . . . a hawking bag . . .'. Many peers kept a full-time falconer, and one of the gifts most frequently exchanged amongst them was a pair of hawks. Over the years the Duke acquired a good many hawks from friends and relations, and if he needed still more he would write to a northern acquaintance like Lord Reay to see if any could be had there.

Hunting and hawking both had their useful side, since the day's bag could supplement the household provisions. Other sports were purely recreational. Golf had been popular with the nobility ever since Mary Queen of Scots played at Seton. The Duchess's grandfather was buying two golf clubs and four balls back in 1603, and her uncle had been an enthusiastic golfer. The Duke himself played from time to time. Throughout the winter of 1658 he was golfing every week on the sands of Leith, paying 6/– a day to the man who carried his clubs for him, and almost fifteen years later Sir John Foulis of Ravelston made several entries in his account book, recording, for instance, '30 November 1672 . . . Lost at golf with the Chancellor [Rothes], Duke Hamilton etc., £4:15/–.'[13]

Probably as a result of their travels on the continent, many noblemen were keen tennis players. Tennis was at this time an indoor game resembling squash, and the Duke often played when he was in Edinburgh. He had several games with Rothes on 24 December 1657, and he played with the Master of Cochrane the following February. After a series of matches in the summer of 1661, he seems to have given it up. He tried his hand at curling, too, when he was young, and he was always willing to have a game of bowls. Long before he laid out the fine new bowling green beside the Palace, bowling had been popular with the Hamiltons. The Duchess's grandfather had laid out a bowling alley at Kinneil in 1604, and in 1616 he had been gambling 'at the bowls in Hamilton'. Many of the great houses of the time had their own bowling alleys in the gardens, and so when the Duke visited Tyninghame or Tullibardine he was able to bowl in the company of his hosts.

Tennis, golf and bowling supplanted at least some of the pastimes familiar to an earlier generation. Archery and football, both mentioned in the accounts as recreations of the Duchess's great-grandfather and grandfather, occur in her own time only as games for children. Cockfighting had also become the prerogative of children, and when the Duchess's sons were at school in Glasgow, money was paid on their behalf when they 'set their cocks down to fight.' Tilting, in which her father had taken part at Whitehall, had died out completely, but horse-racing had gained immensely in popularity. There had been regular races in Scotland for many years, at such places as Lanark and Cupar, but it was not until the reign of Charles II that the sport became really popular with the nobility. The Duke of Hamilton was a devotee, not without some family disapproval. One day as he was about to set off for the races at Leith he wrote apologetically to his wife to assure her that although 'you will think this world should put these things out of mind, but whatever world it be, without my former promise to you, I believe I shall quickly weary of this sport.' In fact he never did weary of it. In the 1670s he was racing his own horse at Leith, and twenty years later he had a special groom to look after his racehorse 'Aberdeen'.

Most of the recreations in which the Duke indulged took the form of outdoor sports, for he was an active, energetic man who was glad to spend his leisure in the open. When he was inside, business kept him occupied for most of the time, and although he played the occasional game of cards and billiards, he usually found better things to do when bad weather kept him in. Even Bishop Burnet had been obliged to admit that the Duke was an expert on Scots law, and he had a passion for history. When the Duke makes one of his rare appearances in Evelyn's *Diary* it is to keep the company entertained with 'many particulars of Mary Queen of Scots and her amours with the Italian favourite etc.'[14]

Admittedly the interest on that occasion may not have been purely historical, but his enthusiasm for the past was very real. Genealogy fascinated him, and he copied out for himself many family trees of quite remote connections of the Hamiltons and the Douglases. He listed all the errors in a manuscript history of his father's family, and he was an expert on heraldry. He compiled memoranda 'for the right ordering of the arms and successions' of the houses of Hamilton and Douglas, and when he read Sir George MacKenzie's work on heraldry he made out pages of criticisms of it, pointing out inaccuracies in coats of arms and basing his corrections on his knowledge of seals. In his day palaeography was already a serious study: in 1700 Sir David Dalrymple the King's Advocate paid 45 livres to an Edinburgh merchant 'For a book Mabillion',* bought at Paris and sent to him via Rouen and Le Havre.[15]

Nor was the Duke a mere dabbler in family history. His organisation of the Hamilton estates led him into a study of early charters, and he collected innumerable notes on fifteenth- and sixteenth-century land grants. The Hamilton rentals he annotated with comments as to the origins of various tacks or leases. Throughout, his many notes and memoranda display an admirable precision and a strict regard for historical accuracy.

His enthusiasm did not arise solely out of a desire to settle his family affairs, for he took the trouble to copy out twenty-three pages of Hawthornden's history of the Stewart kings of Scotland, made 'notes out of Samuel Daniell and other histories of England' recounting events from the time of Caesar to the twelfth century, and collected a library which contained a good many history books.

No inventory of the libraries at Hamilton and Kinneil exists for the Duke's own lifetime, but the list drawn up on his son's death includes many books collected by the Duke himself. Ironically enough, these two men who could never agree about anything showed very similar tastes where reading was concerned, and their combined library contains many works on history. There were histories of England, ranging from Blackmore's *Prince Arthur* to biographies of Cromwell and Charles II. There were universal histories and histories of Sweden, Italy, Poland and the East Indies, written in French, Italian and Latin. Most of all, though, there were histories of Scotland and treatises on Scots law and the Duke's accounts reveal that it was he who bought several of the works of Sir George MacKenzie, the famous Scottish lawyer, including his *Institutions*.

The Duke made a point of buying all the latest parliamentary papers — collections of the acts of parliament, topical pamphlets and the like, and he seems to have had a fondness for maps. Over the years he collected maps of almost every known country in the

---

* Mabillon was the author of *De Re Diplomatica* (1681), the standard work on Latin palaeography.

world, and he subscribed to a handsome coloured atlas being brought out by Moses Pitt in London in the 1680s. He did have his lighter moments too. The memoirs of the Ducs de Guise and Rohan cost him £6 one winter, and another time he picked up in Edinburgh 'a little book entitl'd Cara Mustapha.' On the whole, his tastes were entirely typical of his age. His fellow peers in Scotland were busy assembling libraries of four and five hundred volumes, predominantly on history, the law and the classics, with a few works on estate management, some poetry, and the occasional music book by way of light relief.

Equally typical were the books bought by the Duchess. Women of the seventeenth century were preoccupied with religious books. Lady Eleanor Montgomerie owned *The Abridgement of the Scots Chronicle* but otherwise her library was given over entirely to religious treatises. Similarly when Lady Calder had a list of her books drawn up in 1704 they were exclusively theological. Some ladies did interest themselves in practical publications as well, collecting works on midwifery and cookery, but theology remained their favourite subject.[16] It is not surprising, then, to discover the Duchess buying books like Wedderburn's *Heaven upon Earth* and Hamilton's *Commentary on Romans VIII*, and on one occasion she purchased no fewer than '100 small books against popery'. She took no personal interest in cooking, but she did buy works on medicine for the benefit of her family. *The Country Physician*, 'Mr Boyle's Book of Physick' and Dr Willis's treatise on scurvy were all on her shelves, and so was *The Treatise on the Gout*. No doubt she read some of the books bought by the Duke, and to the end of her life she subscribed regularly to *The Flying Post, The Post Boy* and the London gazettes.

As for entertainments of other kinds, the Duke and Duchess did not ever go to the theatre although their predecessors had been regular playgoers. This was presumably because of their puritan outlook, but even the strictest Covenanters do not seem to have disapproved of gambling away small sums of money at cards, and very often it was the ladies of the family who whiled away the time at the card table. After all, the range of activities available to them was restricted. Certainly the Duchess's grandmother was often 'at the falconing in Avendale' and on one occasion paid almost £3 Scots for 'a laverock [lark] net', but there is no evidence that the Duchess herself ever took part in hawking. She did ride a great deal, of course, and she liked a game of bowls, often losing small sums of money to the ladies she played with. She lost money at cards, too: £12 one day in 1657.

A more conventional occupation for ladies was sewing, both the sewing up of linen garments for the men of the family and embroidery. Many ladies of the time undertook extensive tasks such as the embroidery of complete sets of bedcurtains, and a set embroidered by the Duchess's youngest daughter Margaret exists to this day.[17] Mary Hay of Park apparently preferred tapestry, for 'a tent' was sent to her from England along with embroidery silks, pins, and cards on which the silk was to be wound, and the Duchess herself ordered embroidery silks from London. On one occasion these were conveyed to her husband's secretary with a message from the lady who had bought them for the Duchess to the effect that he should 'have a care that the silks be put near no sweet smells nor yet no dampness for either of these will change the colour.' She may also have done some lace making, for in 1683 her ladies bought an ounce of thread and a dozen needles 'for My Lady Duchess's point.'

As well as occupying themselves with their sewing, ladies could entertain themselves with music, and could keep pets for company. Apart from her parrot, the Duchess kept various animals and her early accounts record the spending of money 'for milk and meat to My Lady's pets.' Possibly these were dogs. There is no mention at all of cats in the Hamilton papers, but this was either because no expenditure was necessary, or because they were kept more as farm cats are today, for the purpose of catching mice and nothing more. When the Duke of Lauderdale stayed at Holyrood as the King's Commissioner he certainly made payments 'for milk to the cats in the wardrobe.'[18]

Even with these amusements life must have seemed dull at times for the ladies of the household, and they must have welcomed the occasional diversion provided by a travelling entertainer. Minstrels and jugglers sometimes called at the Palace, but in 1706 even more exciting visitors arrived. In April of that year David Crawford paid two guineas 'to the man who brought the

Elephant to show Her Grace', and in the following month no less than £73:18/– Scots was paid 'to Mr Higgins, posture master, who came and acted before Her Grace and several persons of quality'. Mr Higgins was a contortionist who had been appearing at the Nether Bow in Edinburgh every evening at six o'clock after proudly advertising in his printed brochure that he could perform 'those postures of the body that posture clerk nor any other posture master ever could attain to: he extends his body into all deformed shapes or postures of statues, makes his hips and shoulder bones meet together . . . with several other wonderful postures that never any other men attain to but himself.'

The children must have enjoyed these exotic visitors to the Palace too, and of course they had their own entertainments. Whenever the Duke visited Edinburgh or London he would bring back with him 'bonny things for the bairns'. His sons had toy drums, swords and trumpets, and John Muirhead the tailor solemnly sewed up gowns for Lady Katherine's doll. Children's toys and games were imported into Scotland in large quantities at this time, the Edinburgh merchants shipping from London boxes and barrels 'with children's toys' and then selling in their shops such items as '1 wand rattler . . . 1 supple Andrew . . . 1 leaping beast . . . 1 hobby horse . . . 1 wagon . . . 1 timber crane for a child . . .'.[19] A surprising variety of pets was kept by children as well, ranging from the Earl of Arran's squirrel to William Tollemache's otter;[20] then they were permitted to watch puppet plays from time to time, and their birthdays were marked with due ceremony.

There were relatively few celebrations by this time, though. To the Presbyterians the frivolous enjoyments which had once marked the great occasions of the ecclesiastical year were inappropriate, and by the middle of the seventeenth century Christmas was not celebrated at all in most places, although the traditional festivities lingered on in the northern half of Scotland. In 1691 the Episcopalian Marchioness of Atholl urged her son to come and spend Christmas with her at Dunkeld, since it was no longer celebrated in Fife but was still observed in her Perthshire home. Even so, the festivities were of a restricted nature, and a year later she wrote to him describing how the family at Dunkeld had spent Christmas Day with a sermon and devotions in the morning, adding apologetically that these had been followed by some 'innocent mirth.'[21] In a similar vein, Lord Montgomerie invited a friend to Christmas dinner in 1694 with the words 'I hope [that] to eat a goose that day will give little offence to Presbytery.'[22]

New Year, on the other hand, was usually marked with some rejoicings and the exchange of gifts. (In Scotland the New Year had begun on 1 January ever since James VI altered the calendar in 1600, whereas in England the New Year did not begin technically until the end of March.) If the Duke and Duchess happened to be in Edinburgh on 1 January the town hautboys would come to Holyroodhouse 'to wish Their Graces a good new year', and tradesmen and servants expected a 'handsel', in other words, a small gift of money.

There was now also the feeling that baptisms should be private, family affairs. Gone was the fashion for the sort of splendid christening which had marked the Duchess's own arrival into the world. Her babies were baptised either in the Palace itself or in the conveniently near parish church, very often on the same day that the child was born. Because of this, the ceremony was a simple one, and it was held before a few close relatives and friends. The only details available of any christening relate to the baptism of Lord Basil's children. His son William was born on 16 September 1692. David Crawford recorded five days later, 'Lord Basil's son was christened William. My Lady Panmure [the baby's aunt] cary'd the child to church and my Lord Panmure, Sir William Maxwell, Earnock, Barncluth and Barntoun were gossips [godparents].' A month after the child's birth he noted, 'The Lady Baldoon was kirked.' A month was the conventional period to wait before the churching of women service took place, but this interval could be shortened if necessary. After the birth of one of her children the Duchess's daughter Susan recovered quickly and planned 'to go to church yesterday though her month was not out, that she might go to Edinburgh before the parliament sat down.'[23]

Birthdays of adults as well as children were usually observed, and when the Duke was in London in the winter of 1693 he wrote home to his wife telling her, 'I shall be glad to hear . . . you have eat a good barren doe and remembered my birthday as I intend to do yours.' Soon afterwards he told her that he had bought 'a suit of new clothes for your birthday and shall drink your health with your friends here', and on the actual day he, four of his sons, and his brother-in-law the Earl of Cassilis drank her health. Not everyone was as punctilious as the Duke, and his eldest son could be regrettably remiss about such matters. He forgot all about the birthday of his own little son one year until the Duchess wrote to remind him that 'This is your son's birthday, which he is much taken up with.'

The real occasion for family celebrations was, of course, a marriage. Preparations for a wedding had to begin weeks beforehand, for the occasion had to be a memorable one: not only must the family honour be upheld, but the bride's new relations must be impressed. When Katherine was to marry Lord Murray on 24 April 1683 the catering arrangements were begun early in March. Servants were sent out to see about provisions, a special list of extraordinary expenditure was drawn up, and a great box of sweetmeats was brought out from Edinburgh. The Duke advised the Duchess to ask their old master household John Hamilton to come out of retirement for the occasion so that he could 'set the meat on the table, as he is fittest', and Katherine was kept busy with fittings for her trousseau. All manner of extra household goods were then bought in, ranging from wine glasses to chamber pots, and as the day approached wild fowl were brought, more sugar plums were sent for, and no fewer than thirty cows were killed. The wedding celebrations were liable to go on for as long as a week, with dancing and feasting, and the whole affair cost hundreds of pounds.

Perhaps the most expensive ceremony of all was the very last, the funeral, for the Hamiltons went in for all the funeral pomp so dear to the hearts of the peerage, both English and Scottish. The funeral of the Duchess's grandfather in 1625 had been typical of the kind of burial accorded to a nobleman throughout the seventeenth century. The honour of the family demanded that the dead man should be accompanied to his grave with dignity and grandeur, and so it was that the heralds and pursuivants, trumpeters and soldiers followed the 2nd Marquis of Hamilton to his grave, accompanied by a great crowd of mourners led by the dead man's younger son. So many guests had been invited that they could not all be accommodated in Hamilton Palace but were boarded out in the town: so many poor from the surrounding area tried to force their way to the church in hope of alms that six halberd men were needed to keep them back; and so grandiose was the funeral feast that the Earls of Morton and Wigtown had to lend their cooks to help with the catering, and extra cooks and bakers had to be hired from Edinburgh. The whole occasion cost over £2,000 Scots.

Even when a child died, the ceremony was not a private one. When the Duchess's little brother William passed away at Hampton Court in the winter of 1638 a solemn procession accompanied by over eighty Londoners bearing torches carried his body to Westminster Abbey, where the dean and subdean, four prebendaries, two vergers and a 'chanthor' were waiting to take part in the service, with the organist and his singingmen and ten young choristers to provide music.

The Civil War brought about a change in the attitude of Presbyterians towards funerals as well as towards clothing and festivities. Not only was there a feeling that lavish expenditure on such an occasion was hardly justified, but many began to feel that it was also inappropriate. Their sentiments were summed up by a request made by Anne, Countess of Lothian, at the end of her Will. 'I desire no ceremony at my burial', she wrote firmly.[24] It became common practice to insert a clause of this sort in one's testament, and women were particularly emphatic upon this point, sharing the English ladies' repugnance at the notion of embalming. 'My body I desire may be carried to the grave without any ceremony and not bowelled, only wrapped in cerecloth and buried in a few days after merciful God grant my change', the Duchess's sister Susanna wrote in her Will, expressing the sentiments of many of her sex.[25]

Such pious wishes were to be admired, but they did present the relatives with something of a problem. While carrying out the wishes of the deceased, they must at the same time uphold the honour of the family. There therefore grew up a somewhat ambivalent attitude to the whole subject, and while a nobleman might desire for himself a plain burial, he thought that friends and relations should go to their grave with all the ceremony befitting their social status. The Duchess herself, who always expressed the desire to be buried 'without pomp or ceremony in Hamilton Church', nonetheless wrote to an uncle's widow, the Countess of Denbigh, offering her condolences on the Earl's death but regretting what she called 'the meanness' of the funeral, and on another occasion David Crawford wrote critically to the Earl of Arran about the unimpressive burial of the Duke of Queensberry.

Usually the matter was resolved in a compromise whereby the women and children of the family received simple burials while the head of the house had a grandiose funeral. Wives and children were buried at night, by torchlight, in a simple wooden coffin made by a local carpenter and with only a few friends in attendance. When the Duchess's father invited an old friend to Lady Anna Cunningham's funeral he explained that 'because it was her own express pleasure that there should be neither solemnities nor shows used at her funeral, I shall desire you would be pleased to come only accompanied with your own domestic servants, for I intend not to have any there but your Lordship and her own children.'[26] Children were sometimes still embalmed, but usually because they had been 'opened' for medical reasons, it being felt that if the cause of death could be ascertained, precautions could be taken to prevent other offspring from succumbing to the same disease.

The funeral for a lady or a child cost from £200 to £500 Scots, but far more had to be expended when the head of the family died. A contemporary engraving of the funeral procession of John, Duke of Rothes in 1681 gives a graphic impression of exactly how grand such an occasion could be. Rothes was Chancellor of Scotland when he died, and archbishops, bishops, the Lords Treasurer, Register and Advocate, the Lords of Session and the Edinburgh magistrates all walked in his procession. There were trumpeters and standard bearers, noblemen and servants, and fifty-one poor men in hoods and gowns. The coffin, magnificently decorated with the symbols of mortality and coats of arms, was carried along under a canopy borne by ten noblemen, including that assiduous attender of funerals, the Duke of Hamilton, and the dead Duke's mourning coach, horse of war, saddle horse and parliament horse were all there.

After the interment there was always an elaborate banquet, nor did the ritual of mourning end there. When the head of a family died, part of the church was painted black – the minister's and elders' seats, the church door, railings and stairs – and in the dead man's home a similar transformation took place. Funeral escutcheons were hung up outside, all the window curtains were dyed black, special black hangings were put on the walls, and the cushions, beds and chairs were all covered in black. Moreover, the entire family and servants had to be fitted out with black clothes. Letters sent out were edged with black and sealed with black wax, and relatives were given mourning rings containing locks of the dead man's hair. Strict etiquette governed these outward trappings of grief, and the whole ritual of mourning was an expensive and elaborate reaffirmation of the family's status and prestige.

PART 2

The Great Design

CHAPTER 6

The Education of the Children

By the 1670s the Duke and Duchess were completely settled in their Palace. The sufferings brought by the Civil War were fading into the past, and the pattern of life had been re-established in a manner which few would have believed possible. By little short of an economic miracle they had put their finances on a sound footing once more. The Duke had spent long hours in his study poring over the family papers, calculating debts, sorting out leases, counting, numbering and listing. The evidences of his industry exist to this day. He sold Chelsea for £19,000 sterling and persuaded the English Exchequer to pay back £30,000 owed to the Duchess's father. The sale of furnishings and pictures in Holland had brought in £10,000 sterling and, of course, there was the £25,000 paid back by Charles II. As a memorandum of the time noted, 'By these great sums of money received and others, and by the Duke's most prudent and diligent management of the affairs of the estate, the debts of the family are not only discharged but a great part of the tailzied [entailed] lands sold off are acquired again and some other lands and rights purchased which did not formerly belong to the family.'

But it was not enough to have restored the way of life destroyed by the Cromwellian occupation. The world was changing, and the Duchess was very much aware of the future. The House of Hamilton had been preserved in her, and as guardian of its interests she must make certain that never again would its fortunes sink so low. From the very beginning she was concerned with the survival and prestige of her family, and for this reason she and her husband gradually evolved a plan for the future, their 'Great Design'. Even when money was hard to come by, when religious and political difficulties were a continual threat to stability, she and the Duke knew what they wanted to do. A fine new Hamilton Palace would rise from the rambling, old-fashioned house. Extensive new parks and gardens would be laid out. The estates would be improved, the townspeople and tenants cared for as never before. The head of the House of Hamilton would be in his traditional position of pre-eminence, a protector of the people of the west, a defender of the Presbyterian Church, an influence for good on the destiny of Scotland, and the heir to this great inheritance would be an educated, compassionate man who would be a worthy guardian of his noble heritage.

Of course, the Duchess was no impractical idealist. One of her most outstanding qualities was her practical grasp of reality, her innate common sense, and it was this very attribute which permitted the realisation of her ambitions. As she once remarked to her eldest son, there was no point in undertaking anything 'upon pretence of doing that for our posterity which will not signify anything to them.'

In the 1660s all this was a half-imagined hope, something which might be achieved eventually, but even so it was possible to make a start. The Duchess was genuinely unconcerned with her own situation. What she was doing was for the family, for future generations, and so when her children came along she gave a great deal of thought to their upbringing, and particularly to the education of James, her eldest son.

From the beginning, James was a very special child. He was the first male heir to the House of Hamilton to live in the Palace for nearly forty years, and after all the dangers of the 1650s his birth had been greeted with even more rejoicings than would normally have marked such an occasion. The result was that, from his earliest days, he was petted and indulged by the women of the household. When he was an infant his mother's cousins were still in the Palace, as well as her sister Susanna and Lady Margaret Kennedy. Then there were all the Duchess's ladies, her nurses and the nursery girls. It was small wonder that they were entranced by the charming little boy, and that he became the centre of attention. The Duchess herself was firm enough with him, but she loved him dearly, all the more so because he bore a striking resemblance to her own father. As for the Duke, although he often chose to play the heavy father with his sons, his pride in them was evident and James soon learned how to win him over when he was annoyed.

The Earl of Arran's early years were spent in the first floor nurseries, but these formed no enclosed world of their own. The children passed a good deal of time in their parents' company, and they had the entire Palace to explore when they were old enough, with exciting visits to the stables and to the gardens. When he was five or six, James was sent daily to Hamilton Burgh School. This was the normal procedure for the sons of Scottish noblemen. Almost all Scottish peers sent their sons to begin their education at the local grammar school: the Marquis of Atholl's sons went to Perth Academy, the Earl of Annandale's children attended school in Haddington and the Earl of Airlie's son was taught in Dundee.[1] There was much to be said for sending the boys to be educated locally, for they could stay at home under the moral and religious supervision of the family and yet have some contact with the outside world. When the Earl of Arran sat at his desk in the school founded by his Hamilton ancestor, he had for companions the sons of the burgh shopkeepers, the Palace servants and the local farmers.

At Hamilton School the Earl of Arran learned to read, write and count. As was customary, he also had his own governor, Mr Bannantyne, and by 1666 Mr Bannantyne was buying 'Latin books to my Lord Arran to learn upon.' Two years later, the Earl had progressed to a study of Ovid, Cicero and Erasmus. Nor was life all a matter of hard work. In the summer he was allowed to take his books and study with Mr Bannantyne in the Palace gardens, and there were sometimes agreeable opportunities of watching cockfighting and puppet plays.

Hamilton School provided no permanent solution to the problem of his education, though, for he could not stay there forever. By the time he was eleven the Duchess was giving serious thought to the next stage in his education. There were two alternatives. He could remain at home, taught by his governor, or he could be sent to University. The Duchess decided to seek the advice of her old friend Sir Robert Moray, and in the winter of 1669 she wrote to him tentatively outlining her plan to send James on to Glasgow Grammar School and from there to Glasgow University. Sir Robert did not approve, and wrote back at once expressing his low opinion of children 'being bred in a college.' He was even more censorious when the Duchess explained that she did not mean her son to take ordinary lodgings in the city, but would send him to board with their mutual friend Gilbert Burnet, by that time Professor of Theology in the University. Sir Robert declared that he did 'not see how your son can be well boarded as you propose, since Gilbert is unmarried . . . Nor do I at all commend a grammar school.' In his opinion, the boy should stay at home with Mr Bannantyne.

Certainly it must have been a temptation to keep him at home, but Sir Robert's long stay in the south had resulted in his opinions being given in the context of English rather than of Scottish society. Scottish noblemen's sons went to University. It was what was expected and, really, a young man's education would be incomplete otherwise. The Duchess's own father had gone to Oxford, and her uncle had been a student at Glasgow. Glasgow was only ten miles away, and there was already a longstanding link between the University and the family. James, Lord Hamilton had in 1459 bequeathed a tenement in the town to the college of arts, and the Duchess's father had not only promised 1000 merks for the new library, but had become the University's first lay chancellor.[2]

All these considerations weighed strongly with the Duchess, so in the end she decided to disregard Sir Robert Moray's advice, and the Earl was duly installed in Mr Burnet's house. Few details of his education at Glasgow Grammar School have survived. He certainly continued his classical studies, indeed, Latin was the only language officially in use in the school, and he read theology and Scottish history. Finally, in the late autumn of 1671, he was ready to begin his University studies.

Mr Bannantyne had accompanied him to Glasgow, and his accounts for the period begin on 17 November 1671, the day when the Earl entered the University. He attacked his studies with initial enthusiasm, and on 16 December Mr Bannantyne was able to reward him with £5:6/- 'for expounding Caesar's

Commentaries to me in twelve dayes space.' He was soon reading Isocrates and Homer in both Greek and Latin, and he received instruction in logic, geography, theology and French. The social graces were also included in his curriculum. He had a singing master, was fined 12/– 'for breaking the laws of the dancing school' and for some time he even had lessons in the military arts, learning how to handle pike and musket. It is perhaps significant that a week after he began his military lessons, a glazier had to be summoned hastily to mend one of the windows in his chamber. He attended church regularly, witnessed a 'boar killing', viewed a 'monstruous fish' and he paid £2:6/– to watch the dissection of a dog.

Unfortunately, these diversions occupied his attention far more than his studies did and Mr Bannantyne was finding him difficult to control. He was ready enough with his protestations of obedience and a desire to please, but his sudden enthusiasms soon faded and it was hard to persuade him to concentrate on serious matters. He was showing a deplorable preference for low company, and his family had already noted with dismay his deceitfulness. There was, for instance, the distressing incident of the map. One summer his father lent him an illustrated book, no doubt with strict admonitions to take care of it, but when James returned to Glasgow after the holidays it was discovered that one of the maps had been torn out. The Duke prized his books, so he was furious, and the Duchess had the difficult task of trying to conciliate him, at the same time writing her son an urgent letter instructing him to send the missing map back at once, since it was all too obvious what had become of it.

This in itself was a trivial incident, but it was symptomatic of what was to come. In 1674 the Earl was hotly denying Mr Burnet's accusation that he had been wasting his time, and he wrote to assure his mother that his days were fully occupied. Each morning, he declared, he rose between five and six, and spent the next three or four hours with the professor of scripture. From nine until ten he was preparing disputes, and from eleven till twelve he had a class. Certainly he had an interval for dinner after that, and 'diverted himself' until three o'clock, but he spent the rest of the afternoon reading, and from five until seven he did his history. The effect of this recital was somewhat spoiled by his admission that he had indeed gone out without permission in the past, so his family's fears were not allayed. 'Pray consider,' the Duchess begged him a year later, 'what credit it will be to you that after four years being at the college you come from it a dunce.'

By this time, she and the Duke were already planning the next stage in the education of their heir. As early as the mid sixteenth century the idea had grown up in England that a period of study in France and Italy was an excellent preparation for future life,[3] and as time passed an increasing emphasis was placed on the acquisition not only of learning but of culture. The Grand Tour therefore became an indispensable part of the courtier's training, be he English or Scottish. True, the Scots with their more limited resources did not travel abroad in such style as did their English counterparts, but already in the second decade of the seventeenth century the Earl of Mar's sons, the Master of Roxburgh and the Earl of Morton were improving themselves in France, and in the 1630s Lord Lindores and the future Earls of Southesk, Leven and Airlie were but a few of those who undertook the Tour.[4] Lesser men like Sir John Kennedy of Culzean and Sir Alexander Carnegie of Pitarrow were likewise to be found in the academies of France. All those who could afford to do so sent at least their eldest son abroad. Expensive though the Tour undoubtedly was, those peers whose sons went to study in Paris or Rome or Amsterdam were reconciled to the financial loss by the expectation that their heirs would return home accomplished gentlemen who could ride well, fence well and dance well; who could reminisce about the splendours of Versailles and point to the paintings and antiquities collected during their travels; who could converse fluently in French and Italian. Such accomplishments were immediate indications of social status, and what might seem to the twenty-first century to be mere sports and diversions were regarded by the seventeenth as serious and worthwhile occupations. The most frugal or puritanical of fathers would be perfectly satisfied to hear that his son was spending his time singing, riding and playing the lute. It is true that the young men studied mathematics, philosophy and history as well, but by the middle of the seventeenth century these were of secondary importance, unless in the case of some younger sons who studied law or military matters with a view to their future career. The primary object of the Grand Tour was to fit the young nobleman to take his place in society, and there to display all the necessary social attributes. The Duke and Duchess therefore decided that, expensive or not, it was vital that their son should undertake the Tour.

In the summer of 1675 the Earl himself had been writing urgently to friends asking them to persuade his parents to send him abroad. In fact, their minds were already made up, and they were anxiously debating the choice of a governor. In the end, they decided to send Mr Bannantyne, although he himself was reluctant to accept the responsibility. He was newly married, he did not want to leave his wife, but the real truth of it was that he foresaw trouble ahead, and emphasised that he could not think of going unless not only the Duke but the Earl himself desired his company. His objections were overruled, and in the middle of October the Earl, Mr Bannantyne and young William Hamilton the page sailed for France.

On 1 November they arrived at La Rochelle, where, after visiting the church, they toured the King of France's great magazines and inspected all the ships which were in port. Altogether, they spent nearly a week at the coast, before setting off overland through Saumur to their ultimate destination, Angers. This last was a favourite stopping place with English and Scottish visitors, because it allowed the young nobleman to avoid the temptations of Paris while learning the pure French spoken in the Loire towns.

Unfortunately, the Earl's stay in the town was not a success. Free at last of his father's restraining influence, he decided that he could now really enjoy himself. Certainly Mr Bannantyne was constantly at his elbow, complaining bitterly of home-sickness and droning on about diligence and industry, but he turned a deaf ear to the governor's admonitions and set forth on a spending spree. He returned home that night with a silver sword which had cost him £39 and a hat priced at £27.

Mr Bannantyne did his best. He hired masters of geography,

history, dancing, fencing and the guitar, but all was in vain. Instead of devoting himself to serious study, the Earl developed a passion for tennis and after a day spent at the courts he would return to his lodgings to spend the evening entertaining his dancing master to dinner. None of this was calculated to please the Duke of Hamilton, and when in Mr Bannantyne's accounts for 4 February 1676 he read the words, 'For the expenses of a ball given to Mademoiselle Chimery, £100; for masquerades £12', his reaction was as swift as it was predictable. He wrote back at once to his son rebuking him for having spent far more than was justifiable, 'and in things very unfit for you, as balls, masquerades, unnecessary clothes and tennis.' At the same time, he recalled both Mr Bannantyne and William Hamilton.

No doubt the governor was relieved by this decision, but the Earl was appalled. He felt that it was very hard of the Duke to insist on the return of Will as well, and he wrote home painting a pathetic picture of himself left 'in a strange place, destitute of any whom I can presume has tenderness for me.' His pleas failed to move his father, who remained adamant, but of course he had not the slightest intention of leaving the boy alone in France, and he had already found a replacement for the unhappy Mr Bannantyne in the person of Mr James Forbes, to whom he now remitted full and absolute charge of his son. The latter was to obey his new governor as if he were his father, and he was warned by the Duke that 'if you do not regulate your expense better and leave these vanities, your abode abroad will not be long, for it was to improve you in useful breeding you was sent there, and not to follow vanity and folly.' The Duchess added her warning that 'if there should fall the least difference between you [and Mr Forbes] it will prove an irreparable loss to you, and upon the first notices of it you will immediately be called home, and what the consequences of that will be, I shall not here enumerate.'

This letter was sent by the Duchess with Mr Forbes, who arrived in Paris in the middle of April 1676. He must have been in some trepidation as to what he should find at Angers, for it was with obvious relief that he was able to report to the Duchess on 6 May that 'His Lordship's humour and disposition ... is much better than either I did expect or was told of.' The Earl

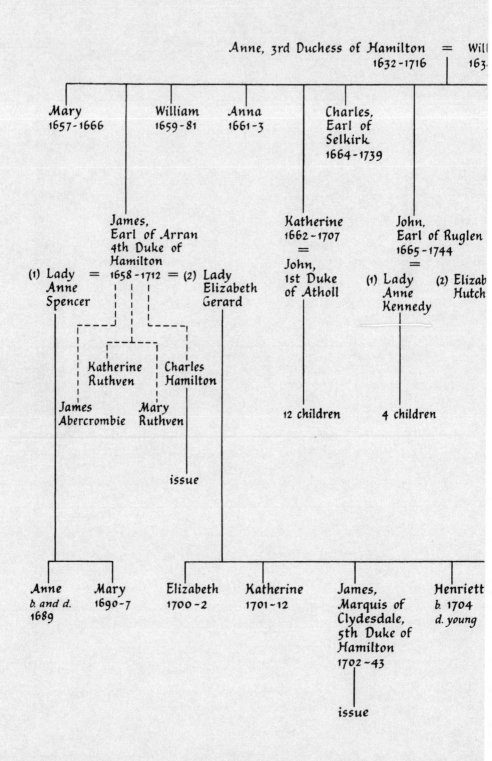

Anne, 3rd Duchess of Hamilton = Will
1632-1716   163.

Mary   William   Anna   Charles,
1657-1666   1659-81   1661-3   Earl of
                                        Selkirk
                                        1664-1739

              James,   Katherine   John,
              Earl of Arran   1662-1707   Earl of Ruglen
              4th Duke of   =   1665-1744
              Hamilton   John,   =
(1) Lady =   1658-1712 = (2) Lady   1st Duke   (1) Lady   (2) Elizab
Anne   Elizabeth   of Atholl   Anne   Hutch
Spencer   Gerard   Kennedy

              Katherine   Charles
              Ruthven   Hamilton

James   Mary
Abercrombie   Ruthven

                                        12 children   4 children

                          issue

Anne   Mary   Elizabeth   Katherine   James,   Henriett
b. and d.   1690-7   1700-2   1701-12   Marquis of   b. 1704
1689   Clydesdale,   d. young
                                                      5th Duke of
                                                      Hamilton
                                                      1702-43

                                                      issue

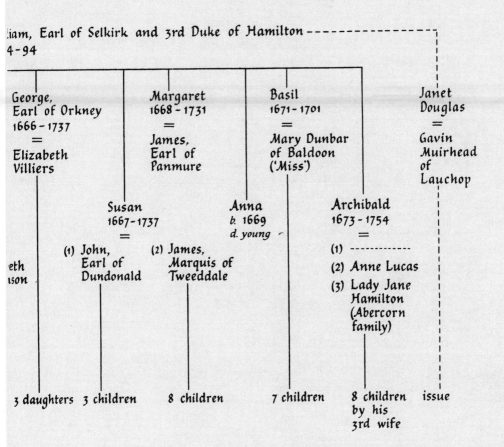

...iam, Earl of Selkirk and 3rd Duke of Hamilton - - - - - - - - - - - - -
...4-94

George,
Earl of Orkney
1666-1737
=
Elizabeth
Villiers

Margaret
1668-1731
=
James,
Earl of
Panmure

Basil
1671-1701
=
Mary Dunbar
of Baldoon
('Miss')

Janet
Douglas
=
Gavin
Muirhead
of
Lauchop

Susan
1667-1737
=

Anna
b. 1669
d. young

Archibald
1673-1754
=

...eth
...son

(1) John,
Earl of
Dundonald

(2) James,
Marquis of
Tweeddale

(1) - - - - - - - - - - - -

(2) Anne Lucas

(3) Lady Jane
Hamilton
(Abercorn
family)

3 daughters   3 children   8 children   7 children   8 children   issue
                                                                      by his
                                                                      3rd wife

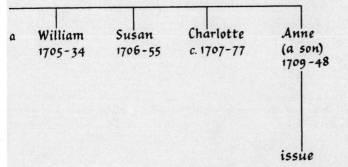

a   William   Susan   Charlotte   Anne
     1705-34   1706-55   c. 1707-77   (a son)
                                                       1709-48

issue

seemed sensible, spirited and vivacious, and on the previous day he had demonstrated his good nature when seeing off his former companions. 'He did cry mightily', Mr Forbes noted, 'expressing a great deal of sorrow to part with them having attended him so long and so well, and notwithstanding all the little quarrels between him and Mr Bannantyne.' That same day, the new governor and his charge left Angers for Blois, where his Lordship's improvement could now begin in earnest.

After a pleasant journey by way of Richelieu, where they saw the great house and paid £1:10/– for a description and drawing of it to send home to the Duke, the travellers arrived at Blois, and settled down in a house near the King's Walk, 'a garden of simples just before our door', where Mr Forbes hoped that the Earl would 'endeavour to learn the art of gardening and the virtue of plants, and love them as well as Your Grace [the Duke] does.' More important, the town afforded a variety of good masters under whom the Earl could pursue his studies. Although he had picked up a good many French words at Angers, he could not write the language or speak it correctly, so a French master was engaged. The Earl also claimed, somewhat surprisingly, that he was altogether ignorant of even the first principles of mathematics, and so Monsieur Bonhart, an excellent teacher, was hired, along with masters of fencing and dancing.

During his few weeks in Blois the Earl made gratifying progress. He mastered the four rules of arithmetic, studied geometry, navigation and fortification and continued to play tennis. With the advent of the hot weather Mr Forbes thought it wise to replace the tennis and fencing lessons with something less strenuous, and found for him a singing master. His Lordship was then discovered to have 'a good tunable voice' and a knowledge of little French songs would 'give him a good ear for dancing and make him more acceptable among the ladies at his return to England.' Despite this success Mr Forbes soon began to think of moving on. The main reason for this was the customary desire of a governor to avoid the company of his fellow countrymen, whose presence meant that the young noblemen did not need to exert themselves to speak French. At first Blois had been agreeably free from Englishmen, but they now began to arrive in force and it was reported that the Earl of Plymouth would soon be coming from Saumur. There was also the fact that only in one of the Parisian academies could the Earl's improvements be perfected. On 16 July, they therefore left Blois and, pausing at Orleans for two nights, made their way to Paris. On 19 July they had their first meal in the city.

Mr Forbes now set about choosing a suitable academy in which the Earl could pass the winter. The Duke of Hamilton's brother George, Earl of Dumbarton, was at the French Court, and he suggested Monsieur de Vallé's, but Mr Forbes rejected this on the grounds that it had neither good horses nor good masters (the order of precedence is significant) and had as its pupils some young English noblemen who would be undesirable companions for his charge. Instead, he preferred Monsieur Faubert's in the Rue Ste Marguerite, off the Faubourg St Germain, a favourite area for Scottish visitors to Paris. Its proprietor was a Protestant and its reputation good; moreover, although the sons of Lord Halifax and the Earl of Bath were already there, they were sober and discreet youths and they were accompanied by their governors.

Before entering the Earl in the academy, Mr Forbes sensibly permitted him a short period of sightseeing, during which they visited the Tuileries, the Opéra, the Louvre and Versailles. After that, they went into residence at Monsieur Faubert's, where the Earl was to spend the next few months riding, fencing, dancing, drawing and improving his French. At week-ends he left the academy, attended the famous Protestant church at Charenton, paid visits and continued his sightseeing. This pleasant routine was somewhat disturbed towards the middle of August by the arrival of an irate letter from the Duke of Hamilton criticising the move to Paris. In common with many of his contemporaries he was obviously of the opinion that Paris was too expensive and too full of temptations for his heir, so Mr Forbes hastened to appease him with descriptions of James's good progress and with assurances that his clothes would be 'neither rich nor gaudy, but plain and fashionable.' A further danger was averted in October when Lord Bruce's son Charles arrived from Holland, but was dissuaded from entering the same academy as the Earl, because Mr Forbes 'on account of their being so long together at Glasgow . . . was afraid their school acquaintance and too much former familiarity, might oblige them to play the little tricks they learned there over again here.'

The rest of the Earl's time at the academy was uneventful, although enlivened by seeing the dissecting of an anatomy and by visits to firework displays and fairs. The most important occasion of that winter came in December when James was presented to the King of France, who took particular notice of him 'and made him more than an ordinary return of his civility with a smile, which is not very common to that king to do.'

Finally, on 4 May 1677, term ended and the Earl left the academy. Mr Forbes had at one time had thoughts of taking him to Caen that summer to study civil law, but in April a letter from the Duke of Hamilton had arrived bringing the totally unexpected but altogether delightful news that he wished his son to visit Italy. Italy was not invariably included in the Tour, for reasons which were financial, political and religious, but a number of Scotsmen always had gone there. As early as 1618 the Earl of Mar's sons had toured Venice, Padua, Rome and Naples, while in 1632 Lord Lindores had declared that he longed to visit that country 'avec telle passion que si quelque malheur m'empêcherait je passerais le reste de mes heures en amertume et tristesse.'5

It was customary to wait until autumn before going south, and because of the arrival of the great heat it was necessary for the travellers to leave Paris and spend the summer elsewhere. After much deliberation Mr Forbes finally chose Bourges as the next stopping place so, taking with them Cassell's *Book of the Voyage of Italy* (a copy of which was still in the Earl's library in 1712), they made their way south through Orleans and Fontainebleau. For the next few weeks the Earl studied civil law. No mathematics or Italian masters could be found in the town, but he continued to apply himself to French, under the tuition of Monsieur Grudeh, who taught him how to write letters in that language and to read French history. He also prepared himself for the autumn by purchasing a *Journal d'un Voyage de France et d'Italie*.

Armed with this, two Italian grammars bought at Lyons, *The Prince of Condé's Voyage into Italy* and a book called *Le Guide des Chemins*, all of which were to end up in the library at Kinneil, the travellers at last set out in late September. Unhappily, it was to be several months before they were able to cross the Alps into that country, for when they reached Turin Mr Forbes fell seriously ill of a tertian fever. The Earl was greatly upset, and, fearing the worst, declared that 'never governor has taken of any gentleman [such care] as he has done hitherto upon me.' For several weeks Mr Forbes was critically ill, able to take only oranges by way of nourishment. Fortunately the Duke of Savoy's excellent physician was put at his disposal, and the Earl was befriended by the French ambassador at the Court of Savoy, the Marquis de Vilar, who was a close friend of the Earl of Dumbarton. Although he now had to keep his own accounts and write home himself, the Earl had two servants to attend him and he was soon being treated like a son by the Duke and Duchess of Savoy. As he spent his days at their Court in hunting, playing tennis, visiting the comedy and dancing, he soon became convinced that this was 'the prettiest and most civilized Court of Italy.' Meanwhile, Mr Forbes was making good progress, although it was not until January that he was well enough to travel.

After his happy time in Turin it was with mixed feelings that James moved on, but a very pleasant two weeks were now spent in Venice, during which time the visitors toured by gondola round the arsenal and the other sights, with an Irish priest as guide. From there they went to Florence, where they saw 'the Great Duke's galleries . . . and . . . the lions', St Laurence's Chapel and the Bibliothèque, before moving south to Rome.

On 20 February they arrived in the city, and were to spend the next three months there, involved in a happy round of visiting and sightseeing. Almost every afternoon Mr Watson the language master carried the Earl off to see some of the antiquities: on 26 February it was the Capitol, on 21 March the tomb of Bacchus, on 7 April 'the relics of Aaron's Rod' and on 4 May Prince Borghese's Palace. The Earl made friends with the English Cardinal Norfolk, attended a carnival and went frequently to the baths. He visited Naples, bought more Italian books, and he paid £55 to have his portrait painted by 'Ferdinando'[6] (Jacob Ferdinand Voet).

The stay in Rome was prolonged by the political situation. Mr Forbes could not contemplate travelling north because of 'the uncertainty of war or peace', and when they finally left Rome on 26 May they made their way to the French border as quickly as possible. The only real stop was made at Bologna, where Mr Forbes suffered a recurrence of his fever, but he soon recovered and by 20 July they were in Paris once more.

The Earl of Dumbarton now suggested that his nephew might stay on in the city for the purpose of promoting his family's claims to the French duchy of Châtelherault. This honour had originally been conferred on the Duchess's great-great-grandfather, but it had afterwards been revoked and bestowed upon a French nobleman. The Hamiltons still claimed the actual title, however, along with a pension in compensation for the loss of their French lands. The pension had been paid from time to time, but it was very much in arrears, and the Duke and Duchess wished to obtain payment, along with recognition of their claim to the duchy. This would certainly have been an opportunity to press these claims, but James's parents were anxious to see him again after his two and a half years' absence. More important, he was now of marriageable age, a suitable bride must be found for him, and in any case his parents simply could not afford to keep him on the continent any longer.

The Earl's tour had undoubtedly been expensive, though it did not compare with the huge sums spent by some of the English nobility. The English nobleman set off for France with an entourage of at least ten attendants and only a mere gentleman would move around with just one or two servants. Expenditure was correspondingly high. In the 1630s the Earl of Salisbury gave his eldest son £1,500 sterling a year and his two younger boys £1,200 each, while in 1629 the Duke of Lennox had been claiming that he could not live on £2,000 a year, and had been asking for more.[7]

In contrast to these large sums, the Earl of Arran was expected to spend no more than £600 sterling a year, so economy was one of Mr Forbes's main preoccupations. He asked his employer to send bills of exchange from London rather than from Edinburgh, as Scottish bankers exacted more and were less obliging than the English and French. He allowed the Earl only two servants, and in Paris managed to save money by borrowing the Earl of Dumbarton's coach. The fees of the academy had themselves been high: a contemporary 'Memoire de ce qu'il coûte à un gentilhomme qui entre pensionnaire à l'académie' estimated a quarter's fees at 790 livres with another 150 or so for master's fees and domestic expenses, and James paid more than £150 a quarter, what with 700 livres to Monsieur Faubert, the cost of clothing, servants' wages and the Earl's own pocket money of two crowns a week. As Mr Forbes pointed out, a gentleman of the Earl's status was expected to live in a certain style, and during the previous session of the academy the sons of Lord Bath and Lord Halifax had each spent over £800 sterling but were not more in company than the Earl. Mr Forbes did in fact manage to keep almost within the limits imposed, and by May of 1678 he could boast that since he had entered the Duke's service he had spent only 15,565 livres or £1,203 sterling. From the Duke's point of view, however, the £7,200 Scots a year spent on his eldest son was a severe drain on his finances, and it was only to be hoped that James would return from his foreign travels improved beyond all recognition.

The Earl and Mr Forbes stayed in Paris for six weeks only on their second visit. On 23 September 1678 they embarked on the yacht *Merlin*, which that day sailed for Gravesend. Back in Scotland, an anonymous poet anticipated James's return with delight:

> 'Six times more welcome than returning light
> To Greenland men, after six times more night . . .
> Illustrious Arran, thou art welcome home,
> Fraught with improvements from all Christendom',

he declared, and initially the Earl's family shared these sentiments.

The Duke was in London when his son returned, and at first he was favourably impressed. Outwardly he found little difference in James, despite his long absence, and he was able to write home to the Duchess, 'You will see little change in his face and he is scarce so tall as my brother James [Lord James Douglas]', adding, 'I hope he will have sense enough, and he carries himself discreetly and I use him as a comrade.' A fortnight later he was less optimistic. Not only had the boy returned home with very few clothes, but 'I find also that he has neglected even his exercises and not followed them so as he should have done, and even spent his time abroad as he did at home at Glasgow by conversing too much with idle company, which is his great satisfaction still . . . and for his sincerity I fear he retains too much of the way he had when he was a child.'

The real effect of his Grand Tour upon James is difficult to assess, but perhaps its most enduring influence on him was that it transformed him into a lover of all things French, and was at least to some extent responsible for his later Jacobite sympathies. On a happier note, it may well have been in the galleries of France and Italy that he developed his life-long love of paintings, and it was certainly there that he acquired his fatal passion for fencing and duelling. All in all, he returned with a taste for a far more sophisticated way of life than Scotland could offer, so that thoughts of settling down there were, in his father's words, 'much the same to him as to go to the galleys.'

Despite this unsatisfactory state of affairs, the Duke and Duchess followed the same pattern for the education of their younger sons. Lord William, only a year younger than James, was delicate. No specific account of his malady is given in the correspondence, but it seems that he suffered from some serious physical handicap. His stay at Glasgow Grammar School was interrupted by ill health, and he was late in entering the University there. His delicate constitution made it plain that he would have to 'win his livelihood by his pen and by the endowments of the spirit', and so his parents decided that he should study law. His expertise in this subject would be of great value to the family, and he could stay at home and advise his parents in all their multifarious legal affairs.

He was accordingly sent to the Low Countries to begin his legal studies there. Patient and hardworking, he kept a note of all his own expenditure in a beautiful, neat hand, for he went abroad without a governor. 'He gives me very exact and perfect accounts what he does', the Duke wrote to Mr Forbes, 'and tell James if he saw his letters he would think shame of his own.' William travelled on to Poitiers, where he spent a year, before entering one of the Paris academies. He even ventured to take up riding there, and he was on the point of returning home when, in the late spring of 1681, his health broke down completely.

He lay ill with dysentery throughout the summer, consoled by the fact that his uncle Lord James Douglas was lodging in the same house, and his cousins the Drumlanrigs were in Paris with their governor, Mr Fall. As autumn came on, Lord James himself contracted a serious fever and died. The Drumlanrigs, like all the rest of the English and Scottish gentlemen, were preparing to move south, and Lord William feared that he would be left alone, 'destitute of those helps and comforts he has received from his fellow countrymen . . . and . . . it very much weighs his spirit to be left among strangers', as Mr Fall reported to the Duke, begging him to send out one of the Hamilton servants to keep Lord William company. There was to be no need for such an arrangement. Lord William died on the morning of 23 September, as calmly and uncomplainingly as he had lived, cheered by his mother's last letter to him which had arrived the night before and was found beneath his head after his death. His cousins attended his funeral in the Protestant cemetery near the Hospital of the Charity in the Faubourg St Germain,[8] and his few pathetic belongings were shipped home to Scotland in the care of a young Scots merchant called Hamilton. The Duke had at first kept the seriousness of their son's condition from the Duchess, but when news of his death came, he could not conceal it. They had been on their way from Edinburgh to Hamilton, and the Duchess stayed on at Kinneil for some days, too overcome by grief to travel.

Happily, the other members of the family were of a different constitution. After Glasgow University, Lord Charles, the next brother, was sent to France with his governor Mr Fenton, and after a few months in Blois, went on to Paris where he reluctantly entered one of the academies. His stay in France was somewhat interrupted by the presence of James, who had lately arrived again at the French Court. He proved a grave source of distraction, and finally carried Charles off to watch the siege of Luxembourg, despite their father's irate commands that Charles be made to resume his studies at once or return home, 'for it's not a soldier I intend him, and so long as he stop there he shall not have sixpence from me.' Repeated threats of this nature were without avail, but Luxembourg finally surrendered, and the Duchess wrote to James to tell him that she was pleased to hear it, 'both that there was less blood shed and for my particular concern in you and your brother . . . I hope you will not expose yourselves so needlessly again, but make haste to England with your brother whom you may tell from me that if ever he offer to dispose of himself again without his father's allowance [i.e. consent] and mine he shall never get anything from us, and that this he has done shall on his return be pardoned . . . He writes to his father that he as well as you are looked on more favourably than others, which if he prefer so airy a thing to the favour of his parents he must be very simple . . . I will not say how great a disquiet your being at Luxembourg has been to me, but I am sure in duty you both ought not to have given me such perplexities.'

When Lord Charles did return home, Lord John and Lord George were immediately dispatched with their governor and 'some pills to take to sea.' Unlike the older brothers, they had attended St Andrews University, where they had studied mathematics, fortification, gunnery and geography. Lord John now gave up these military subjects and read law at Poitiers: he was to replace Lord William in the role of the family's legal expert. Lord George continued with his military training, though, and eventually entered the army.

As for the two youngest sons, Lord Basil and Lord Archibald went to Glasgow University, but that concluded their cultural education. It would have been far too expensive to send them abroad as well. Lord Basil remained at home to help manage the estates, and indeed he did not even go to England until he was in his early twenties. Lord Archibald, on the other hand, professed a desire to enter the Navy, and in spite of their misgivings, his parents allowed him to do so. The Duke took him to London where he spent six months studying with the Astronomer Royal: the accounts record that the Duke paid £30 sterling 'to John Flamsteed in London . . . for expenses, diet and tuition.' Even then, the Duke had doubts about sending him to sea, and told the Duchess 'I have vexation and trouble enough with the rest of our sons here and does not know what to do with Archibald. He will be great charge to send him with some of these fleets that is going to the straits or West Indies and it will be long enough befor[e] he gets command to free us of charge. He looks still so like a boy.' In the end, though, he arranged for Archibald to join *The Resolution*.

While their brothers studied at Glasgow and toured on the continent, the three surviving Hamilton daughters stayed at home. Just as the education of a nobleman may be said to have been vocational in that it was designed to fit him to take his place in society and, to some extent at least, to manage his estates, so too his sisters would be trained for their future place in life. Marriage was the most likely destiny for a Duke's daughter, and as the wife of another peer she would be expected to run her household, keep accounts and display a variety of social accomplishments.

The girls were accordingly taught to read and to write an elegant italic hand. Learning arithmetic came later. The eldest daughter, Lady Katherine, was a tall, black haired young woman with a serious disposition. When she reached the age of eighteen her father gave her £66:13:4 and told her to keep an exact account of how it was spent. The payments noted down were mainly small, personal disbursements for gloves, stockings and little presents for the family, but she included £2:18/– given to her brothers' writing master for teaching her arithmetic. For the next two and a half years she continued to keep her accounts, and her father gradually increased the money he gave her until she was entrusted with £250 for four or five months. Her early training in household management was to stand her in good stead. In later life she often checked her husband's accounts for him and on one occasion, looking over the chamberlain's calculations, she jokingly told her husband 'I make you but about a groat in his debt, which he was convinced of himself.'[9]

Lady Susan, the second daughter, was more interested in the social side of the girls' education. Tall, elegant, and as fair as Katherine was dark, she was fond of clothes and she particularly enjoyed the dancing lessons which formed a part of her curriculum. For a number of years she and her sisters had regular lessons from Mr Edward Founteine, the dancing master, and they were also taught to sing and to play the harpsichord.

There are indications that their education went farther than the basic reading and writing, singing and dancing. Margaret, the youngest daughter, was artistic, and from an early age she was fond of painting and of writing poetry. Among her surviving verses are four lines marked by herself as being 'made when I was 10 years of age, which my father always wore in his pocket.'[10] More than that, one historian has recorded that her 'acquaintance with the classics . . . is evinced by the remarks and notes in her own handwriting which appear upon Latin books in the Panmure Library'.[11] Certainly by the time of the next generation it was regarded as being desirable to teach girls languages, and the Duchess's granddaughters had lessons in Latin as well as in French from an early age, 'because it helps them to spell and understand the English.'

As daughters of a Duke, the girls were much sought-after prizes in the matrimonial market, but the Duchess was a firm believer in the principle that a girl should marry only someone to whom she was attracted: if she did not like the proposed bridegroom, her family should take the matter no farther but should seek a husband for her elsewhere. She was therefore very careful where the marriages of her own daughters were concerned, and when in 1682 the Marquis of Atholl proposed that his eldest son Lord Murray should marry Lady Katherine, she and the Duke at first did nothing. However, the quiet, serious Katherine was soon won over by Lord Murray's ardent wooing, and the following year they were married. They were delighted with each other, and their happiness endured for the rest of their married life. Early on Lady Katherine told the Earl of Arran that he would never regret any kindness he did Lord Murray, 'for he deserves it all, better then I do; but perhaps you may think it is partiality in me which I do assure you [it] is not, for if you knew him you wou'd say it all and more', and a letter of about 1690 gives a pleasing glimpse of their life together: in the course of writing to the Earl, Lord Murray mentioned that his wife 'has been feeding me with my breakfast while I have been writing this.'

A year after Katherine's marriage, Lady Susan became the wife of an Ayrshire nobleman, Lord Cochrane. They began their married life in the household of the bridegroom's grandfather, and Susan was not very happy at first. She told her mother that she 'never knew what it was to be bid to do everything my self before', but she soon settled down and enjoyed a few years of happiness before her husband's premature death in 1690. He left her with three young children under the age of five, but seven years later she remarried and had eight more children.

Lady Margaret, the youngest sister, married in 1687. Her husband, the Earl of Panmure, came from a strongly Royalist family, and both he and his bride were pleased with the marriage. 'It's a rich one', the Duke of Hamilton told the Earl of Arran, 'and that's all and she is pleased and he is in haste to be married before Lent.'

By this time, all the Duke's sons had completed their education, and the Duke and Duchess could reflect that they had made sure that their sons and daughters were as well educated as any of their contemporaries. Nothing had been omitted in a programme designed to give them all possible advantages. The sons had studied at the University and had received a grounding in the classics. The Earl of Arran had been given the opportunity of profiting from all that travel in France and Italy had to offer in the way of personal improvement: whether he would take advantage of it remained to be seen. Lord Charles was a cultivated, civilised gentleman who had found favour with the King. Lord John's legal studies would stand the family in good stead. Lord George was successfully launched upon a military career which would culminate in his becoming Britain's first field-marshal. Lord Basil was proving invaluable in assisting with the estates, and Lord Archibald was enjoying life in what he termed his 'little wooden world' at sea. The three daughters were accomplished young brides, and if the achievement of all this had been expensive, it had certainly been worthwhile.

CHAPTER 7

The English Influence

When the Earl of Arran had returned from his Grand Tour, he had found his father in London. The Duke was visiting the south with increasing frequency and, apart from their political implications, these visits had another significance. There is little doubt that in their aspirations and ambitions the Scottish peerage were influenced by what they saw in England. The effect of the union of the crowns on the Scottish aristocracy has often been exaggerated. In 1603 the Scottish King went to live in London but the Scottish Parliament and Privy Council continued to meet in Edinburgh, the nation's central law courts were there, and every peer had business which took him to the Scottish capital each year. It was to be the union of the parliaments in 1707 which was to bring about a real change in the situation, not the union of the crowns, and throughout the seventeenth century only a handful of peers like the Earl of Dysart and the Duke of Lauderdale actually took up residence in England. Nevertheless, noblemen with any political ambition at all found it necessary to visit Court from time to time, and naturally enough when they were in London they made purchases of goods not available at home, noted the latest fashions in clothes and furnishings and generally brought back with them new ideas about the style in which life should be lived.

On the whole, their attitude towards London was an ambivalent one. There was the feeling that it was a place full of moral temptation, and in his last letter of advice to his wife, the Duchess's uncle had urged her to 'forget and hate the empty pleasures of a licentious Court, or of London, and with David pray, "Turn my eyes from beholding vanity, and quicken Thou

149

d lodgings in town. These
sive, but in a fashionable
of Tweeddale to bespeak
thereabouts . . .', Lord
1673, 'where Mr Cole
lton. See they be good and
good lodging. The Earl of
that street next Whitehall,
dchambers above for your-
loor as can be had.'[2]
ngs was to ask a friend to
rst visit to London in 1660
that the Duke of Hamilton
eafter he had Andrew Cole
him in advance. Whenever
hall or St James Park as you
house and stables as part of
en he was at Mrs Rugley's,
ble his horses and leave his
's Head in Haymarket.
y the week, since he never
town. During the 1670s he
he oddly named Mr Imp in
it he really preferred to be in
in Leicesterfields. There was
hen he arrived at a house in
ext day, 'His Grace not being
cause in great disorder.' Mrs
re satisfactory, and the Duke
reasonable rate there'. His
rs Nepho's. Not only was it
household in comfort, but it
o herself was on hand to help
ed.
a week, which was the highest
ugley took £4 a week, Mrs
e asked £3:10/- and Mr Imp
se this would include furniture,

bed-linen and table-linen, although the occasional item was hired from elsewhere: the Duke borrowed a clock from Mr Knibb in 1694 for the Leicesterfields lodgings.

The weekly rent did not include board. Very often the Duke had his meals out, dining almost every evening with friends or at Court, and sometimes he would eat at a tavern, 'The Rose' in Bridges Street, 'The Fountain' or 'The Horseshoe' in Charing Cross. Sometimes he would arrange to have meals sent in from a nearby eating house, but in later years he had to be careful what he ate and he brought his master household with him from Scotland, to supervise a temporary cook hired in town. He was not always as fortunate as he was in 1693 when he 'got a very good cook and seems to be a very honest fellow', as he told the Duchess, adding 'I give him 10/– a week beside his entertainment [lodgings], and a maid under him. He makes the bills for dinner as we used there [at Hamilton] and writes a good hand and understands the buying of meat much better than Lamb [the provisor] ... I drink broth every morning and eat jelly every night, which the cook makes very well.'

Not only the cook and the cookmaid but another maid to help with the food and sometimes a porter and footman would be hired in town. By far the greatest part of the household, however, consisted of the Duke's own Scottish servants, for when he travelled south he was accompanied by his secretary, his grooms, footmen and his valet. The cost of maintaining this household in London was high. Food was expensive, there were many purchases to be made, and there were always extra items like coach and horse hires, flambeaux and 'pocket money' for the Duke himself. On average he would spend £6,000 Scots a month while he was in London, and this could rise to as much as £400 sterling, as when he came south in 1686. Most of this money he gave to his secretary before they set out, and it had been derived from the rents of the estates. Sometimes it was possible to defray the cost a little by selling something in London, but this formed only a fraction of the total charge. In 1686, for example, the Duke provided over £3,000 Scots for the coming visit. An additional £21:14/– was received from the Earl of Arran as the balance of an old account, and later the sale of an old grey gelding raised a

Above left: 'One of My Lord's Six Children', possibly Duchess Anne as a child, by an unknown artist (The Hamilton Collection, Lennoxlove)

Above right: 'One of My Lord's Six Children', possibly Lady Susanna as a child, by an unknown artist (The Hamilton Collection, Lennoxlove)

Below: William, 2nd Duke of Hamilton, Duchess Anne's uncle (on left) and John, 1st Duke of Lauderdale, by C. Jonson, 1649 (The Hamilton Collection, Lennoxlove)

The north front of Hamilton Palace, drawn by Isaac Miller, 1677 (Crown Copyright: RCAHMS)

'The Colledge of Glasgow', engraved by J. Slezer (Crown Copyright: RCAHMS)

The south front of Hamilton Palace, built by James Smith, 1693-7 and photographed in 1919 (*Country Life*)

The old north front of Hamilton Palace, from an engraving of 1807 (Crown Copyright: RCAHMS)

James, 4th Duke of Hamilton, painted in Rome while on the Grand Tour, by Jacob Ferdinand Voet (The Hamilton Collection, Lennoxlove)

Lady Elizabeth Gerard, the 4th Duke of Hamilton's second wife, by Maria Verelst (National Trust for Scotland)

John, Earl of Ruglen, Duchess Anne's fourth son, by G. Kneller (The Hamilton Collection, Lennoxlove)

George, Earl of Orkney, Duchess Anne's fifth son, by G. Kneller (The Hamilton Collection, Lennoxlove)

Lord Basil Hamilton, Duchess Anne's sixth son, by G. Kneller (The Hamilton Collection, Lennoxlove)

Lord Archibald Hamilton, Duchess Anne's seventh son, by G. Kneller (The Hamilton Collection, Lennoxlove)

The monument to the 3rd Duke of Hamilton, now in St Bride's Church, Bothwell (Crown Copyright: RCAHMS)

The silver communion cups presented by Duchess Anne to Dalserf Church in 1700 (Dalserf Parish Church)

Gold chatelaine hook worn by Duchess Anne, from which her watch was suspended (The Hamilton Collection, Lennoxlove)

further £4:10/– sterling. Once, the Duke received an allowance of £400 sterling from the Scottish Privy Council 'for his journey to and from London on the King's service',[3] but this was exceptional because he was usually in opposition.

Most of the Duke's visits to London lasted for about two months, although there were those occasions when he stayed on longer, and he was often delayed by the fact that it was necessary to obtain the King's permission before departing. Only on rare occasions did the Duchess accompany him. Her visit to the town in the summer of the Restoration to pave the way for her husband's reception at Court was the first time she had been there since childhood, and although she took the Duke to see round Chelsea Place, she found most of the familiar places in town too painfully evocative to visit, the royal palace at Whitehall having the most tragic associations of all. She therefore usually declined to accompany her husband to Court, although she sometimes went with him to Tunbridge Wells or Bath.

The purpose of these trips south was, of course, political. At one time the Scottish nobleman could use his influence in Edinburgh, but now the Court was in London and that was where all the scheming and manœuvring for places went on. With his growing significance as a statesman, the Duke associated more and more with fellow politicians, and he took rather a touching pride in this evidence of his own importance. 'All the great men about the town and Court has made me visits', he told the Duchess in 1693, and he was always careful to record any noteworthy invitations: 'I met this day with the Archbishop of Canterbury at Whitehall, who invited me to dine with him on Saturday', 'I was particularly invited to My Lord Mayor's feast on Monday' and so on. His companions during the later years were men who, like himself, were supporters of the 1688 settlement. At least once a week he would dine with the Duke of Bolton, an almost exact contemporary and a strong Whig. Almost as often he saw the Duke of Devonshire, another leading Whig, and Hans Bentinck, otherwise William of Orange's close friend the Duke of Portland.

Not only was London now the seat of the Scottish Court and the centre of political intrigue, it was also the great centre of conspicuous consumption. The English nobility who flocked to

Court each autumn spent large sums there on the latest clothing and jewellery, and could purchase all manner of luxuries not available elsewhere.[4]

Not to be outdone, the Duke of Hamilton took time to make expensive purchases too, many of them designed to enhance and modernise Hamilton Palace. The clothing which he bought for himself and his wife formed only a proportion of his purchases in the south. Whenever he set off for London without the Duchess, she saw to it that he was equipped with a memorandum which was in fact a shopping list, so that he was involved in all manner of domestic complications. Sometimes the list itself was at fault, as in September 1689 when the Duke wrote home to complain that her memorandum was 'so general you put me to it, for you neither tell the fineness you would have the damask napkins nor the length or breadth of the tablecloths and I have no skill what to say.' The Duchess did elaborate to some extent, but in his next letter he was still asking 'what rate the damask napkins and tablecloths should be at and the length and breadth of them . . . Let me know also where you got the cherry dishes, for I can find none but what is either much coarser and as dear or much finer and none under a crown a piece.' It was not surprising that on one occasion he was driven to remark, 'I confess I like this trade of buying things worst of any, for I see I do not understand it.'

Apart from all the petty irritations involved, his main reason for disliking 'this trade of buying things' was that it entailed a good deal of expense. He was always very much aware that there was no room for extravagance, and every item of expenditure had to be justified – all the more so because goods in London were so much more expensive than at home. He could buy a periwig in Edinburgh for £11 Scots, but in London it would cost him the equivalent of £84 Scots. A suit made in London could cost twice as much as one made in Edinburgh, and £29 Scots spent there could pay a carpenter for two bedsteads and a table, whereas in England the equivalent sum would buy only one small table. These differences in price can in part be attributed to the more elaborate materials used in London, but any item purchased there was liable to have an inflated price simply because there was always a flourishing market for luxury goods.

Because of this situation, the Duke worried constantly about whether he was being overcharged and thought carefully before he bought anything. If silks had gone up in price since his last visit, he would have his new bed hung with a dark coloured cloth instead. He would remind the Duchess that she herself had been of the opinion that a copper warming pan would be better than a silver one, and although he admired some real Indian cabinets in the city, because the cheapest of them was forty guineas he would tell his wife, 'For my part I think a counterfeit one looks as well and will so there, so let me know if you will take such a one or give the forty guineas.'

One method of economising was to give in part exchange an article no longer of any use. When the Duke wanted a new silver sword he could hand in his old one and so have to pay only the £1:10/– balance. Similarly, his old gold watch could help to pay for the new one, and some useless plate could be exchanged for a new silver tea kettle and a chafing dish. Then again, part of an old article could be used in the making of a new one, as in 1688 when he had the glass from a coach he had bought from the Duchess of Monmouth put into a new one he was having built. On another occasion, he instructed the coachmaker to convert his chariot into a travelling coach.

Because of this financial stringency, the Duke did not purchase in London articles which could be had at home. Disregarding those items bought for consumption in town – fuel, food and so on – the goods he bought to send home to Scotland fell into definite categories, despite any impression to the contrary given by the bills of lading. Certainly these last record a heterogeneous collection of articles. In 1691, for example, the Duke sent to Bo'ness in James Boutchart's ship *The Rose* six firkins of soap, six weather glasses, a tin box with tea in it, *The Scots Acts of Parliament*, two pamphlets, several pairs of shoes, a pound of chocolate, some harness, six maps of the Holy Land, a quantity of sweetmeats, a looking glass, an iron grate and Montaigne's *Essais* in three volumes. Nevertheless, his purchases were far from being random or capricious.

Much of the money spent by the Duke in London went on the purchase of clothing, but the most costly single item in the accounts was undoubtedly a new coach. Whenever he needed a new one, it was in London that he placed his order. In 1660, he was having made a new coach with taffeta curtains and red and white ribbons, and Evan the coachmaker worked regularly for him over the years. These coaches were for use in Scotland, and they were shipped home as soon as they had been completed. Sedan chairs were also bought in town. The mourning sedan bought by the Duchess in the summer of 1685 was probably used by her in London, for the Court was then in mourning for Charles II, but a sedan ordered in 1693 was chosen with a view to impressing friends at home. The Duke reported having seen a very pretty one 'lined with blue flowered velvet with blue and gold fring[e] and white damask curtains.' Lined with red flowered velvet it would cost forty shillings less, but in any case it had gilded nails, fine glass and, in the Duke's opinion, was 'finer . . . than your son Arran's.'

As well as the actual coaches, the Duke sometimes purchased horses in London. Presumably Smithfield could offer a better selection than anywhere at home, and there was always a brisk trade amongst the nobility themselves. Over the years the Duke bought a succession of black geldings, white geldings and grey nags, and his most expensive purchase of this sort was made in the month before his death, when he paid almost £60 'to my Lord Paulet for two grey Flanders coach horses.' Some of his dogs came from London too, selected from the doghouse at Knightsbridge.

Much of what the Duke bought, however, was designed to enhance Hamilton Palace. He and the Duchess wanted their residence to be furnished in the latest fashion, and so the Duke would spend £7 sterling on 'a pair of silver candlesticks of the new fashion', or 'a new fashioned screen' and 'four large double new fashioned beer and wine glasses.'

Most of the impressive beds which were in the Palace had also been bought in London. When the Duchess wanted a new one, her husband usually paid a visit to Jean Paudevin in Pall Mall, cabinet-maker to Charles II. In the winter of 1688 the Frenchman was at work on a magnificent 'crimson mohair bed lined with green satin, fringed with silk fringe and quilted mohair cushions.'

The draperies were embroidered with scarlet silk thread and it took seven hundred and thirty-eight ounces of scarlet silk fringe to make the trimmings. Eight black arm-chairs upholstered in green accompanied the bed, along with eight walnut chairs covered in crimson serge and a walnut easy chair upholstered in striped plush and edged with gold and white silk fringe. There was a walnut couch to match and Paudevin even supplied the four quilts and two pairs of blankets that went with the bed. The complete set cost the Duke over £326 sterling.

Beds were no problem to send home because they were easy to dismantle, but the purchase of other furniture was to some extent limited by the difficulty of transporting it. Large items were too heavy and cumbersome, and small goods might be broken in transit – a consignment of chairs was badly damaged at sea in 1678. Nevertheless, chairs were perhaps the item of furniture most frequently bought, and each time he was in London the Duke acquired several dozen more. One bill mentions 'the chair embroidered with gold' but usually they were the more mundane '3 bundles chairs' or '18 cane chairs.' He bought small tables almost as often, on one occasion sending home as many as six Spanish tables at a time.

If London could offer a wide range of well-made furniture, it could also provide a fine selection of entrepôt goods. With the Court creating a continuing demand for luxuries, the city became a flourishing market for foreign wares. A wide variety of textiles from the Far East and the Levant, household goods from the Low Countries, fruits and spices, dyes and medicines – all could be purchased in London. The Duke took advantage of this fact to buy a number of foreign articles. Whether or not he bought the real Indian cabinet or the counterfeit one remains unknown, but he did purchase fifty-three yards of crimson Indian cloth and forty-two yards striped with gold to be made into curtains for the Palace. The box of tea and the figs that he sent home had probably come by way of Holland, and the chocolate which the Duchess enjoyed was certainly brought to Europe by the Dutch.

There was a great vogue for drinking chocolate in the mid seventeenth century. Pepys tasted it as early as 1664 and Evelyn mentioned it nearly twenty years later. Purchases of chocolate occur in the Hamilton accounts in 1667, but the Duke nonetheless thought it best to offer some advice when he sent some to the Duchess in 1694. 'Two cups of chocolate, they say, clogs your stomach', he warned her, 'and puts you from your dinner, so if the cups be big you should take but one.' He purchased it in fairly large quantities – twenty-five or fifty pounds at a time – paying about four shillings for a pound. (In 1682 it was advertised in *The London Gazette* at from 2/6d to 5/– a pound.[5])

Some of the other goods in the Palace had also originated in Holland. In 1689 the Duke bought from John Greene at the King's Arms in the Poultry a variety of bottles and crockery, including 'four very fine blue Dutch cups' and 'eighteen very fine Dutch painted saucers, several fashions.' Table-linen and bed-linen came from Holland too. Much of the linen used in the Palace was made in Scotland, but occasionally there were purchases of '6 yards of fine tabling damask' or '112¾ yards of fine napkins' from London merchants. On the whole, though, any linen not manufactured in Scotland was bought direct from abroad, for, as the Duke had found out, it was much dearer to buy it in London. 'It's very troublesome to me to get all the things bought', he complained to the Duchess, 'and I am sure I shall be cheated, especially as to your damask table cloths and napkins, for I can see none good and they say they are twice as cheap got from Holland.'

Harassed as he was by the need to choose all these household goods, the Duke turned with relief to another import from Holland much nearer to his heart – garden seeds and plants. On his very first trip south he had paid £7 'to the Frenchman for seeds to the garden', making a further payment of £1:10/– to him 'for two garden knots drawn on paper.' Later on, both he and his brother-in-law the Earl of Cassilis patronised Edward Fuller, the seedsman at Strand Bridge. From him, the Duke bought seeds of marigold, gillyflower and nasturtium, as well as vegetable seeds. He ordered tuber rose roots, cypress seeds, and one year purchased 2/6d worth of 'sensible and humble plants.' Of course, not everything for the garden came from abroad. He visited Brompton Park when he wanted new fruit trees, buying from Mr London the gardener there such items as three peach, three apricot, three pear and three cherry trees, and later he was to acquire fig trees and vines from the same source.

Nor did the Duke forget his cellar when he was in London. Generally he obtained wine direct from France through the Edinburgh and Glasgow merchants but this was supplemented by casks shipped home from London, so he occasionally bought canary, Rhenish wine and claret when he was in town. He chose comparatively few provisions of other types: sometimes a flitch of bacon, barrels of pickles and sweetmeats or a large cheese, but most foods were readily obtainable at home.

Not only were foreign goods available in London. There were foreign craftsmen too, and from time to time the Duke availed himself of their services. He rather liked the occasional pair of shoes made by Louis Leclerc, had his hats made by a Monsieur Chaigneau and his periwigs came from Monsieur Laborde. It is interesting to speculate whether or not the Duke preferred to patronise another group of 'foreign' merchants and craftsmen in London – his own fellow countrymen. Certainly the names of several people with whom the Duke dealt suggest that they may well have been Scottish in origin. He patronised James Heriot the goldsmith, bought muffs and chocolate from James Donaldson and went to a tailor named Munro, while the Duchess had some of her gowns made by a John Ramsay.

If London could offer the Scottish peer the services of skilled foreign craftsmen, it could also provide those of native specialists. Plate and jewellery were often acquired there. Early in the 1670s the Duke spent £155 on a set of silver plate, and the following spring he had engraved three dozen plates, along with salvers, basins, pepper boxes and other silver articles. From time to time he added another piece or two, like the great silver cooler which cost him £100, but this remained the basic family plate for the next thirty years.

As for jewellery, this was entrusted to Richard Beauvoir at the Silver Ball in Pall Mall when any alteration was to be made. In 1660 the Duke had a new diamond set in his 'bracelet' when he was in town, and the Duchess and her daughters often asked for pieces to be reset. Lady Katherine in 1682 sent up a diamond clasp for that purpose, and Lord Basil sent a diamond to be combined with those which formerly surrounded a sapphire in a brooch, so that a locket could be made for his fiancée, Mary Dunbar. It was from Beauvoir, too, that the Duke purchased his great George costing £610 sterling and his little George costing £52 sterling when he became a Knight of the Garter.

Clocks and watches also came from London. A new repeating watch cost the Duke £60 sterling in 1693, and some years before he had bought an eight day spring clock in an ebony case, a little thirty hour clock in a walnut case, a thirty hour clock marked with the minutes and the days of the month, and even 'a little pendulum alarm'.

These purchases made it plain that from the early days of their marriage the Duke and Duchess were very much concerned with seeing that Hamilton Palace was furnished in a modern and in a suitable manner, with all the latest luxuries as far as expense would allow. Similarly, it was the custom to fill the gallery of one's great house with family portraits, and the seventeenth-century nobleman sat for his portrait as a matter of course. To be painted by a fashionable artist was a well-known ambition among the aristocracy, and at this period the most fashionable artist of all was Sir Godfrey Kneller.

At one time or another, Kneller painted every member of the Hamilton family, mainly at the instigation of the Earl of Arran. The Earl had a passion for paintings of all kinds, he was a protégé of Charles II, and he knew the Duke of Monmouth well. These two were the first important patrons of Kneller, so it was only to be expected that the Earl would soon be introduced to his work. When exactly he sat to Kneller is unknown. The existing portrait of him* has been assigned to a much later date on stylistic grounds but it would be surprising if he had not also sat about 1680.[6] Kneller arrived in England in 1676 but it was not until three years later that he obtained real recognition. In 1679 he painted Monmouth, then Charles II, and with the death of Lely in 1680 he became the pre-eminent Court painter.[7] It is therefore interesting to note that it was in 1679 that the Duke and Duchess of Hamilton sat to him. The Duke was painted in the summer of that year, and in the autumn several payments were

* In the Collection of the Duke of Hamilton.

made for the Duchess's portrait. Hers was particularly successful. Kneller's portraits of the young Court beauties have often been criticised as being lifeless and lacking in individuality, but he obviously found in the Duchess's features a strength of character worthy of his talents.*

Throughout the 1680s Kneller painted a galaxy of important clients, including Louis XIV, James II and Mary of Modena, but lists of his major works do not mention any of the Hamilton family. In the following decade, however, the younger generation of Hamiltons all sat to him. When the Earl of Arran eventually married he persuaded his wife to sit, and she wrote him a letter telling him that she had, 'according to your commands been at Kneller's this morning'. This remark was echoed by Lord Archibald in 1691 when he told the Earl, 'According to your desire I have been at Kneller and am to sit for my picture on Wednesday next.' He wore armour for the occasion, and was painted with a ship in the background, as befitted a sailor. Lord George, who was painted in the same year, was portrayed against an equally suitable military background, as was Lord Charles. Lord John also sat in 1691, after some delay while waiting for a new wig, and when Lord Basil came to London for the first time, he too sat to Kneller. Finally, in 1700, the three sisters were painted. According to Lord Basil, Lady Susan's picture was 'very well done' but he declared, 'I don't like the other two sisters' pictures.' All of the portraits were sent home to hang in Hamilton Palace.†

Fashionable painters were to be found at Court and so too were fashionable doctors. Although the Duke always declared that he had 'ill will to meddle with the doctors', he was in middle age distinctly valetudinarian, and he quite often sought their advice for bouts of sciatica, gravel and the like. Normally the Edinburgh and Glasgow practitioners served him adequately and he could buy his medicine in Hamilton itself, but he placed a good deal of reliance on the medicinal value of a visit to Bath or Tunbridge Wells. No doubt he enjoyed the society there, but his health was

---

* See frontispiece.

† Lady Katherine's portrait is in the Collection of the Duke of Atholl: the other portraits are in the Collection of the Duke of Hamilton.

his main concern and on such visits he bathed and took the waters assiduously. In 1678, for instance, he paid £1:6/– sterling in Bath for 'a bathing suit' and gave ten shillings to the man at the pump in the King's Bath. He went to the baths in Maiden Lane while he was in London, and he regularly shipped home consignments of 'spa water' and 'Bath water', three dozen bottles at a time.

If he felt unwell while he was in town, he called in Sir Edmund King, who had been Charles II's personal physician, and towards the end of his life he consulted William of Orange's doctor, Sir Thomas Millington. The latter had been recommended to him as 'a very discreet man, and good physician, and will not try experiments on his patients for which', the Duke told the Duchess, 'I like him much the better.' Not only did he consult these doctors personally. He shared with his contemporaries the alarming habit of seeking long distance treatment. When taken ill in Edinburgh he would write to one of his sons in London describing his symptoms so that they could be relayed to Sir Edmund King for his advice. A method of treatment in which the patient was separated from his doctor by four hundred miles was, to say the least, unsatisfactory, and it was not perhaps surprising that in the end while the London doctors were confidently predicting the Duke's speedy recovery, their patient lay dying in Holyroodhouse.

Medicinal advice was also available in the form of books like *The Compend of Willis Physick* which the Duke bought in 1685. Books could supply advice on other subjects too, and he bought in London *The Mystery of Husbandry*, *The Expert Farrier*, *The True Conduct of Persons of Quality* and 'a book of gardening' which, he told his wife, 'will teach us all to be good gardeners.'

It is interesting to note that the Duke was not the only person in his household to do shopping of this nature. When he went to London he was always accompanied by his secretary David Crawford, and it seems that whenever news spread that the Duke was planning another trip south, all David's friends and acquaintances hastened to beg him to do errands for them when he was in London. So many and varied were the requests made that he found it necessary to record them all in his personal memorandum book lest he forget anything.

First of all, the Duke's relatives would have commissions for him. The Duchess gave him her fan to be mended, Lady Katherine's husband might want a stone of gunpowder, two pairs of stockings and a book, Lady Susan's husband would need fruit trees and deer, and she herself would want dress material. Then there were David's legal acquaintances, like Sir Alexander Gibson, who gave him careful instructions about buying for him 'Sir Matthew Hale's *Life and Death of Pomponius Atticus* in octavo', and Arthur Nasmith who asked for a black-framed looking glass costing no more than a guinea. Finally, there were his own relations and fellow servants. 'A pair of good strong Bristol stoned buttons . . . and a pair of spectacles' were to be found for his cousin William Crawford. Mr Cornwall of Bonhard would like to know how much a cornelian ring would cost, and Mrs Darlo gave him a carolus and a half to buy her some yards of sad coloured stuff. John Lamb the provisor often went with the Duke to London, but one time when he did not, he told David to bring him back some grey cloth, a pair of good stockings and a hat costing 16/–. John Spens asked for '2 pair worset stockings to a little gentlewoman' and James Moffat the groom had a notion for a green apron for his wife. The English influence was obviously not confined to the immediate members of the ducal family, and it is not altogether surprising to detect a hint of affectionate impatience in David Crawford's note reminding himself to buy a magnifying glass with a case, six cravats and a pair of buckles 'to my graceless friend James Nisbet.'

Although the Duke brought David and his other servants with him to London, he also took the opportunity of hiring new servants to take back to Hamilton. It was not that he and the Duchess preferred English servants; indeed most of the household staff were Scots, and the Duchess often expressed her preference for them. The Duke also entertained a certain prejudice against English servants, based on the fact that servants hired in London were, like everything else found there, highly expensive. As he remarked, 'Here such as we have need of will be hard to be got and not under great fees.' Nevertheless, England could supply experienced men of a kind not always to be found at home. In the autumn of 1678 the Duke sent north 'a boy I have feed to be a warrander. He understands that employment well, and seems an honest fellow. I got him on the road to Bath.' The boy in question was Abraham Holywell, who was still warrender at Hamilton Palace nearly forty years later. Nathaniel Jennings the butler who stole the fifty dozen bottles had been hired in London, and the names of Harry Wickliffe, William Dinsdale, Joseph Topping and Benjamin Swain suggest that they had been taken on there too.

As well as Englishmen, there was a variety of foreign servants to be had in London, mostly French. In 1689 a French wine merchant in town recommended a confectioner, Daniel Gazeau, who had been in England for the past five years and was skilled in setting up sweetmeats. The Duke duly hired him, and although he had to pay out £10 or £12 'on the man's behalf for things to make dry sweetmeats and counterfeit cherry things to make pyramids and other ways of serving sweetmeats to the table, he told the Duchess with some satisfaction: 'He will learn you all to make dry sweetmeats, so the keeping of him it were but one year is worth something.'

A fortnight after he hired the confectioner, the Duke was able to report that he had 'taken a French page, the son of a gentleman that's a refugee. He is a very pretty boy and speaks good English, so you have two French servants comes home with your goods, who I hope shall prove better than the English.' Unfortunately for the Duke's plans, when the page's mother heard that her son was to travel to Scotland by sea, she flatly refused to let him go. The Duke was considerably put out. French servants were fashionable, and this one had been even prettier than Lord Murray's page. However, a few days later, the Duke found another French boy whose family were undeterred by the thought of his voyage north.

Having hired his servants and purchased his goods, the Duke was then confronted with the problem of sending them home. Almost everything went by sea, including the servants, as the French boy's mother had discovered. Arranging for their passage home was simple enough. In 1675, Robin Gilmour the groom set off happily for Scotland, his wages paid to him in advance, an extra ten shillings provided for him to buy provisions during the voyage, another ten shillings in his possession 'for a coat to him on the sea' and five shillings in his pocket for any personal expenses. Thus equipped, he sailed for home.

The servants could look after themselves, but where the goods were concerned it was a different matter. First of all, a ship had to be found, usually a Scottish one. Most convenient would be a vessel bound for the Duke's own port of Bo'ness. James Boutchart's ship, *The Rose*, used to sail from the Thames to Bo'ness, or alternatively, James Law, James Forrester or Andrew Burnside might be sailing from London to Leith. On one occasion the Duke sent his belongings by sea to Newcastle and then had them carried by road to Edinburgh, but this was exceptional, and he normally entrusted his possessions to a Scottish ship sailing to a Scottish port.

When he had found a suitable vessel, he had his goods packed up carefully in hampers and boxes, the latter marked in nails with his initials and a number: 'DH 1', 'DH 2' and so on. David Crawford then took them down to the docks, paid the necessary customs duties and saw that the sailing papers were in order. Sometimes the Duke took special precautions with his purchases. When he sent down a box of glasses in 1661 he paid 5/– to a man to look after them, and in 1694 when he was shipping ten baskets of growing trees he gave 5/– extra to the seamen for carrying them carefully into the ship and for watering them and taking care of them during the voyage. On these occasions when he was sending home the family plate he was particularly anxious. He made sure that the vessel carrying his goods sailed with a convoy to avoid the danger of privateers, and one year his belongings were sent north 'in the man-of-war called *The Centurion*, Captain Bridges commander.'

Even if the ship were not carrying such precious cargo there was no guarantee that it would arrive safely. In the spring of 1691 David Crawford noted a payment, 'To James Forrester, skipper, for bringing His Grace's hat from London in a box, and the ship being lost he paid 4/1d sterling salvage for each £1 sterling, so

His Grace's hat being valued at £3 comes to 12/4d.' Again, a rough passage might damage the cargo but there was little that could be done about that, apart from ensuring that the goods were packed up carefully in the first place.

The Duke was equally particular about what was done with them on their arrival in Scotland, and if they were to arrive home before he was there to supervise the unloading, he gave detailed instructions on how to deal with them. The Duchess was told to 'cause ding [knock] out the head of the barrel with the 2 dozen of bottles of Loupain wine, and cause set it in the best cellar, and taste it how you like it, and if it be beginning to spoil, dispose of it to friends.' She was also to make sure that his new coach 'be carefully brought up and set in the best coach house, for I assure you it is a dear one.' When he sent home some peach trees she was to 'cause inquire for them and haste them out to Hamilton', and as for the seeds he sent in 1678, 'the names are with them and are excellent kinds, so cause Hew set them in the best places in the garden at Hamilton as soon as they come to him.' He added that he had 'ordered the skipper to cause the chamberlain at Kinneil send them over as soon as they landed, and the seeds to be kept till I come home. The flowers in the pots must be kept from the snow water.'

After the goods had been sent off, the Duke would refrain from buying anything else, other than a few small items which could be taken back personally. He was in the habit of bringing home with him presents for the family, although he experienced some difficulty in choosing them. 'I have ill skill of these things', he declared. When his children were small he brought them back playthings, and his female relatives usually received silk stockings, gloves or ivory combs.

Finally, a week or two after his goods had gone, the Duke himself would set off for home. Expensive and time-consuming his purchases had undoubtedly been, but as he jolted northwards in the hired coach, he must have reflected with considerable satisfaction on the elegant acquisitions awaiting him at home. When he drove down the High Street of Edinburgh in his fine new English coach, clad in his splendid English clothes, he would look around him with pleasure at the envious expressions on his friends' faces. More than that, the furniture, the dishes, the clocks and the curtains would enhance the appearance of Hamilton Palace, and the careful plans for future improvement laid by himself and the Duchess would be a little nearer realisation.

CHAPTER 8

The Marriage of the Heir

Although the English influence in Scotland was gradually increasing in the seventeenth century, it remained largely peripheral to the way of life and certainly to the main line of thought of the Duke and Duchess of Hamilton: they did not envisage a time when the head of the House of Hamilton would make his permanent home in London. Since Chelsea Place had been sold to pay the English debt, the Hamilton estates were entirely in Scotland, and the future of the family must lie there. For this reason it was imperative that the heir to the family should marry a Scottish lady and settle down at home. The Duke and Duchess had prepared Kinneil expressly as a residence for their eldest son, and until he eventually succeeded to his inheritance he could live there and learn the complicated business of running the estates. It was true that by this time approximately one Scottish peer in seven was marrying an English bride, for reasons which were not far to seek. English ladies invariably had larger dowries, and the need for a wealthy bride was an accepted fact of the time. Be that as it might, the Duke and Duchess remained firmly convinced that, as far as the Earl of Arran was concerned, 'a Scots wife is by far the preferablest.' Unfortunately, their heir had other ideas.

Ever since his return from the Grand Tour, the Earl had spent most of his time at Court. He had arrived back from France full of resolutions never again to live in the boring north and, unluckily, he had found an ally in the King, who took an immediate liking to him. Charles II had known the Duchess's father and uncle well, and he saw in her son a close resemblance to his old friends. 'Madame', he told the Duchess, '... your son has so much in his looks of your father and uncle as I cannot choose but be very kind to him upon that score and I am confident [he] will deserve no less of me upon his own.' Added to that, there was the fact that whatever other qualities the Earl lacked, he possessed an undeniable charm which pleased the King and captivated the ladies of the Court. His father was most anxious to take him home and the Duchess was longing to see him again after his long absence, but the idea of a prolonged stay in Scotland was totally abhorrent to him. He spoke vaguely of going home, avoided committing himself to any particular date, and thought hard for a few days. He then announced that of all things in the world, he should like to go to sea – at once. His parents were astounded. Such an idea had never entered his head before, and in any event, it could not have been more unsuitable. A younger son with no prospects might enter the Navy, but no heir to a dukedom would ever contemplate becoming a sailor!

The Duke of Hamilton lost no time in making his disapproval felt, but James had his answer ready. The King and the Duke of York both approved of the plan, he said. Here indeed was a complication, and his father was thrown into a state of understandable confusion. He could not think of letting the boy go to sea, but how could he refuse the King? Perhaps a spell in the Navy might even be good for the Earl of Arran, and yet . . . Tortured by doubt, he made up his mind at last. He would write home to the Duchess telling her that the final decision rested with her.

The Duchess was even more appalled than her husband had been. James's choice of career was extraordinary, and she was all the more distressed because it seemed that he was to join a ship without even coming home to see her after his long absence. However, she knew where her duty lay. Suppressing her own feelings, she wrote a dignified letter to the King agreeing to the proposal since it was what His Majesty wished, and then she waited sadly to hear that James had gone abroad once more.

The news never came. Instead, she had a letter from the Duke telling her that it was all off. James no longer wished to go to sea. All thought of the Navy was forgotten. Instead, he had told his father triumphantly that he was about to be made a Gentleman of the Bedchamber to Charles II, nor was he slow to point out that this position involved constant attendance at Court. Shortly afterwards, the Duke returned to Scotland alone, and it was not until the end of the year that James paid a brief visit to Hamilton Palace.

By this time his parents were seriously concerned with the question of his marriage. While he was in France, the Earl of Dumbarton had put forward the names of various prospective brides. The most promising of these was Mademoiselle de Roussi, a niece of Turenne and the granddaughter of the leading Protestant nobleman, the Comte de Roussi. Not only were her religious beliefs satisfactory, but she would bring with her a dowry of 50,000 crowns. Both Dumbarton and Mr Forbes had pressed this marriage on the grounds that it would strengthen the Hamilton claims to Châtelherault, but the Duke and Duchess would not hear of their son marrying a foreigner. Marriages with foreign ladies were extremely uncommon for Scottish peers, and as the Duchess pointed out, such a match would lead James into journeys and expense when it seemed that in any case he did not know how to manage his money. The idea was therefore dropped and although some years later there were rumours of the Earl marrying a wealthy French lady, no serious negotiations for a foreign bride ever took place.

Usually the heir to a noble house was expected to marry the lady of his parents' choice, and as one historian has remarked, the eldest son had as little say in the selection of his wife as his sisters did in the choice of their husbands.[1] This may have been true for the peerage in general, but the Earl of Arran never did adhere to these matrimonial conventions. Throughout the years which followed his arrival at Court, he pursued a series of prospective brides, happy in the knowledge that the four hundred miles which separated him from his father gave him an unusual measure of freedom. His parents for their part knew that there was little they could do. As long as he enjoyed the King's favour at Court there was no way of bringing him back to Scotland, and as long as he remained in London there was little likelihood of him marrying a Scottish bride. Scottish ladies remained at home with their mothers, they did not go south for the season each winter, and as

visiting her in person. The aforementioned ladies of the Court could not spare him, but he did decide to send an emissary, his friend Sir John Coplestone. Sir John accordingly set off for Wells, but when he arrived there he met with a distinctly cool reception. Seeing a strange gentleman alight from a coach outside her door, Nellie hid herself in the nearest closet. Her aunt and uncle showed Sir John into the house with profuse apologies, and then they all stood outside the closet and tried to reason with Nellie. They pleaded and they shouted and they cajoled until at last she emerged with a very ill grace.

As they all sat down to a meal together, Sir John studied Nellie covertly. He was not impressed. Her expression could only be described as mutinous, her hair was untidy and her clothes left a great deal to be desired. However, while she toyed sulkily with her lunch, he embarked on an enthusiastic discourse about marriage, telling her how scarce good husbands were and emphasising the Earl's 'unspeakable affection' for her. Nellie listened in silence, and at last she replied that she was young, she was a stranger to the world, and she would need time to consider. Sir John withdrew to his lodgings in some exasperation and spent the rest of the day playing cards.

Next morning he arrived at her home bright and early. He was admitted by the aunt, and when Nellie appeared he noted with satisfaction that she was dressed in a much more becoming manner and that she even seemed quite cheerful. He did not lose a moment, but repeated his remarks of the previous day. His optimism evaporated when Nellie replied with a sweet smile that she was young, she was a stranger to the world, and she would need time to consider. After that, she refused to say another word, and Sir John retreated once more to the card table.

Not only did Nellie refuse to give him a proper answer that day: when he called on the following morning her attitude was exactly the same. He came to the conclusion that he was getting nowhere, and so he decided to return to London to report in person to the Earl of Arran. When he did so, the Earl seemed scarcely interested, but he did remark that a little persuasion by himself was obviously needed. Sir John had no doubt done his best, but of course he lacked the Earl's own irresistible charm.

James therefore started plying Nellie with letters. These she received with 'a great deal of sourness and moroseness', and later on she even refused to look at them or to have them read to her, despite her aunt's efforts to intervene on the Earl's behalf. At last, in the summer of 1680, the Earl failed to put in a definite proposal by an agreed date, and the treaty was at an end. As Mrs Paulett informed the Earl afterwards, Nellie confessed that 'she with pleasure told [counted] the hours as they drew on to the conclusion of your limited time that she might be at liberty . . .'.

One of the reasons given by Nellie for her reluctance to accept the Earl had been that she did not wish to 'marry to a foreign estate', in other words, live in Scotland. The prospect of sending his daughter to live so far away must have deterred more than one father, and it was certainly the excuse given by the Earl of Rochester when he refused to let his daughter marry the Earl of Arran, or so Arran said. The Duchess of Hamilton had put forward the suggestion that the young girl might come and stay with her for a little before the wedding, so as to become acquainted with Scotland. His mother's insistence that the couple settle in Scotland, the Earl told her, 'will absolutely put an end to this treaty, for I know her friends will never consent to it', and he added peevishly that 'at this rate I am like to be an old bachelor, for if you continue positive nobody that has parents and that is to be married by treaty will marry me without your consent, and if living in Scotland be one of the first articles I believe they who have such a fortune as will be necessary to provide for my younger brothers and give me a suitable allowance will be apt to think they can do much better nearer hand.'

This line of argument made little impression on the Duchess, who told him plainly that neither his persuasions nor those of his father would convince her. She quoted her 'grandfather's living off of [sic] his estate at Court though in so advantageous a post that it is not to be expected you will arrive at, yet brought his family to the very brink of ruin', adding, 'This is not that I am such a fool as to think Scotland a finer place or near so good as England, but being the country where your interest lies cannot but be most your advantage to set up your residence in', and 'as for that you write you are like to be an old bachelor is your own fault, not mine.'

His parents were fast reaching the conclusion that such reasons for their son's failure to marry were merely excuses. Having initiated proceedings with the Pauletts, his deliberate procrastination had ruined his chances there, and his behaviour with regard to the Duke of Newcastle's daughter Arabella had been even more deplorable. Although marked by smallpox, the lady was 'fine shaped otherwise' and likely to make a good wife, but the Earl's arrival at her father's house a good deal the worse for drink put an end to that particular opportunity and caused his father to tell him that 'it's no wonder at the rate it's talked that his daughter nor any other discreet person ever desired to match with you . . . Unless you change your way people will be feared to meddle with you.'

Undeterred, James now paid court to Lady Conway, but before anything could be decided he was sent to Paris as Charles II's ambassador extraordinary. Despite the disapproval of family and friends he stayed on as the French King's aide-de-camp, and soon had 'in prospect one of the finest ladies in France with a million.' There was no future in that, of course, and when he came back his exasperated father noted that 'his head is on the Duchess of Monmouth, which I believe will come to as little as all the rest.'

To make matters worse, the Earl did not allow any of his marriage negotiations to interfere with his other attachments. It was during this period that he became the father of a son, James Abercrombie, who, when he grew up, was given a commission in Lord Charles's regiment and was described by his uncle as being 'very proud to be thought the man's son he is . . . is the greatest ill liar that ever was, drinks like a fish [and is] confident to the last degree . . .'. There were also two daughters, apparently born to the one mother. Katherine and Mary Ruthven were brought up together in London and were later sent to finish their education in France. They were perpetually short of clothing and money and, according to Lord Charles, they were lacking in the social graces as well.

These liaisons were all known to his mother, who in despair

told him that, 'As for your marriage which you term the philo-sopher's stone, it may be so. For my part, I have given over the expectation of ever seeing it, and am sorry you are so much more unhappy than other men that you can find no person fit for you that will be content to live with you where your interest lies, but it is so evident where the fault lies that it is needless for me to pursue it further.' His father was even more blunt. 'Until you marry and that thereby you bring in a portion to the family, I will neither meddle in your transactions nor concern myself in your debts', he declared, adding, 'I have hitherto delayed making any settlements of your mother's estate or my own, hoping before this you would have come to [have] understood your own interest, but finding you are like to continue in your old ways, I am now about making settlements of our estate which I hope to complete next session. If therein you meet with a disappointment of what you might have expected, blame yourself, and believe what I have been at so much pains and trouble to recover, I will not leave in your power to destroy, so far as the laws of Scotland can prevent.'

It was not surprising that the Duke and Duchess were worried. Their son's refusal to marry was bad enough, his way of life was an embarrassment, to say the least, but the worst of it was that he was steadily falling deeper and deeper into debt. Tradesmen and others were willing to extend credit to him because they knew that he would one day inherit the Hamilton estates, and he said he would pay off his debts eventually when the lands were his. But after all the Duke's prudent management, after the years spent in careful reorganisation of the family finances, the Duke and Duchess were sickened and dismayed by the thought that their son's improvidence would put them back where they had started. Were he allowed to contract huge debts on the estates as was his desire, the revenues would have to be diverted to pay his creditors. There would be no money to spare to carry out the Great Design and there would be none to provide for their younger sons. Certainly the Duke had resigned his title of Earl of Selkirk to Lord Charles, Lord George was eventually to become Earl of Orkney and Lord John was created Earl of Ruglen, but they were almost entirely dependent on their father's generosity for their income. James's extravagance would jeopardise all the plans for the future and might even lead to the Duke and Duchess having to sell their family lands again. The prospect was unbearable.

Although his parents' threats seemed to fall on deaf ears at the time, in the end it was the financial consideration which forced the Earl into the realisation that he could not go on as he was doing. However much he wished to remain a bachelor, the arguments for his marrying had by 1687 become distinctly pressing. For one thing, he was almost thirty, and most young noblemen in his position had married long since. More important, his debts now amounted to some £10,000 sterling, and he had been forced to pawn his jewels. If he were to settle with his creditors he would have to obtain a large portion and an allowance from his father.

Marriage was the only answer, and at the very moment when he reached this distasteful conclusion, he was approached by that master of equivocation, the Earl of Sunderland, who had a proposition to make to him. James had been a friend of Sunderland's for years, and he knew the whole family well, including the eldest daughter, Lady Anne. Why not, Sunderland now suggested, take the obvious way out of his financial difficulties and marry Lady Anne? She was vivacious and popular, she would make a charming wife, and Sunderland would ensure that she had a large dowry. He would go even farther, and he and James would work together to extract from the Duke of Hamilton the best possible financial terms. Of course, it was as well to keep the plan secret for the time being but James could talk the idea over privately with another old friend, the French ambassador, Barillon, who knew all about it.

The Earl of Arran was immediately taken with the suggestion. Here was a really effective way of wringing a good deal of money out of his father. The Duke would be unable to refuse his demands if they were supported by Sunderland, and there was also the promise of a lavish dowry. Of course, the scheme did mean that he would have to take a wife, but since he had to marry someone it might as well be Lady Anne. He had never paid a great deal of attention to her in the past, but she was attractive enough. She was tall, with soft brown hair, grey-blue eyes and she had a nice figure. People said she was very good company, very amusing. He would marry her as soon as it could be arranged.

Compared with the enigmatic Sunderland, the Earl of Arran was a child where political machination was concerned. He may well have been unaware of the background of intrigue and the manœuvrings for power in which Sunderland was currently engaged, or he may simply not have cared, thinking it better to be used as a political pawn if only it would bring him a powerful ally against his father, for of course political pawns were what he and Lady Anne undoubtedly were on this occasion. Sunderland had long pursued a successful career of opportunism, but he was in difficulties at last. He had survived the changes brought about by the death of Charles II, but he was rapidly losing influence as James II came to rely more and more on his Catholic advisers. Sunderland was Lord President of the Council and he had successfully eliminated one rival, Rochester, but others remained. There was, for instance, the Catholic Earl of Melfort. The latter was Secretary of State for Scotland, and his policies there were opposed by the Duke of Hamilton. The Duke was anxious to come to Court to expose Melfort's mismanagement of Treasury affairs, and the King had at last given him permission to come. James II was eager for the Duke's support. Now supposing Sunderland could effect an alliance with the Hamiltons, the situation could be so manipulated that the Duke replaced Melfort in the King's favour and Sunderland could be all-powerful once more:[2] hence his willingness to back all the Earl of Arran's financial demands.

Unaware of his son's involvement, the Duke of Hamilton arrived at Court that winter and was none too pleased when James suddenly announced that marriage negotiations were already in hand. He wrote home to tell the Duchess that James 'has managed it himself . . . and the terms they demand are very high, which I believe our sons helps well to.' His suspicions were confirmed a few days later when he learned from the French ambassador that James, while pretending that the match was designed for the family interest, 'had been discoursing the terms with the Earl of Sunderland and how to bring me up to give great conditions and have his debts paid.' The Duke was understandably annoyed, and told the Duchess that 'upon this subject you need not doubt my son and I has had reckonings you have heard us have before.'

Despite his annoyance, the Duke now began the long series of negotiations which formed the inevitable prelude to any marriage contract. On this occasion, agreement was reached quickly enough on the main proposals. Lady Anne would bring with her a dowry of £12,000 sterling, a very large sum indeed by Scottish standards, and in return the Duke of Hamilton would provide £1,500 sterling a year for the young couple's maintenance. Left to themselves, the Duke and Sunderland could have concluded the treaty quickly enough, but they had to contend with the Earl of Arran's own demands. Sunderland seems to have been indifferent to the terms of the marriage so long as it was accomplished, but he was willing to put forward any proposal made by James, and James certainly had demands to make. He wanted one third of the dowry to be paid directly to him, and he wanted to be allowed to contract debts of up to £15,000 on the Hamilton estates.

The Duke absolutely refused to agree to either of those terms and a good deal of hard bargaining ensued. Sunderland pointed out that the Duke had already refused to pay James's debts whereas Sunderland himself had promised to entertain the young couple in his family for so long as they remained at Court, be it at London or at Windsor. The Duke remained adamant, so Sunderland and James now decided to exploit the fact that the Duke held his titles only because he had married an heiress. Sunderland urged that, should the Duchess die first, her inheritance should be divided equally between her husband and James. 'This proposition I understand to have been occasioned by our son', the Duke wrote home angrily, 'which I confess I took not very kindly, considering what I had done for the family and what he had done.' He was not unwilling to listen to another suggestion, however, namely that should the Duke himself die first James could become Duke of Hamilton.

This was really most unusual. The Duke had no power of transmitting his title to his heirs and so James could not become fourth Duke of Hamilton until his mother died. Still, there was something to be said for the suggestion. 'It is not in your interest to oppose it', the Duke told the Duchess, 'for I see the necessity of always having a man to represent the family else it would be run down.' Of course, the decision rested with the Duchess herself, and she would not hear of such a thing. 'As for your being Duke of Hamilton on your father's death, I assure you no consideration will make me treat of that at this time', she told James. '[It] will be time enough to speak on when that falls out on which it is proposed, so I desire this may not be more insisted on. It disobliges me who am desirous to express all the tender kindness to you that an affectionate mother can do, but these things must proceed from myself and can't be extorted from me.'

The Duchess's approval was supposed to be necessary before the articles could go through at all. Until her reply came, the matter was to remain a secret. On 21 November the Duke therefore sent his son John north with both his and Sunderland's proposals, and he sent word to his wife to go into Edinburgh to confer with their lawyers.

On the following day, the King and Queen were told of the match and pronounced themselves well pleased. James II went on to arrange a formal reconciliation between the Duke of Hamilton, the Earl of Sunderland and the Earl of Melfort, and Lady Anne became a Lady of the Queen's Bedchamber. Much to the Duke's annoyance, the bridegroom himself was still showing a strange reluctance to marry. His father had already noted him to be 'little desirous to be settled . . . and afraid of that condition of life', and had confided to the Duchess that their son was 'in as much perplexity of thinking to be married as I have been, in fears not to be married to you.' James was furious at an arrangement whereby his wife's pin money was to be paid out of the £1,500 a year allowed to them for their maintenance, and he seemed oblivious to the fact that Lady Anne was attractive and charming.

As soon as the Duchess of Hamilton heard about the negotiations she wrote to James, welcoming the news and gladly giving her consent to his marrying 'so fine a lady for whom I had a particular respect from the first time I saw her.' Nevertheless, she complicated matters by declaring that she would give James her claim to the French duchy of Châtelherault on the understanding that he would not part with it, but that he could contract no more than £5,000 worth of debts on the estates. Moreover, should the Duke predecease her, she would give James no more than £500 a year extra.

Her answer dismayed the Duke, for it added to his difficulties and he even thought of sending James home to discuss the situation in person, but this would have occasioned further delay and so he decided against that course and took it upon himself to offer that if he should die first the young couple could have £1,000 more. He explained this to his wife as tactfully as he could the next time he wrote, remarking, 'I am confident when I meet with you I will convince you that you would have done it yourself had you not been in haste.' This arrangement satisfied Sunderland, who went off to have the articles drawn up by his lawyers, but James remained ill-pleased, 'swears he will be a beggar and is undone', and declared that he would be better off single and had a mind to break the match.

It was now planned that the wedding should take place a week before Christmas, so the Duke began to worry about the expense of new clothes needed by himself and his sons. The Duchess could not come south in time, and so she would have to be absent on the great occasion. 'As you wish me present', she wrote to James, 'so do I, more than ever I did to be in England since I was a wife, for to have been a witness of seeing you so well married would have been a great pleasure to me, which I shall partake of, though at a distance.'

The marriage plans had actually been made public before the news of her approval came, for Sunderland had been unable to resist mentioning them to Melfort. As Christmas drew near, the Duke was still busy with the drawing up of the articles, and found himself confronted by a new series of problems. 'The lawyers here', he complained, 'their terms of law are such and their way of business so different from ours that I have difficulty to understand them, and they I believe more to understand me.' (The Scottish legal system was and still is quite different from the English system.) The Duke could not fully comprehend the draft drawn up by Sunderland's lawyers, so he had a better one made, although he was sure that 'when it comes there [to

Edinburgh] our lawyers will not well understand it unless I be their interpreter.'

To add to his troubles, the Earl of Arran was now demanding £800 to enable him to redeem his jewels, wanted extra money to buy new clothes and insisted that his bride be given an expensive wedding present. He also continued his complaints about the terms of the contract, and 'goes mad that the £10,000 sterling is not allowed him to take on the estate.' On 29 December the Duke was still busy with drafts, re-writing the entire contract many times in his own hand and telling his wife, 'I never wanted you so much, nor has had no friend nor could get no Scots lawyer to help me.' At last, however, the articles were completed and on 5 January 1687 the signing took place.

James was there with a face like thunder, and as soon as he saw his father he started complaining loudly about not being allowed enough money. Some of the company turned away in embarrassment at such unseemly behaviour, but Sunderland himself seemed unaffected. He was looking as urbane as ever and although he did stroll over to the Duke to suggest that when the articles were drawn up more fully James should be allowed to contract larger debts on the Hamilton estates, he did not press the point and the Duke managed to put him off.

As he chatted amicably enough with Sunderland, the Duke's gaze fell upon the future bride. Lady Anne was looking far from cheerful, and he felt a surge of genuine compassion. She 'seemed in some concern today at the signing of the articles', he told his wife later, 'which I thought no wonder of, for she cannot but know his wildness.' He therefore went across to her and 'said some things to encourage her.' Lady Anne replied decorously that if she pleased him she would think herself very happy, and the Duke decided that the more he saw her the better he liked her. She was both 'handsome and personable', she had been carefully educated, and if anyone could reclaim James from his present ways she would do it.

Like it or not, Lady Anne and the Earl of Arran had to sign their marriage articles. The Earls of Middleton and Dumbarton along with Godolphin and Harry Sidney signed as witnesses on the back of the parchment sheets, and then they all celebrated with a ball and supper at Sunderland's lodgings. On 16 March at Holyrood the Duchess of Hamilton added her signature, with Lord Bargany as one of her witnesses.

The very first clause of the marriage articles had ordained that the marriage should take place on or before 15 January 1688, and on 10 January James was able to pick up his pen and write his mother a letter announcing that he had 'been a married man a quarter of an hour'. Up to the very eve of the ceremony he had been threatening not to go through with it, but his father saw to it that he appeared at the Earl of Sunderland's lodgings at the appointed hour. There, in the dining-room, the Bishop of Rochester performed the ceremony. The Duke of Hamilton and two of his sons were present, wearing fine new suits, and James and his bride were both splendidly attired in garments sewn all over with ribbons which were later cut off and given as wedding favours. Seven such knots were sent home to the Duchess, and another recipient was John Evelyn, who recorded in his diary two days later that the wedding had been celebrated with 'extraordinary splendour' and that he and his family 'had most glorious favours sent us.'[3]

Throughout the ceremony Lady Anne looked very grave, but the guests enjoyed the supper which followed and the dinner and supper on the next day. The Duke of Hamilton was certainly feeling satisfied. He had heard that £1,000 had been spent on Lady Anne's trousseau, and he considered that if his son 'could have had his choice of all England he could not had [sic] a finer young woman.' He could also reflect with pleasure on how he had arranged to leave £2,000 of the portion in London, so that when he returned in the summer he would not have rates of exchange to pay as he did when he brought money with him from Scotland. Then he still had plenty of money left to help pay his daughter Margaret's dowry, provide for his younger sons and finance his various lawsuits. The only thing he had forgotten to do was to give the bride a present, and he seems to have been oblivious to the fact that this caused some comment among the guests and a good deal of irritation to his son. Now all that remained to be done was to draw up the final contract in Edinburgh, and that was completed by the summer of 1688.

If the Earl of Sunderland was also congratulating himself on the success of his plan on that January day, his satisfaction was short lived. Instead of remaining in London as a counterpoise to Melfort, the Duke of Hamilton left town a few weeks after the wedding and by 16 February he was back at Holyroodhouse. Before he left Court he managed to persuade the King to allow him to defer giving an opinion on the repeal of the Test Act until that summer, and although the King now sent after him demanding an immediate reply, he managed to avoid committing himself for the time being. Sunderland therefore found that instead of gaining an influential Scottish ally at Court, he was having to make excuses to the King for Hamilton's unsatisfactory behaviour. The Duke did continue to expose Melfort's financial mismanagement, but in the end Sunderland came to the conclusion that his friendship was more of a liability than an asset and in the summer of 1688 he announced his reconciliation with Melfort, thereby abandoning all that he had hoped to gain from the Hamilton alliance. It is interesting to note, though, that he remained on personally good terms with his son-in-law for the rest of his life, and as late as 1696 Lord John Hamilton in a letter to James referred to 'your friend and our patron My Lord Sunderland.'

So much for the political implications of the marriage, but what of its more personal aspect? When he wrote his first letter home announcing his marriage, the Earl of Arran excused his wife from writing too, explaining that 'she is still in so grave a way that I durst not begin so soon to make use of my authority.' Two days later, however, Lady Anne wrote a graceful first letter to her mother-in-law, and this evoked an affectionate and welcoming response. Both bride and groom were already feeling much happier. Gone were all James's misgivings about matrimony. He was pleased with his new wife and, much to her own surprise, Lady Anne now fell deeply in love with her husband. It is consoling to reflect that the coldly calculated match which had occasioned her so much unhappiness in prospect was to bring her a measure of real happiness in its fulfilment.

It was unfortunate that she and the Earl had to endure many separations in their short time together. Certainly the young couple had lodgings at Whitehall beside Sunderland's apartments, but Lady Anne was occupied with her duties as a Lady-in-Waiting, while James had to be away with his regiment a good deal. During one of their first separations Lady Anne wrote to tell him that she 'could not have believed that three months' acquaintance could have made a week's absence so very uneasy to me', and she looked forward eagerly to an occasion when the Queen was to go to Richmond and would pass through the camp to see the soldiers, for Lady Anne would be with her and would have the opportunity of seeing her 'dear lord' again.

In the early summer, she discovered that she was pregnant and she was allowed to withdraw from Court to spend a few weeks with her mother at their country home. 'Althorp is so fine that I have no reason at all to repent me of it', she told James, 'only because I am from you, but indeed that is enough to hinder me from having much pleasure; however, if I could but be sure that you think of me now and then though it were not half so often as I do of you, it would make some amends. Pray send me word where you are and what you do with yourself.' Life was indeed dull without him, and she told him in her next letter, 'I hope you will not be long before you come and make me a visit, for I don't know what to do with myself without you . . . I believe you never saw such a scrawl, but indeed I am almost asleep but I am just enough awake to assure you with all sincerity in the world, whatever you think, nobody ever loved another so well as I do you, my dearest lord. Pray write two words by this bearer to comfort me.'

That autumn, she returned to Court and not long afterwards the Duke and Duchess of Hamilton came to town. The whole family was assembled in London when Lady Anne's first child was born, and on 18 January David Crawford the secretary was able to record in his personal notebook, 'At 1 o'clock afternoon, the Countess of Arran was brought to bed of a daughter in her lodgings in Whitehall, who was christened on the [   ] day of January. Her name Anne.' Although he noted this down in elaborately neat handwriting with many a flourish, there was the usual sense of anti-climax at the birth of a daughter. No doubt the Duchess consoled Lady Anne with recollections of her own first child having been a girl and any initial disappointment was soon changed to anxiety. On 3 February the Duchess's doctor was prescribing medicine for her grandchild, but the baby died soon afterwards.

The death of his daughter was the least of the Earl's troubles. By this time William of Orange had arrived in England, and with the Revolution the Earl of Arran's fortunes took an abrupt turn for the worse. While the Duke of Hamilton welcomed the new King, the Earl remained loyal to James II. Theoretically, this course may have been admirable, but practically it was disastrous. The Duke of Hamilton as a leader of the Presbyterians naturally welcomed the advent of a Protestant king, but in any case he knew that it would have been folly to jeopardise the work of years by upholding James II and risking exile and forfeiture.

The Duke therefore supported the Revolution. His son greeted William of Orange with a defiant message from James II and was promptly sent to the Tower. Even this had its advantages, for as the Duke pointed out, had the Earl been released at once 'he would have been seized by his creditors.' James's finances were as chaotic as ever, and when at last he was prevailed upon to sell some of his silver plate, instead of paying his creditors he bought a luxurious velvet bed and a set of hangings for it.

When he had been in the Tower for almost a year, the Duke managed to obtain an order for his release, whereupon the Earl voiced a preference to stay in prison rather than face the irate creditors. Finally, it was agreed that he would slip out of the Tower secretly on a Sunday morning in order to elude them, and would ride at once for Scotland. This he did on the morning of 12 November 1689, leaving the Duke with the problem of bringing Lady Anne to join him in Scotland. She was five months pregnant, and feeling sick and miserable. The Duke viewed the prospect of accompanying her north with alarm. It was the worst time of year for travelling and the thought of spending a fortnight shut up in a coach with a pregnant girl was far from appealing, but most of his dismay was occasioned by genuine concern for her. 'The more I am acquainted with her I like her the better', he told his wife, and Lady Anne was so determined to accompany him that he had to agree. They set out on 26 November, the Duke, Lady Anne and Lord John Hamilton travelling in one coach with Lady

Anne's serving women following behind in another. Fortunately, the journey proved uneventful, and although they did have to spend an extra night in Doncaster, they were able to make good speed. They arrived in Edinburgh on 10 December, and Lady Anne and her husband were reunited.

Normally, they would at once have taken up residence at Kinneil, but the Castle had been standing empty for a good many years. Certainly there was a small resident staff, and the house had always been opened up in the summer when the Duke and Duchess paid a visit, but a few weeks would be needed to put it in readiness for a whole household to move in. At first the Earl and his wife therefore occupied lodgings at Holyroodhouse, but by the end of the year Kinneil had been put in order and they were able to take up residence there.

Political and financial circumstances had forced the Earl of Arran to return home, and the Duke of Hamilton's warning to his wife that 'neither of them will ever think of living in Scotland though we were both dead and gone' could safely be forgotten. The heir to the House of Hamilton would surely be permanently settled at Kinneil now. There he would raise a family and at last he would be brought to appreciate the value of learning how to manage the estates. With Lady Anne beside him, the future of the family would be safe in his hands.

So much for the nascent hopes of the Duke and Duchess of Hamilton. On 13 March 1690 the Earl's second daughter was born at Kinneil: she was christened Mary. Lady Anne came safely through the birth, but a few days later she contracted puerperal fever and for several weeks she lay dangerously ill. Doctors were summoned urgently from Edinburgh, the Duchess of Hamilton hurried to Kinneil and the Earl of Sunderland wrote anxiously from the south with medical advice. She was treated with syrup of violets, plantain water and 'hysteric plasters', and for a little time she seemed to rally. The Earl of Arran went off to Holyroodhouse, and the emergency seemed to be over. But this was only a brief respite. Lady Anne suffered a relapse and after twelve days of fever and delirium she died at Kinneil on 10 June 1690. She was twenty-four and she had been married for less than two and a half years.

The Earl of Arran was distraught. He had never envisaged such an outcome to his wife's illness and he simply did not know what to do. There is no doubt of his genuine grief. Two years later he wrote sorrowfully to his wife's sister, Lady Clancarty, describing his little daughter as 'the only comfort I have left, yet I can never look upon her without grieving that her dear mother is not alive to share with me the pleasure of that pretty baby. I make no doubt she is much more happy and we ought to submit to God's will, yet I can't think it any crime to wish it had pleased Him to order it otherwise.'

Lady Anne was buried in the family vault at Hamilton Parish Church on 2 July,[4] and shortly afterwards the Earl dismissed all the servants he had installed at Kinneil and closed up the Castle. While his mother brought up little Lady Mary, he went back to London where he sought the consolation of Charles II's illegitimate daughter, Lady Barbara Fitzroy. Nine months later she bore him a son, Charles.

CHAPTER 9

The Great Design

While the Earl of Arran spent the next few years in a renewed pursuit of wealthy heiresses, his parents were very much occupied with other matters. Their daughters were married, their other sons were settled in military and naval careers, the debts had been paid and lands had been bought back. At last the Duke and Duchess could turn their attention to the improvement of their estates and, especially, to the rebuilding of Hamilton Palace.

It was not simply that the rambling collection of different buildings was inconvenient and cramped for a really large household. This was a period of great building activity in Scotland as well as in England. While Montagu, Conway and Buckingham spent fortunes on erecting stately homes for themselves in the south,[1] Scottish peers were also finding it desirable to extend and re-model their houses. As early as the 1650s the Earl of Lothian had made extensive alterations at Newbattle, and his daughter continued the work when she inherited the title.[2] In the 1660s the Earl of Strathmore was busy re-designing his castle at Glamis, while the Earl of Panmure employed John Mylne to rebuild his home at Panmure.[3]

By that time, the celebrated Sir William Bruce was working not only for the King at Holyrood but for the Duke of Lauderdale at Thirlestane Castle and for the Hope family at Hopetoun House. Towards the end of his career James Smith rose to fame. He had worked on the re-modelling of Holyroodhouse and in 1683 he became Overseer of the Royal Works in Scotland. Queensberry employed him at Drumlanrig, Leven at Melville House, and he was responsible for alterations at Traquair and Yester.[4] In all this, the peerage was motivated not only by the desire to have more comfortable homes, but by the feeling that a great family must have an appropriately splendid residence. The rooms in late sixteenth-century houses are charming: small and panelled, with diamond paned windows, they have a delightful intimacy all their own. There are no corridors, however, and where one chamber opens from the next, there is a distinct lack of privacy. Apart from this practical disadvantage, the rooms did begin to seem claustrophobic and old-fashioned to those noblemen who had visited Versailles and the châteaux of the Loire. There was no longer any need for a house to be defensive in function, but it should be a visible symbol of its owner's wealth and power and so it must be dignified and spacious.

The Duke and Duchess of Hamilton shared these sentiments to the full and for many years they planned the transformation of their Palace. They did not, however, begin with Hamilton. Instead, they started in a smaller way at Kinneil, long before the Earl of Arran ever brought his bride there. The Castle inherited by the Duchess was much too small to provide a permanent residence for her son and so in the early 1670s the Duke and she employed masons and wrights to build a fine new wing at Kinneil, dwarfing the old tower house built by Châtelherault. Their new house was five storeys high, classically elegant and surmounted by a cornice and a balustrade. At either side was a pavilion, one storey lower than the main house. The south pavilion accommodated the main staircase, while the north pavilion linked the new house with the old. The principal entrance was through a simple Renaissance doorway which led to a large hall. Immediately above this hall was the Great Salon, a huge room occupying the entire length of the first floor, and above that were bedchambers and drawing rooms.[5]

How much all this cost the Duke and Duchess does not emerge from the Archives, for the building accounts for Kinneil have not yet come to light. The Duke did, however, mention to Queensberry that the pavilion containing the staircase was 'dearer than the other, being 1,000 merks Scots for the workmanship of the stone work only.'[6]

When the rebuilding at Kinneil had been successfully completed, the Duke and Duchess felt that they could turn their attention to the immense undertaking of rebuilding their Palace – what the Earl of Arran once named their 'Great Design'. Apart from having gained experience from the building work done at Kinneil, the Duke had for many years made a point of visiting other great houses. On his way south to London, he would stop at 'my Lord Sandwich's house of Henshenbrook near Hunting-toun' to go 'through yards and house', or he would pay the porter five shillings to be shown round 'My Lord Salisbury's house at Hatfield'. He purchased books on architecture and he and the Duchess pored for hours over the plans of the great French houses visited by the Earl of Arran on his Grand Tour. As early as 1678 the Duke had promised his wife that he would have the draft of a new house drawn up while he was in London, thinking it wise 'to have such a thing by us against we be able to build it', but in the end they were to settle for a Scottish architect, and on 30 March 1682 a payment of £14 was made 'to Mr James Smith for drawing drafts.'

Whatever drafts Mr Smith drew that spring, they were certainly not the final designs for the new Hamilton Palace. In such an immense undertaking it was years before all the details were worked out and indeed the final plans had still not been settled when the Palace was well on the way to completion. Probably the Duke and Duchess now agreed with Mr Smith on their general strategy. As it existed, the Palace consisted of the main building round the quadrangle, with the office houses clustering round the Back Close. First of all, the offices would be changed – some altered, some demolished. When the Back Close had been reorganised, the Palace itself would be tackled. The idea was to demolish three sides of the quadrangle, leaving only the north front standing. As the portion of the house containing the principal public rooms, it would be retained. Two entirely new wings would then be built on to this, on the site of the former east and west wings. The main entrance would now be from the courtyard formed by the two wings, so that the entire building would face south towards Edinburgh instead of north towards Glasgow. Of course, it was unthinkable to demolish all three wings at once. The household must continue to live in the Palace throughout the alterations, and in any case the expense might be such that when one wing had been completed no more could be undertaken. Everything would have to be done gradually and many modifications might have to be made, but in essence those were the outlines for the Great Design.

Work on the office houses was not particularly complicated and so it could be entrusted to the local masons. A start was made in 1684 when John Boyd from Glasgow was hired to build a new stable. This was to be two stories high, with a doorway wide enough to take a coach. The Duke promised to provide all the necessary stone, sand, lime and scaffolding, and he paid Boyd 600 merks and eight bolls of meal for his work. Three years later John Lochore from Birkenshaw was given the task of converting the old stables into kitchens and he was also to put up two entirely new dovecots, each with over a thousand pigeon holes. When that had been done, the Duke decided to erect a new building for the other offices. John Lochore the mason was engaged to take down the existing north-south building and replace it with an entirely new house, with a large bakehouse alongside. The latter was to have two ovens 'to be built after the fashion of those at Kinneil or in His Grace's lodging at Edinburgh.' They were to be raised four feet from the ground, with spaces underneath where the ash could collect.

This new set of houses could have been fairly expensive, but the Duke managed to economise by using a good deal of existing stone. The old houses in the Nethertoun of Hamilton had recently been pulled down and sixty-three cartloads of stones were brought from there. The house once occupied by Hew Wood supplied another 414 cartloads, and the rest of the stone was brought from Hamilton quarry.

Finally, the Duke needed three more new stables. This involved the enlargement of the Back Close, and so he bought some adjoining land from John Lang, a shoemaker in Hamilton. By the summer of 1691, Robert Nasmith, one of the masons in Hamilton, was busy putting up the three new stables, each two storeys high and running from the existing new stable to the new office houses.

By this time, more exciting plans were in hand. In October of that year Mr James Smith came out to Hamilton once more and drew some more drafts. The Duke and Duchess were ready to begin work on the west quarter of the Palace, and on 23 November 1691 the Duke and James Bryson signed a contract whereby 'the said James is to take down the whole stone work of that west quarter of the Palace of Hamilton, both within and without, and that from the top to the bottom . . . He is carefully to do the said work and lay the hewn stones by themselves, the wall stones by themselves and the rubbish by itself to the inner court that all of them may be carried away by His Grace to the outer court.' The fireplaces from the west quarter were carried carefully through and stored in other parts of the house.

While the demolition of the west quarter went on, the Duke and Duchess were involved in anxious consultation with a variety of experts. The Duke sought the advice of his friend Sir William Bruce and in March 1692 Tobias Bauchop was sent by Sir William 'to engage concerning His Grace's new house at Hamilton.' The Duke had a long discussion with Bauchop, who went out to look at the Palace itself the following month, although he was not actually employed by the Duke and Duchess. In August, the Duke and his son John went to visit Sir William at his own house of Kinross and in October both Sir William and Bauchop went out once more to Hamilton. By this time, 'young Mr Smith', the cousin and colleague of the older James Smith, had also supplied drafts, and finally on 10 March 1693 the Duke and Duchess paid £58 Scots 'to Mr James and James Smith, masons, in earnest when their Grace[s] and they entered in a contract of agreement for building the west quarter of the Palace of Hamilton.'

In all the building work which followed, it is plain that the Duke and Duchess played a leading part in planning how their Palace was to be transformed, and when the Duke went to London that winter he took the opportunity of having further architectural discussions, taking with him Mr James Smith and also the wright, James McLellan. 'I am now consulting it with one Banks that carries on the buildings at Hampton Court, who is the best at contriving of any in England', he wrote home to the Duchess, 'and Mr James Smith is going out there tomorrow, and you will think you are a better contriver than I am when I tell you he is against that stair you was . . .'.

No detail was too small to merit their attention, and a few weeks later they were discussing a carving which was to be placed on the south front of the Palace. 'I am of your mind', the Duke wrote home, 'that our cipher without the Garter will be better than a sundial . . . but it must be large with the year of God under it and a flourish or a laurel about, so the place to put it must be left till we agree on the cipher.'

Early in 1694 he paid £11 sterling 'to Mr Banks the King's carpenter for drawing some draughts of the Palace of Hamilton at several times' and the Earl of Arran was later to refer to Sir Christopher Wren as 'one whom my father used to consult with.' At the same time, the Duke arranged to have sash windows made. These had first been seen in England in about 1680 and towards the end of the decade they had been installed in one of the office houses at Windsor Castle.[7] Before that, windows were of the mullioned variety, with thick, leaded lozenges of glass. That there were other types of window in use earlier is suggested by one payment made by the Duke of Hamilton in 1661, when he ordered 'a new window of Normandy glass is 57 foot and a half foot' and paid 12/– 'for carrying the same up from Glasgow upon a man's back.' Sash windows were certainly introduced into Scotland at an early date, and the assertion that they were unknown throughout the first half of the eighteenth century is patently false. As early as 1674 the Duke of Lauderdale bought '4 pairs of clock strings to make strings for the sash windows' at Lethington and in 1690 the Duke of Hamilton gave £29 'To James McClellan, wright, for a new sash window and his own charges in coming out to Hamilton to put it up.' McClellan may not actually have made the window himself, however, for when he was in London in the winter of 1693/4 the Duke sent him to watch the carpenter making sash windows, presumably so that he could learn the English technique.[8]

Back at Hamilton, the stonework of the new west quarter was rising rapidly. By March 1694 the workmen were beginning to slate the roof, and although the Duke had warned the Duchess to 'tell Mr James Smith that I desire no provision of stones for any new building that only they may provide to finish that building now in hand, for I do not intend to pull down a stone more until we be living in that now in hand and until we see a little more appearance of peaceable times', there was little doubt that when he saw the handsome new west wing with its fine stonework and its large plain windows he would give immediate orders to begin on the east quarter. The outlook was optimistic and his family were eagerly anticipating his return from London, little knowing that the Duke was destined never to see his fine new Palace.

Throughout the winter he had been far from well, and disquieting reports had reached the Duchess of his thinness and general appearance of ill-health. Worn out with affairs of state as well as with personal concerns, he longed to be home and wrote to her with every post telling her that he would 'not willingly be so long asunder [from her] again, and shall not easily be persuaded to make this journey again.' The truth of it was that, whatever his reasons for marrying the Duchess, he had come to rely on her more and more. They had enjoyed an affectionate working partnership for almost forty years of married life and he valued her judgment and depended on her advice. As he grew older he frequently expressed the hope that he and she would 'be happy together in our old age after all the difficulties and turmoilings we have had in this world', and when he was about to leave for home on 3 April 1694 he ended his letter with the words, 'God send us a good meeting and I hope we shall never be so long asunder again.'

He left London that same day, in company with his daughter Katherine and her husband, his son John and his secretary David Crawford. He was hoping that the journey would improve his health, but things went badly from the start. Lady Katherine had a fall on the stairs of Bugden Inn, injuring her leg so that she could not put her foot to the ground and had to be carried from room to room. Worse was soon to follow, for on 12 April the Duke himself suffered what must have been a stroke, and lost the use of his left leg. His companions were very much alarmed, fearing 'a palsy', although they dared not say so to him. Although 'much disheartened', the Duke insisted on continuing his journey, and on 13 April he wrote to the Duchess from Darnton describing his symptoms but telling her not to be too alarmed about him, although he himself did not know what would come of such an illness.

When the packet of letters arrived from England the Duchess was in Edinburgh for the General Assembly. She took one look at her husband's strangely shaky writing and knew that something was very wrong. The accompanying letters from Katherine, Lord John and Lord Murray confirmed her worst fears, and she decided to set out at once to meet them. First of all she summoned the Hamilton minister, who was also in town, then she sent for several eminent doctors. They set out together on the road to England.

It was an agonising journey. At last, just north of the border, the Duke's coach came into sight. He was obviously far gone, but he was able to greet his wife with a relief which was reflected in the anxious faces of his companions. In spite of the Duke's critical condition, he was determined to get home. They managed to reach The Biel that night, where Lady Belhaven did all she could to make him comfortable, and the doctors were able to minister to their patient.

They sat up with him all night. By morning he was no better, but he had himself carried out to the coach, and he asked weakly to see Lady Belhaven once more. She hurried over to him, leaning in at the coach door to catch his parting words. He thanked her for all her kindness to him, then begged her to do what she could to see that his sons carried out the settlements he had made in his Will and lived peacefully together.

By the time the little cavalcade reached Edinburgh, news of his illness had spread throughout the city and the Abbey Close was thronged with people. Amongst those who pressed forward to catch a glimpse of him as he was lifted from the coach was the Earl of Sutherland. He was near enough to murmur a few words of sympathy and, recognising him, the Duke whispered a reply, urging him not to mourn for him.

He was taken up to his own chamber and laid in his bed. The Duchess had not left his side since their reunion at Cockburnspath, and Lady Katherine, Lord John, Lord Murray and David

Crawford had been with him constantly since the onset of his illness. They were now joined by Lord Basil and by other relatives, while a crowd of noblemen and friends waited outside the door. Once in Holyrood, the Duke sank rapidly. He talked a little with the Duchess, begging her once more to see that their sons lived peacefully together. These were the last words he ever spoke. He lost consciousness shortly afterwards, and at about half past five on the morning of 18 April he died.

The Duchess was heartbroken. In an age of high female mortality when women half expected death each time they had a child, it was an all too common occurrence for a man to lose his wife. The Duchess had always accepted the fact that she might die young, but never had she imagined for one moment that she would outlive her husband. Throughout their marriage she had loved the Duke dearly, and this love had been strengthened by all the 'turmoilings' they had endured together. Certainly the Duchess was in many ways a highly independent woman, and the Duke had sometimes despaired of her venturesomeness. He had worried about her constantly when he was away from home, for in spite of all his warnings she would set off on exhausting journeys in bad weather, calmly ignoring his prudent advice. Although she paid no heed to his exhortations of caution in little things, she relied on him in all other matters and he had been at her side when financial ruin seemed inevitable, when Abercorn had threatened her inheritance and when their son William and their small daughters had died. Now she was alone again, for although she had her sons and daughters to comfort her, she was once more the sole representative of the family, the only head of the House of Hamilton.

Usually self-contained, she admitted that 'my tears . . . are but too frequent both in the night as well as day', and her desolation was all the greater when, only a few months after she lost her husband, her sister Susanna died. Her family found Hamilton Palace a sadly altered place, and the Duchess herself was reported as being 'pretty well but most extremely melancholy.' As she said herself, many months later, 'The great grief that still possesses me for that loss of my dear lord makes other troubles not have so deep an impression', and, referring to the anniversary of her husband's death, she told her daughter Katherine, 'That day . . . I shall not forget while I live, and now I am writing where he used to do it and everything I see is marks of his industry. I fear his son will not leave such behind him, but it's like he thinks he is too long agetting it.'

The death of his father made no alteration to the Earl of Arran's position. The Duke had held his honours personally, with no power to transmit them to his children. In a way, his dukedom had been almost a courtesy title. The lands and honours of the family remained in the possession of the Duchess and only on her death would her son inherit. She herself could find little comfort in the contemplation of her heir. Although he had quarrelled constantly with his father and had publicly criticised him up to the very last, he wrote an extravagant letter to his mother as soon as he heard the news, declaring, 'It's for my sins that I am punished . . . Oh, how it grieves me that ever I offended my dear father, but for all my failings it comforts me that I never in my life but wished him well.' He would leave London at once, 'the sooner [to] be at my dear mother's feet' and would spend the rest of his life serving her. After that, he delayed his return to Scotland for several weeks and although he did arrive at last, it was felt in many quarters that he could have come sooner.

In her grief for her dead husband it was the Duchess's devotion to the family which was to sustain her. It would have been simple to give up. She could have resigned her titles to the Earl of Arran, leaving him to do as he wished with the estates while she lived in retirement. After all, she was now over sixty and she suffered agonies from arthritis. However, she knew very well that she could not take this easy way out. Perhaps in the future James would be ready to assume his responsibilities, but that time had not yet arrived. To allow him control of the estates would have been to ensure their financial ruin, and so the Duchess rejected the notion of having him made 4th Duke of Hamilton on his father's death.

Difficult though it was for her, she turned her attention to practical matters. There remained several duties which she could yet perform for her husband. First of all, the funeral had to be arranged. The doctors who had attended the Duke embalmed his body a few hours after he died. 'Dead linens' were bought for him, and James McLellan made 'an extraordinary fine wainscot coffin, well varnished.' For the next month a constant stream of messengers went between Edinburgh and Hamilton in connection with the funeral preparations, and on 24 May, to the sounding of guns from Edinburgh Castle, the funeral procession left for Hamilton Church. There the burial service took place with customary pomp. All the dead man's sons walked in the final procession except for Lord Archibald, who was at sea. The coffin was surmounted by a gilded ducal coronet, the relatives of the family bore standards with the dead man's coat of arms, and noblemen, heralds, townspeople and the poor from the Hospital followed the hearse to the church. After the service, the mourners returned to a Palace draped with black for a magnificent banquet. The entire household was in black, from little Lady Mary, the Earl of Arran's daughter, to the youngest kitchen boy, and for the rest of her life the Duchess wore deepest mourning and had her bedchamber and her dressing room permanently hung with black.

After the funeral, the Duchess returned to Edinburgh and on 1 June she presided at Holyrood over a meeting of family, friends and lawyers. 'After regretting the sad occasion of the meeting' she produced various documents left by her husband. There was a disposition by which he left her all his belongings and money, and there were bequests to his sons. The Earl of Arran was handed the deed of entail made by the Duke and Duchess the previous year. Although this settled the estates on him, the entail had been a bone of contention between the Earl and his family ever since it had first been contemplated. It limited his powers of contracting debts on the Hamilton estates, which infuriated him, for it meant that he could not use his inheritance as a means of raising credit for himself. When the entail was publicly registered in Edinburgh, he was beside himself with rage, and he now accepted the actual document with a very ill grace.

The other bequests were less controversial. The Duchess handed to Lord Charles the key of a small trunk, which contained the title deeds of the lands of Crawford, his father's gift to him.

199

To Lord John the Duchess passed over a document providing him with £40,000, along with several bags containing the title deeds of Riccarton. Lord Basil was given a bundle of papers which cleared off debts on his wife's lands of Baldoon. Lord George was now abroad as well as Lord Archibald, so the Duchess kept in her custody the bonds of provision settling 10,000 merks on each of them. All the title deeds were then examined and sealed up in trunks, after which the meeting was at an end.

There was then the question of a suitable memorial for the Duke, and as well as deciding to erect a monument to him, the Duchess planned to endow a series of bursaries at Glasgow University in his memory. Apparently the Duke himself had intended a mortification of this description and three months after his death the Duchess had a memorandum drawn up outlining the conditions for the bursaries. She would gift £1,000 sterling for the use of three students of theology who were to study for two years at Glasgow University and for a further year at some Protestant University abroad. The Duchess was most definite that the money must be used in no other way, for 'to destinate any part of it to other uses, such as the library or fabric, is neither needful, nor would it redound to the honour of the family, but would be swallowed up among other mortifications or improvements already bestowed that way.' After all, her ancestor had provided premises for the original college and her own father had made his generous donation to the library.

She was equally determined that the money should not be used for bursaries in philosophy. Not only were there too many of these already, but 'it is not for the interest or honour of the church or nation to encourage any upon foundation of charity to lose their time at philosophy.' Only those well-qualified would be considered for the bursaries, 'it being evident that all the learned professions are too much burdened and crowded already with idle and insignificant persons', and when the students had successfully completed their courses it was stipulated 'that the House of Hamilton shall have the first offer of well-bred and learned men for serving in those churches wherein they have interest, and in time there may come to be a set of the best men in the church who shall have an obligation of gratitude and consequently a dependence on the Family.' In conclusion, the Duchess felt that it would 'be honourable to the Family to have given the first example in Scotland of a noble and regular foundation of this kind which may be followed by others to the great advantage of both church and state', and on 30 October of the same year she signed the formal deed of mortification.

Concern with the family was also in the Duchess's mind when she turned to the planning of a suitable monument for her husband. The obvious person to design and execute this work was Mr James Smith, who was already at hand, and on 10 December 1694 the Duchess gave him £70 sterling 'for sending to Holland to buy marble towards the erecting of a monument upon His Grace the Duke of Hamilton in Hamilton Church.' By the following autumn Mr Smith was busy sawing up the marble. There then ensued some delay, occasioned mainly by the Earl of Arran's tardiness in sending back the draft lent to him for his consideration, and it was not until 12 February 1696 that the Duchess and the two James Smiths formally signed the building contract.

Specific instructions as to how the tomb was to be made were laid down in the contract, which was accompanied by a pen and ink draft of what it should look like.[9] The entire monument was to be of black and white Dutch marble, forming a tall rectangle enclosed by pillars decorated with coats of arms, Hamilton cinquefoils and with capitols carved 'according to the rules of architecture.' At the base were to be panels cut with the trophies of war and honour, and the emblems of mortality 'exactly like the draught or better.' The centre of the tomb was to consist of an inscription on a large block of black marble, with a mourning boy at either side and a flaming urn on top. Above the urn was a small angel blowing a trumpet, and at the very top, outside the main rectangle, was to be a large coat of arms surmounted by another urn.

So huge was this monument that the whole aisle had to be altered to accommodate it. Marquis John's[10] monument had to be temporarily removed, the vault enlarged and new flooring of black and white marble put above it. The entire roof had to be lifted off so that the aisle could be heightened, the north wall was rebuilt, windows blocked up and a new stair put in.

The Duchess paid £600 sterling to the James Smiths for the work, and the finished monument is indeed highly impressive. Removed from its original situation when the burial aisle was demolished, it now stands in St Bride's Church in nearby Bothwell, and the towering marble structure with its life-sized cherubs and its imposing urns and draperies still evokes a feeling of awe in the beholder. In planning this monument, the Duchess hoped that it would provide a permanent memorial not only to the man she had loved but to the honour of the House of Hamilton. Those who came to gaze at the white marble would not simply remember the man who had died, but would be impressed by the dignity and splendour of the family he had represented.

Her concern for the family and for the continuance of her line was, if anything, strengthened by her husband's death, and in the months which followed she spent more and more time actively planning for the future. The most pressing question was, of course, the Great Design for the rebuilding of the Palace. The west quarter was all but finished. Now, the Duke himself had half decided to let the matter rest there, and so the simplest course for the Duchess to have taken would have been to see to the completion of the new wing and then to dismiss Mr James Smith and all the workmen, leaving the Great Design to be executed by her successor if he chose to do so at some future date. After all, the expense was well nigh prohibitive and the trouble involved was tremendous. No one would have been surprised had she abandoned the ambitious plans for the Palace then and there.

The Duchess was, however, a woman of courage and vision, and she did not hesitate. For the sake of the future Dukes of Hamilton she was resolved to continue with the building programme even although she was convinced that she would not live long after her husband's death. Nor was her task an easy one. No longer able to consult the Duke, she tried to draw the Earl of Arran into the plans for the new Palace, but he was depressingly casual about the whole business. Not only did he fail to appreciate the expense involved, but when his mother sent him the drafts of the proposed buildings he did not return them promptly and his vague comments made it all too clear that his interests lay elsewhere. Realising that it was useless to wait for his advice, the Duchess went ahead on her own.

Throughout the autumn of 1694 cartloads of Swedish timber were brought from Leith to Hamilton, and in the months which followed more timber arrived from Bo'ness and Glasgow. The west quarter was duly completed, and within the space of two years an identical east quarter was constructed at the opposite side of the courtyard. Since the plans had already been success-fully worked out and completed for the west quarter, the building of the east wing presented no difficulties and went ahead unin-terrupted.

Arrangements had been made to obtain from England glass for the windows of both new wings, and on 18 February 1696 Samuel Antrim and William Goddard, glaziers of London, loaded thirteen chests of window glass aboard *The Christian and Mary* of Bo'ness, then riding at anchor in the Thames. At that time the window frames were not yet ready, but by July they were in place, and John Frank, another glazier, travelled up from London to set up 'a parcel of glass at the Palace of Hamilton'. By then Thomas Warrander the painter had come out from Edin-burgh and was busy on the west quarter, painting the walls of the bedchambers a fine walnut tree colour and doing panels and cornices in 'fine marble and all the styles with varieties of Japan fancies on a black ground.'

In the meantime, the Duchess was busy consulting with the two James Smiths about the draft of the north quarter. This was to be the main part of the new Palace, the idea being to retain the walls and floors of the original Palace but to remodel the interior. From the end of 1695 onwards there were endless discussions as to what should be done and how the finished building should look. In January 1696 the Duchess sent a draft to the Earl of Arran for his consideration. The usual delays ensued, but by May Mr James Smith had produced an amended design which he declared 'is the result of all that we can think upon, either relative to our invention or by comparing the designs that came from London with the work which is already done. This design is thought by all concerned here to be an improvement of all these that were sent from that place, and of that which was sent there.' He added that 'My Lady Duchess has ordered us to go on vigorously with the work and accordingly the foundation is digged and we are building the rock work under ground.' As for the external stonework, 'Her Grace is content that we should make it as fine as possible so as the same be not gaudy or exceed the rules of proportion and true symmetry with the rest of the work', and so, 'since Her Grace takes the advice of none in this place but of my cousin and me', he entreated the Earl of Arran to send back his opinion of the revised draft with all speed.

Everything seemed to be going ahead splendidly when a radical difficulty was encountered. As the work proceeded, Mr Smith and his cousin realised that it would be impossible to retain the shell of the original building as they had intended. The Duchess wrote to tell her son that 'I was surprised yesterday by finding a necessity to lose the roof and all the rooms in the middle quarter, so what charge this will be and disaccommodation to me I leave you to judge', and Lord Basil explained more fully that the roof was in so bad and dangerous a condition that the whole building would have to come down except for the wall on the garden side and the two towers.

In a way, this new setback was to prove a blessing in disguise as far as the finished appearance of the Palace was concerned, for it now meant that all the floors in the central wing would be on the same level as those in the two side wings, and instead of being eighteen feet wide as formerly, the central block could now be twenty-two feet in width, like the wings. The eventual Palace would be much more of a unity now that this more extensive rebuilding had to be undertaken.

Of course it did mean a good deal of dislocation of the household, and when the Duchess's widowed daughter Lady Susan decided to marry again in the autumn of 1697 the Duchess explained that she could not have the ceremony at Hamilton as she would have liked to do, because 'the house is in such a condition as renders it impossible', many of the rooms being shut up and out of use altogether. The work was going ahead vigorously, though. By the end of July the new building had risen to the height of the tympanum, and on 6 October the Duchess was able to go up to the roof, where she rewarded the masons and wrights with '2 ducatoons of drink money.'

'The Palace at Hamilton is large . . . the front is very magnificent indeed, all of white freestone with regular ornaments according to the rules of art . . .'. This was how the new Hamilton Palace appeared to Daniel Defoe when he visited Lanarkshire in 1706[11] and the completed building was truly impressive. More French than English in its conception, its nonetheless rather heavy classicism might not appeal today, but there is no doubt that in 1697 it was an example of the most fashionable good taste. Viewed from the south, the front was somewhat overshadowed by the two deep wings, but it combined elegant simplicity with some pleasingly decorative detail. The ingenious, carved pillars, the large, plain windows and the intricately carved coat of arms on the tympanum gave an interesting accent to the general impression of dignity and grandeur.[12]

Not only was the building externally handsome. The Duchess went on to employ the best craftsmen available to work on the interior. In the 1660s a plasterer named Thomas Aliborne had worked in the Palace, and either he or his son of the same name had been employed by the Duke of Lauderdale: in 1673 the 'master plasterer' at Thirlestane Castle was 'Thomas Alburne in Caskieberrie.'[13] Now Thomas Aliborne came back to Hamilton to put up ornate plaster ceilings in all the main rooms. When he had been at work for over a year, David Crawford, Hew Wood and the latter's son Alexander were ordered to measure all the plasterwork that he had done, estimating the area of the cornices, mouldings and clam shells, 'which cannot be wrought by measure, being so troublesome and small tedious work.' He was paid a total of £185:19:4 Scots, and began again at once on the walls of the Great Dining Room and Drawing Room and on the friezes in the Gallery.

At the same time, Thomas Warrander had moved on to the main block and was busy painting the staircase in a wainscot colour and ornamenting fireplaces with imitation marble and festoons of fruit and flowers. Not all the fireplaces were merely imitation marble, of course. The finest rooms in any great house could boast fireplaces of real marble. The Duke of Lauderdale had installed six marble chimney pieces at Thirlestane, which he had picked up as a great bargain in London. 'I lighted on them by chance in an Italian merchant's hand, who let me have them as he paid for them in Italy with the customs and charges' he had told his brother Hatton triumphantly. 'And that poor Lethington [now Lennoxlove, his house near Haddington] be not forgotten, I have bought a brave one for the hall.'[14]

The Duchess of Hamilton also obtained marble fireplaces from London, but not without some difficulty. After much thought, she decided on a white marble one for the Great Bedchamber, a black marble one for the Great Dining Room and one 'of any other pretty colour' for the closet. The Dining Room chimney piece was to be the largest, at six feet and a quarter of an inch broad, and the one for the closet was the smallest at a width of four feet eight inches. As usual the Earl of Arran was acting as an intermediary and as usual the results were unsatisfactory. Lord Basil wrote to complain to him that the drawing-room and bedchamber chimney pieces were 'pretty near to the measure but not exact, and they were desired to have been different colours and they are one.' The one for the closet was even farther out in measurement, though it could be made to serve, 'but the black for the dining room is entirely wrong and can't serve at all and has no ways the proportion according to the rules of architecture but sure has been some old thing that has lain in the man's hand that he could not get off and so it seems has been thought good enough for Scotland. My Lady is much displeased at it and says since you was not at the expenses you might have been at the pains to have seen the chimneys compared with the measures that were sent up.'

Perhaps the most magnificent feature of all was the panelling in the principal chambers. The carving on these panels matched the plaster ceilings in intricacy of execution. William Morgan was the carver employed and he transformed the plain oak panels into amazingly elaborate and decorative works of art. In the Dining Room the wooden chimney piece was carved with fish, fowl and flowers, and a hundred and eighty Hamilton cinquefoils and stars decorated the panels along with a hundred and seventy-six medallions. More medallions, cinquefoils and stars decorated the Drawing Room walls, where flowers and coronets rioted over the chimney piece. The chimney in the bedchamber was similarly ornamented, and in the closet two small carved boys supported the Duchess's cipher. As for the staircase, ten large folding panels had boys and beasts, flowers and festoons, and the monogram of the Duke and Duchess, an 'A' intertwined with a 'W'. It was small wonder that Lord John declared when he saw it all, 'My Lady is making the finest things here in the world: the finishing, carving and pillars go beyond anything in this kingdom.'[15]

The magnificent new Palace was virtually complete by 1701, although the craftsmen continued to work there throughout the decade, and as late as 1713 the Duchess paid £15 sterling to Mr James Smith 'in part of payment of the balance of what is due to me on account of the building of the Palace of Hamilton.' One reason why Mr Smith was receiving payment as late as that was the fact that once he had finished with the Palace itself he was employed on various tasks in the grounds. The plans for the Great Design did not end with the actual building: the Duchess had thoughts of re-modelling the entire area around the Palace. During the first decade of the eighteenth century her daughter Margaret had working at Panmure Mr Alexander Edward, a local man who had originally been a minister. In the religious troubles of the 1680s he found himself without a parish and from that time onwards he was fully employed as an architect and gardener. He had worked for Sir William Bruce at Kinross and he was frequently found in association with Sir William's friends the Bauchops.[16] In 1708 the Duchess commissioned him to draw up a scheme for the complete landscaping of the Palace grounds.

The enormous plan which he drew is extremely detailed, and shows formal gardens, plantations, vistas, walks, and even two mounds cut in the shape of cinquefoils. In the event, Mr Edward died before this scheme could be put into effect, but it is doubtful whether it could ever have been carried out, so great would have been the expense involved. Nevertheless, the Duchess continued her improvements of the grounds by planting and laying out avenues of trees, and even if this final part of her Great Design was not fully accomplished, she had effectively brought about the complete transformation of the Palace and her policies in a way which might have seemed impossible when she and the Duke first discussed their plans for the future fifty years before. Everything was now ready for the heir to enter into his inheritance.

CHAPTER 10

The Fatal Flaw

'My Lady is building you a fine house so that you will have nothing to do but to get a rich wife', his brother John told the Earl of Arran in 1694, voicing a theme which was to preoccupy the family for many years. 'Marry!' urged the Earl's mother, brothers, sisters and friends: even his little daughter wrote to bid him find her 'a good Mama'. In the context of seventeenth-century society it was virtually inevitable that a widowed peer would remarry, especially if he were left with no heir. It was high time the Earl settled at home and provided a son to continue the family line, for his relations were beginning to fear that he had 'given over thoughts of being a Scotchman.' Be that as it might, the Earl of Arran had as little intention as ever of marrying. He was perfectly well aware of his family's expectations, hence his renewed pursuit of wealthy heiresses, but he had no intention of completing any of his marriage negotiations or of allowing them to interfere with his other liaisons.

On his return to London after his wife's death, both he and his brother Charles sought the hand of Viscount Lisburne's only daughter Lucia, who in the end married neither of them. The Earl then turned his attention to the Duke of Devonshire's daughter, but she declared that Scotland was too far away and she could not consider settling there. At that, he thought of Newcastle's daughter Arabella whom he had wooed four years before. This time he went so far as to make a proposal to her, but nothing came of that either. Similarly, disquieting rumours to the effect that he had 'sent to King James [II] to have liberty to marry My Lord Portland's daughter' seem to have been ground-less.

Really, he was much more taken with Lord Crewe's daughter, a former Lady-in-Waiting to Mary of Modena. He described her as being 'tall, well shaped, a good skin, very well fashioned and has been carefully bred.' More to the point, she had a portion of £17,000 sterling, which he hoped might be raised still higher. He seems to have harboured some real affection for this lady, to judge by the persistence with which he put forward her name, but his father was still alive at this time and did not think much of his choice. The Duke had seen her walking in the Mall and declared her to be no beauty, in addition to which she did not come of a good enough family. The Duke preferred Anne Thomas of Wenvoe and Ruperra, a granddaughter of Lord Wharton. Anne was the heiress to extensive lands in the Bristol area, and her only dependant was her mother. The Duke had taken the precaution of inspecting her first, and he told the Duchess, 'I saw her yesterday at the King and Queen's dinner, where I believe she was scarce ever before. She was with the Countess of Denbigh your cousin's relict, whom I stood and spoke with a little a purpose to observe the young lady who I [was] pleased [with] extremely. She is about seventeen [she was eighteen and a half], tall and well shaped, brown hair and a very white skin. Her face has good features but a little pale and green. She hears many good Presbyterian prayers at My Lord Wharton's, so her education is what I believe you would like.'

The Earl was displeased by the suggestion. Anne Thomas would be 'much difficulter to be had' because of her large fortune, and in any case he preferred Crewe's daughter. His father promptly pointed out that, according to the marriage contract with Lady Anne Spencer, his consent was necessary before his son could remarry, whereupon the Earl retorted that if that were so he would not marry at all. However, with many complaints he turned his attention to Anne Thomas.

From the beginning he met with small success, for Anne's relatives did not approve of him, and, as the Duke found out, 'the pretence is that her mother nor herself has no mind she should go to Scotland.' Lord Wharton told the Duke that this was the reason for their attitude, but the Duke suspected that 'anybody that is anything well at this Court has no mind to meddle with him for there is no alteration in him as to his politics.' The Earl's Jacobite sympathies were too well known. In the end, the problem was resolved when Anne contracted smallpox and died within the week.

In the meantime, the Duke himself had died, and his family hoped that they would now see an alteration in the Earl's behaviour. Perhaps he would return home at last. He had made no attempt to conceal his dislike of his father, but he had always professed a deep affection for his mother, very often asking her to intercede with the Duke on his behalf. She, for her part, saw her son's faults all too clearly, but she always treated his requests with patience and forbearance. In spite of this, it soon became obvious that nothing had changed. The Earl wished to live in London, and he wanted the family estates so that he could afford to do so. His protestations to the contrary deceived no one, least of all his family. 'Don't think your saying ... that you are wearied of London will make the world believe it till you alter your course of life', his brother Basil told him, 'you now having lived, I suppose, the half of your time out of your own country and too much a stranger to the affairs of it', while the Duchess confided sadly to her daughter Katherine that James's behaviour 'is liker a man that's out of his wits than in them, God in His mercy pity him, and me who has him thus for the punishment of my sins.'[1]

His entire family wrote to him over and over again urging him to marry and return home. He met these pleas with peevish ill humour. Although 'there are several matches to be had ...', he told his mother, 'it is not easy to get one with all the qualities that my inclinations and circumstances require, so it is much easier said "Marry" than to do it. I am sure I wish it, and longs myself more to be settled than I can express. Great portions requires great settlements and a small one is not able to extricate me out of my difficulties.'

That was in October 1694, and he went on to list the matches then available. Lord Rochester's daughter was 'one of the prettiest young women that I have seen of a great while. She won't have above ten thousand pounds and is very young though sufficiently a woman and very pretty, but they expect great terms.' His old friend Lord Crewe's daughter was still unmarried, and finally 'there is another talked of . . . a maid of honour, Mrs Henrietta Villiers, the old Knight Marshal's daughter. I have had some insinuations made to me that I might get twenty thousand pounds there, but that would lead to engagements that I am not very fond of at present.'

His mother was horrified at the last suggestion. 'I beseech you', she wrote back at once, 'not to think of the Knight Marshal's daughter. You have by my mother the honorablest part of that aliah [alliance] and I admire you ever took that into consideration, knowing how mad the father was.' (The Earl of Breadalbane was not so particular. In the following May he married the lady.) The Duchess favoured Rochester's daughter, but she left the final choice to the Earl himself, warning him that he should come home as soon as he did marry, otherwise 'I should never consent to the match or any other. Those that will not come to Scotland's not for you.' She followed this up a month later by telling him that even if he had all her lands and titles, they 'would not afford you and an English wife to live high in England, so I must return to my old opinion that a Scots wife is by far the preferablest, where you may live comfortably on what you have and pay your debts by degrees as your father and I did before you.'

Her remarks fell upon deaf ears, and months later she was to tell him in exasperation that she had given over all expectation of ever seeing him marry again. She could only beg him, 'not to trifle away your time longer, but if the young lady is a virtuous person, that you go on and make an end of it, though her fortune were less than what you mention,' for even so the marriage would surely solve his financial problems. Lord Basil summed up the feelings of them all when he told the Earl, 'Staying at London, losing your time, consuming your health, unprofitably spending your money, neglecting your affairs and a stranger to your friends and country, still treating marriages and never marrying, give me leave, dear brother, to say it: that's unaccountable.'

Before this letter was written, however, the Earl had already begun to negotiate for the lady whom he was eventually to marry. For several years he had vaguely considered Elizabeth Gerard as a possibility. The only child of the late Baron Gerard, she was the heiress to considerable estates in Lancashire and Staffordshire.

She was only half his age – she was still a minor when she married him and he was forty – but she was of a very good family, and she was extremely rich. With his mother's approval the Earl began discussions with the widowed Lady Gerard, whom he described as being 'a most extraordinary woman for understanding, but very stiff.'

The negotiations were to drag on for three years, during which time the Earl made continual excuses for not coming to the point. At first he declared himself dissatisfied with the financial terms of the contract, and wanted his mother to give him more money. This was out of the question. The rebuilding of the Palace was a tremendous drain on the Duchess's finances apart from all her other commitments. She accordingly replied that she could not do as he wished, pointing out that he already had over £6,000 sterling a year from Kinneil, and all that she was doing in the way of building, estate improvements and litigation was designed for his benefit. Apart from that, there was no reason to suppose that at her age she would 'live long to stand in the way of your full possessing of the whole estate.'

The Earl therefore abandoned this line of argument and hinted instead that the jointure lands could be altered. He was still hoping that the Duchess would resign all her lands in his favour, but she knew full well that if she did so before he married, no marriage would ever take place. She explained patiently that Kinneil was perfectly suitable, and there was really nothing else available – 'Arran would be thought very ridiculous, and Avendale has no habitable house, and if there were one there yet the place would be very unfit for an English lady.'

When he had digested this, the Earl announced that legal difficulties occasioned the delay, 'for here in England things of this kind are very intricate.' That was true enough, as his father had discovered in 1687, but the Duke had managed to overcome similar obstacles in the space of a few weeks. The Earl followed this up with the assertion that the wedding was delayed because Lady Gerard did not have enough ready money to pay the portion at once, to which the Duchess replied that he could accept the sum in goldsmith's notes or in banknotes.

By this time she was convinced that he intended to use such

excuses to break the match altogether, a conviction which was strengthened when he wrote her a letter asking her to be a signatory to his marriage articles and speaking of coming to Scotland on a visit. The former suggestion indicated to his mother that he would end the negotiations and lay the blame on her, and as for the latter notion, 'I am sure', she told him, 'you would never attempt it without the design of breaking the match, whatever pretence you can make, and that you would so fain have broken your first marriage even the very day before, and if your father had not hindered you, you had made yourself so ridiculous at that time.'

In spite of her urgings, no marriage took place that winter and in the following January the Earl was saying that everything was at a halt because of the general scarcity of money. Much to her dismay the Duchess then received from him a letter in which he declared that there had been so many delays to his marriage plans that he was almost ready to give them up, complaining that 'it's a cruel thing when one's circumstances are such that one must prefer money to other things when the whole happiness of one's life is concerned.'

The Duchess despaired of him, but there was nothing she could do other than continue her persuasions, telling him that if this marriage did not go through, 'I blush to think of your disgrace in it, for I think you are too far engaged in honour ever to retreat.' To her daughter Katherine she confessed that James 'is the strangest man that ever I knew or heard of in my life,' and urged 'all of you that are his friends, do what you can to make him end [*i.e.* accomplish] his marriage, otherwise he is utterly ruined.'[2]

Not long afterwards occurred an event which emphasised more than ever the need for him to remarry. Since the death of his wife, his daughter Lady Mary had been brought up by the Duchess at Hamilton, and as the Duchess herself said, if anything could have diverted her after the loss of her husband it would have been her grandchild. Lady Mary was an enchanting, precocious child, 'in wit her mother's very apprehension'. She kept the entire household entertained with her adult ways and comical sayings, and she would give David Crawford no peace until he took her on his knee and guided her hand so that she could 'write' to her father. By the time she was seven she was not only learning to read and write for herself but she was beginning French and Latin. It was not long before she had attained 'great proficiency in her writing', to an extent where 'pen and paper must be kept well out of her hands, for if she get to the letters she will soon learn to answer them, being abundantly forward always', and the Duchess joked that she would make Lady Mary her secretary when she grew up. It was not to be. That same winter the little girl contracted smallpox, and she died. As Lord Basil wrote to the Earl of Arran, 'She was indeed a dear, engaging, witty creature, as ever was seen, far beyond her years, and if it was allowable to be fond of anything on earth, she was it . . . had she been my own, it could not have gone nearer to me.'

The Earl was genuinely upset by the news of her death, all the more so because his fortunes were at a low ebb. He had been in trouble once more because of his Jacobite sympathies, his debts were greater than ever, and he was still half thinking of extricating himself from the match with Elizabeth Gerard. He had one more objection to this marriage to put to his mother. It now appeared that his only desire was to return home and settle down, but where Elizabeth was concerned, 'it's death to talk of living in Scotland.' It is difficult to estimate how sincere he was in this new notion. Hitherto he had viewed the prospect of life at home with unconcealed repugnance, and he was in the habit of writing to his mother what he knew she would like to hear. In replying to her letter of condolence about Lady Mary's death, he remarked that his marriage 'yet subsists and will go on, though I am convinced a Scots wife with a thousand merks might give me more comfort: for I can't expect another Lady Arran, though I may get another wife', and he added with characteristic exaggeration that, as for his living in Scotland, 'my heart is more set on that than ever, nay much more. I hope you'll let me be your chamberlain in Arran that I may live there, or let me be your keeper that I may live in the little house in the wood.'

If this objection to his future wife was designed to influence the Duchess, it failed in its intent. In her usual commonsense manner, she told her son Basil that although she remembered her

own feelings on leaving Chelsea as a child well enough to sympa-
thise with any lady who felt unwilling to come north, 'a good
husband with not despicable fortune will make a reasonable
woman content to go where their interest lies.' Lord Basil passed
on this message, and the Earl seemed finally to realise that there
was no point in arguing any further. On 16 July 1698 he wrote
home announcing that he had signed the marriage contract and
would be married on the following day. Also on 16 July, the
Duchess resigned her titles in his favour.

This resignation was what the Earl had been wanting for
years, but it has frequently been misunderstood. The Duchess
did not give up her estates to him and go into retirement as a
dowager. On the contrary, she retained her own position as
Duchess of Hamilton in her own right, and she continued in full
control of the estates as she had always been, as head of the
House of Hamilton. What had changed was that her son would
now style himself fourth Duke of Hamilton, and as such he would
be entitled to sit in the Scottish Parliament.

This was the main reason for the resignation. The Duchess had
always shared her husband's view that the family required a male
representative, and in a rapidly changing political climate where
there was more and more talk of union with England, it was
imperative that the Hamiltons should have a voice in Parliament.
To resign her estates to her son would have been folly. Everyone
knew that, and even a casual visitor to Hamilton like Daniel
Defoe had made overt reference to the fact that should the Earl
of Arran ever gain control of the estates, financial ruin would
soon follow.[3] The Duchess hoped that by permitting her son to
become Duke of Hamilton he would come to a better realisation
of the responsibilities of his inheritance. He would be able to
make a fresh start with a new wife, using her dowry to pay his
enormous debts. He could then settle at Kinneil with her, raise
a family and serve his country by attending Parliament. The
Duchess was nearing seventy and it would not be long before he
did have full power over everything, but this interlude would be
of the greatest value to him. After much heart searching she
therefore made the necessary legal arrangements, and then wrote
to congratulate her son, using his new titles. Lady Katherine

asked her afterwards if it had been difficult for her to address her daughter-in-law as 'Duchess of Hamilton'. 'I can name her very well', she replied, 'but your dear father's name I confess to you made the tears come in my eyes. I heartily wish he [James] may do well and then what I have done will be the more comfortable to us all,' and she went on to express the hope that 'he may carry as my Uncle did when he came to be Duke [and] was much more humble and obliging than when he was Earl.'[4]

The tragedy was that all this brought about no alteration in her son. His marriage was successful enough in private. Elizabeth Gerard was very young when she married, but she always seems to have been petulant and wilful, with an excitable nature which matched her husband's volatile disposition. When he eventually brought her to Scotland in 1700 she declared that she liked Kinneil very much 'and says he is the most incomparable good husband that ever woman had, and he praises her as much', the Duchess reported, adding 'I wish it may long continue so.'[5]

Elizabeth did at first profess a great fondness for the Duke and, when he left her at Kinneil to go to Edinburgh, she sent a constant stream of letters to 'my Jewel', sometimes two a day. Along with these, she sent a variety of gifts. One footman after another was dispatched to town. The first would carry a jug of soup, the second a bowl of jelly, the third a pat of butter, the fourth a bunch of flowers and as soon as the first one returned he would be sent off again with a dish of porridge.

When some neighbours sent a gift of partridge, Elizabeth decided that they would be ideal to tempt her husband's far from flagging appetite. The cook went to work, and some hours later presented her mistress with a very tasty partridge pie. Delighted, Elizabeth placed it on a table, the better to admire it. At that moment, Beauty, her pet dog, came bounding into the room, took one look at the pie, made a leap at it and the next moment was running out of the door with a mouthful of partridge and pastry.

With a wail of dismay, Elizabeth bent over to examine the damage. It did not look too bad, really. She picked up a knife and scraped away some of the broken pastry. It would be such a pity to waste it. She would send it to James after all, and so she did, enclosing an artless little note describing the sad accident.

Whatever he thought when he received it, he replied kindly enough, declaring that 'your partridge pie was the best I ever ate, and was a most seasonable morsel. I have good enough meat but I want my dear and she [is] constantly in my thoughts. Believe me upon my salvation I adore you and admire your understanding beyond what I can express.'

Elizabeth's relations with the rest of the family were not so good, mainly because she was jealous of them. She resented his mother's supposed influence over her husband and she particularly hated Lady Katherine, 'your politic self designing sister.' 'I wish I were dead', she told the Duke on one occasion, 'then you and your family would be rid of what they don't care for.' In fact, the Hamiltons treated her with kindness and indulgence. The Duchess was sorry for her, for she was very young and was often obviously unhappy, but they must all have regretted that the Duke had not chosen for himself someone with a more stabilising influence.

Whatever her other deficiencies, Elizabeth did provide the much desired male heir. She and the Duke had three sons, James, William and a third boy whom the Duke scandalised his relations and amused the Court by naming Anne. He was at that time willing to go to any lengths to ingratiate himself with Queen Anne, and after all, to one who had spent several years in France, the name was a perfectly acceptable one for a boy. They also had five daughters, Elizabeth, Katherine and Henrietta who died in childhood, and Charlotte and Susan.

Long before their family was complete they were quarrelling constantly. 'I fear [the] honeymoon is over', the Duchess remarked in 1702,[6] and in 1703 the Duke wrote his mother a long and rambling letter in which he told her 'You would pity me if you knew all my troubles, for I think Job never had so great, for my wife is more intolerable than all the rest. I am afraid we shall part. I can't tell you in this hurry all my reasons, but she's become most insufferably insolent. God knows what I meet with. I am sure it would kill any other man living and I believe it will kill me. For what you wrote concerning her to ease me, it's folly to think of it. I wish to God she would but let me breathe in quiet the few moments I have to rest, but that's disturbed to the last degree and joined to all that the Court [party] is industrious to hound out every creditor I have upon me . . . I have bought the name of a fortune dear, though God has blessed us with children and a prospect of something to leave them. I am sure I am far from enjoying one quiet moment. I protest before God I believe I shall at last run away for I have quiet nor support neither.'

These complaints and protestations were painful for his family to read, but there was never any real likelihood of his separating from his wife. In fact they suited each other rather well. They both had shallow natures and they enjoyed indulging in misery and self pity. It might have been different had either really cared for the other, but neither of them seems to have been capable of deep affection and so in their own way they were happy enough together.

Apart from the purely domestic aspect of the marriage, it was an important one for the family. It brought the Duke vast lands in England, although he continued to claim, 'I am plagued out of my life with duns. They think it has rained a shower of gold upon me but I am sorry to tell you I find more debts than money.' He now spent a good deal of time living on the Gerard lands in Lancashire, but he did come to Scotland for several months each year in order to attend Parliament. With his father dead and his own position so much improved, he could become a leading figure in Edinburgh although his influence at Court remained minimal.

Unfortunately, his behaviour in Parliament left his mother feeling 'so ashamed on his behalf that I know neither what to say or how to look.' It was not just because of those occasions when he attended the House drunk that she declared, 'It passes my comprehension to find out a tolerable face for his actings.'[7] It was simply that his general behaviour was so erratic, and fell so far short of what was expected of him. The Duchess had by now become one of the accepted leaders of what was termed the patriotic party. She had always been an influential member of the Presbyterian party in Scotland, but now she was becoming more and more concerned with the country's economic difficulties. The years at the end of the century were marked by a series of bad harvests, and although the duration of these has often been exaggerated, the economic depression was very real. People were literally dying of starvation by the roadside, and many of her own tenants were in grave financial difficulties.

When William Paterson announced his plan to establish a Scottish colony at the Isthmus of Darien, the scheme was seen as the salvation of Scotland's economy and the Duchess and her family were enthusiastic supporters of it. Lord Basil became one of the directors of the company, and the Duchess was the first to sign the subscription books when they opened in Edinburgh. As she explained to one of her sons, 'Though I may be [a] short while alive to see any success thereof, yet considering it to be a good thing for the nation, I am resolved to give what assistance I can to it, and therefore design to sign for three thousand pounds sterling.' Lord Basil gave £1,000, David Crawford the secretary put down £200 and John Porterfield the page added £100.[8]

In spite of all their hopes, the experiment designed to bring immediate prosperity to Scotland was a disastrous failure. Many Scots attributed this failure to English policies abroad, and the Duchess was among those whose opposition to a union with England hardened. For many years now there had been talk of this possible union, and while some viewed it as a solution to Scotland's economic problems, the Duchess held another opinion. Her whole concern was for 'this poor people that our cruel neighbours would starve, and treats them and our nation with scorn.'[9] She had hitherto insisted that she was above party politics, but she was now openly 'more than can be expressed against this Union.' Although a woman, over seventy and suffering a great deal from arthritis, she felt that she had to do something. 'It's sad to sit still and be ruined', she said, and she set about organising local opposition. 'We have frequent rendezvous here', she reported in the winter of 1706, 'and as long as we have law for it, let them say what they will of me, I will encourage them . . .'. At the same time, she was careful to prevent civil disorder, and she forbade the tenants of other parishes to come to a meeting at Hamilton because she was anxious to protect them from reprisals.

That winter an event took place which confirmed her conviction that the supporters of the Union were determined to intimidate her. Her page John Porterfield was arrested along with the Hamilton burgh treasurer, William Weir. The Duchess wrote at once to the Duke, asking him to intercede for them, since John 'was born and bred up in my family and had been my servant ever since, and carried himself well and soberly. I never knew him guilty of any crime or ill thing . . . and because he is but a tender lad I hope His Grace [the Duke of Queensberry] will not allow him to be put in prison.' Despite her efforts the two men were imprisoned in Edinburgh for a time, and the Duchess was sure that the whole episode was intended 'only to make a noise and to see if they can put a lash on me, which I defy them to do.'

In all this, the Duchess naturally hoped that her son would play his part by leading the opposition in Parliament, and in fact the anti-Unionists looked to him as their leader. The difference in character between the Duchess and her eldest son was to be nowhere more clear than in their behaviour during these last months of 1706. The Duke had certainly come north and was attending Parliament, but his erratic behaviour bewildered all his supporters. He was acting with all his usual irresolution. He was ready enough to declare to his mother that he was exhausting himself in the service of his country, but like so many of his contemporaries his real motive was self-interest. Everyone knew that his English wife had brought him extensive lands in the south so he could hardly be expected to be whole-heartedly against a Union. Then again, he was desperately anxious to insinuate himself into the Queen's favour. He lacked the strength of mind to base his conduct on any one of these considerations, and so he veered continually between opposition, and doubt about the wisdom of opposition, falling victim to anything from a fever to a toothache whenever any really decisive move was required of him.

One of his more curious actions was the drawing up of a protest in the name of his mother and himself, declaring that the Treaty of Union should in no way prejudice their right and interest in the succession to the crown of Scotland. This immediately raised the perennial question of the Hamilton attitude towards the succession. Their enemies never could believe that a family so close to the throne would not grasp any opportunity to secure the crown for themselves. In the sixteenth century the possibility of a Hamilton succeeding had been very real, but there is no evidence that any of the Dukes of Hamilton ever did plot to seize the throne, whatever their opponents might say, and so in the seventeenth century all serious thoughts of a Hamilton succession died away. When the Duke sent his mother a copy of the protest, asking her to sign it, she was amazed, and refused at once. 'I am confident the doing of it now will do more hurt than good', she told him, 'and only expose me to be laughed at.'

There was nothing very sinister in the drawing up of this protest. The Duke was at all times liable to fall victim to sudden violent enthusiasms with a fine disregard for their practicality. He was always ready to snatch at anything which would bring him financial advantage or enhanced reputation, no matter how far fetched the scheme, but it is difficult to believe that even he entertained serious hopes of one day sitting on the throne of Scotland.

Distracted by so many conflicting notions, his leadership of the opposition left much to be desired. At first he supported a plan for an armed rising in the west, then suddenly sent word of a postponement and the scheme fell through. Next, he summoned the country gentlemen to Edinburgh to support a demand for a new Parliament, abruptly decided that unless their petition insisted on a Hanoverian succession he could have nothing to do with it, and in the ensuing argument the plan collapsed. When the twenty-second article of the treaty was being debated, he drew up a protest which he intended to present in Parliament before withdrawing altogether, but on the morning when he was to have given the protest in he suddenly developed toothache and refused to go. His long-suffering supporters at last persuaded him to attend, but he refused to give in the paper. Obviously whenever he had decided upon a course of action, someone had only to suggest to him that this might incur the disfavour of the Queen, of the Hanoverian successor or of any other influential person and he would immediately change his mind or at least fall into his usual state of nervous indecision. Whether his ensuing illnesses were, as his family thought, psychosomatic in origin, or whether they were merely diplomatic must remain a matter for conjecture, but whatever the reason for them they had the same damaging effect upon his cause.

In the end, of course, the Union went through. The Duke remained for a time in Edinburgh, complaining that financial troubles prevented him from moving on elsewhere. He was hoping that his mother would invite him to stay with her permanently at Hamilton Palace, but by this time there were too many differences between them for such a course to be possible. 'Everyone is sparing either to speak or write of your brother Hamilton to me', the Duchess told Lady Katherine, adding, 'Lord God pity him and let him see the ill of his ways . . . anything from me is of no more weight than a straw,'[10] and a few weeks later she wrote 'For my son Hamilton, he has been many a sore heart both to his father and me, and his carriage in this Parliament is no small trouble to me, but all he does is right in his own eyes.'[11]

His behaviour in Parliament made her ashamed, but there were other causes of contention between them. After the death of her husband, the Duchess had relied a good deal on Arthur Nasmith to help with the running of the estates. When he died too, her eldest son suggested that she persuade Lord Basil to live permanently at the Palace to assist her. She agreed, and Basil proved invaluable but this made James jealous and he complained continually about his brother being at Hamilton.

That particular disagreement could be suppressed in public, but less easy to hide were their differences over finance. The Duke was more in debt than ever, in spite of the fact that his father had left him an additional £1,000 sterling a year. Not content with this, he nagged his mother continually until she agreed to give him a lump sum of £8,000 instead of the annuity, and then declared that he must have the £1,000 each year as well. Not only did he pester his mother with constant demands, but he complained to everyone about what he chose to call her lack of generosity. 'How such stuff can come in his head and to set it under his hand is odd', the Duchess remarked to Lady Katherine, 'but alas, he minds neither what he says or what he writes. (However take you no notice of this.) I am sure all I am doing is for the family and if I had not played the fool in letting him have that money, it might have been more for the advantage of the family'[12]

Of course, the real trouble was simply that James was not content with the title of Duke of Hamilton: he wished to have complete control over all the estates. The Duchess spoke of this to no one, but she did confide something of her feelings to Lady Katherine. 'You thought all [difference of opinion] was ended between us,' she wrote, 'but that will never be while [until] one of us is dead. He covets mine so much that it troubles me for his sake. I am sure I wish he may succeed to the estate and be a blessing to the family, but alas, he is not in the way he should, though he thinks all right that he does and that I am both unkind and unjust to him.'[13]

In the end, the Duke and his wife went south again. They had been in the habit of spending part of the year in Lancashire, but even there they could not agree with their tenants. In the Duke's opinion, these were 'litigious knaves' who had been without a landlord for so long 'they had got into a notion that the estate was theirs upon paying what I may call a small feu duty', while for their part the tenants made 'a mighty cry out' against the Duke 'for the racking of the rent.' The Duke soon tired of visiting his Lancashire estates, and shortly after the Union he and his wife decided to settle permanently in London. They rented a large house in St James's Square, and the Duke never went back to Scotland again, although he had left his children behind at Hamilton Palace.

The Duchess was too much of a realist to entertain any further hopes of a reformation in the character of her heir who was, by this time, a man of fifty. The magnificent new Palace was complete, the grounds were beautifully laid out, the finances of the estate were on a secure basis, but instead of being aware of his responsibilities the heir to all this was simply waiting for the time when he could use the lands to obtain credit and have the estate revenues diverted to London to finance his extravagant way of life. The 4th Duke of Hamilton was the fatal flaw in his parents' Great Design.

Life had to go on at Hamilton no matter how insecure the future, and the Duchess devoted her energies to the management of the estates and to the upbringing of her grandchildren. The household at Hamilton had changed greatly since the days when the Duchess's husband was alive, and in her last years she found herself once more at the centre of a group of women and children. Lord Basil was with her until 1701, but in the late summer of that year there occurred a tragic accident. Lord Charles and he went to visit his lands in Galloway and when Lord Charles decided to return home first, calling in at Cassilis on the way, his brother insisted on accompanying him for part of the journey. They had with them the usual group of attendants, including a young French boy, De Tang, who waited upon Lord Basil's son. As they crossed the River Minnoch, De Tang found himself in difficulties, fell and was carried away by the current. David Crawford described what happened after that in a letter to Lady Katherine's husband. 'Lord Basil, seeing him, rode back into the water to save him and finding he could not do it on horseback, dismounted himself and following the boy down the water on foot (such was his kindness to a servant) was overturned himself near a precipice and carried quite away in a minute, for the water was not big, yet it ran strick and was stony and there was no saving of him. They found his body 3 quarters of an hour afterwards about a mile down ... My Lady Duchess takes it most heavily.'[14]

Lord Basil's wife had a posthumous daughter, Katherine, a month later, after which she and her young family stayed on in the Palace. When Lord John's wife died suddenly he sent his children to stay there for some months, then in 1707 the Duchess's beloved daughter Katherine died, worn out with years of child-bearing, and her two youngest daughters were sent into the Duchess's care. Despite her insistence that she was 'too old and infirm to be a nurse to children', James now insisted that she bring up his sons and daughters as well, and she reluctantly agreed to do so, feeling that she could offer them a more stable background than their own parents could do. So it was that in her late seventies she found herself bringing up yet another generation of young Hamiltons.

Her interest in the future of the House of Hamilton was not restricted to her immediate family, even at this late date, and she continued to plan for the improvement of the estates. There was Arran, for instance, a remote island on the very periphery of her lands. Not only did she establish a harbour and a settlement at Lamlash, but she introduced coal mining to the island and set up a thriving salt industry under the supervision of her workers from Kinneil. Parliament was persuaded to grant the island the privilege of holding three fairs a year, to encourage economic activity, and the Duchess gifted a ferry boat 'for the benefit of the Isle.' 'I know nothing I am more concerned in', she had told Katherine, 'than to have that poor island settled with two good ministers that the Gospel may be preached there and schools settled that the sad ignorance may be changed to knowledge and turning to God',[15] and so she rebuilt the old chapel at Lochranza, sent a catechist to act as a missionary in the more remote areas and gifted two fine silver communion cups to the two principal churches. She paid the salary of an 'ambulatory schoolmaster' at Lochranza, and she even arranged for a doctor to settle there with his family.

Her barony of Avendale also held a special place in her affections. She had often stayed in the castle there in her grandmother's time, and she particularly loved the high, airy country up above the Clyde Valley. Even in old age she always tried to attend Communion in Strathaven Church at least once a year. She rebuilt the church in 1699, gifting two engraved silver communion cups to it as well, and she provided the local community with a new schoolhouse and a waulkmill.

At Bo'ness, it was she who granted the burgh their founding charter, and under her patronage the little town became a thriving port. Her greatest activity was, however, in Hamilton itself. Apart from the fact that the requirements of her household provided employment for many of the townspeople, she always took a very close interest in all their affairs. There was no rigid division between the life of the Palace and the life of the burgh. On the contrary, the two were integrated to a surprising extent, and it is significant that maps of the time show the houses of the town of Hamilton coming right up to the Back Close of the Palace. The Hamiltons had always taken an active interest in the welfare of the townspeople. The Duchess's ancestor had founded the burgh school, which she decided to rebuild in 1711. She accordingly purchased some old houses in the town for a site and rented 'a large room' in Matthew Thomson's house 'for the scholars to learn in after the old school was pulled down and before the new one was ready.' At the same time, she built a fine new schoolhouse. Her grandfather and the local minister had established a hospital where eight poor men were to be maintained. The Duchess always provided gowns for the inmates, and in 1715 she went further. The original building was in a poor state of repair, and so to mark the centenary of the foundation, the Duchess gifted an entirely new, larger hospital at the foot of High School Wynd.

It was she, too, who established a woollen manufactory in the town. She has sometimes been credited with introducing lace-making, but there is no evidence to uphold this suggestion, which probably arises from a confusion with a later Duchess, Elizabeth Gunning. Duchess Anne's manufactory made heavy woollen cloth, and she set up in conjunction a spinning school. Two dozen or so girls were installed in a large house in the care of Mary Baillie, wife of one of the woolcombers. An overseer named Archibald Boyd was put in charge of the work, and the girls were paid a small wage. They were also provided with clothing, shoes, coal and candles, and the Duchess paid for medical attention for them and for their New Testaments and Catechisms. Also in the educational sphere, she supported a poor scholar at the burgh school, and she endowed a bursary for a Hamilton girl to be maintained at the Merchant Maiden Hospital in Edinburgh.

Her charity was well known throughout all her estates. She made regular payments to the poor of the burgh and of the parish of Hamilton, and she contributed to a wide variety of other worthy causes, ranging from financing the upkeep of a poor child in Edinburgh to making an annual contribution to the widows and orphans of the Episcopal clergy. She provided the Communion Elements for the churches throughout her estates, and she gave communion cups to Dalserf as well as to Arran and Strathaven. She did not forget the country people either. During the period of bad harvests she allowed tenants to have back rents totalling thousands of pounds each year, and she made little payments to other tenants, like the unfortunate James Hamilton in Middleraw, 'for the great loss he sustained when he accidentally burned John Allason's kiln in Over Crewkburn when he was drying his corn.'

While his mother devoted her time and her money to the welfare of her estates, the fourth Duke of Hamilton was enjoying life in London. Apart from the fact that Queen Anne still regarded him with unwavering dislike – she remembered him as a friend of Sunderland and of her own father – the only cloud on his horizon was his lawsuit. This had begun the moment he had married Elizabeth Gerard. In the marriage contract, he had promised to pay old Lady Gerard £10,000 for her expenses in bringing up Elizabeth, but no sooner was he married than he refused to pay. Lady Gerard promptly took him to court, and the lawsuit which followed was to drag on for years, becoming more and more complicated and more and more expensive. Even the death of Lady Gerard did not end it. In her Will she left to her only child five shillings and a diamond necklace, and so the litigation went on with redoubled fury. Lady Gerard's brother the Earl of Macclesfield took up her claims, and eventually passed them on to his own heir Lord Mohun.

In 1711, the Duke's fortunes unexpectedly took a turn for the better. Queen Anne at last relented, and on 11 September 1711 she created him a peer of Great Britain as Duke of Brandon and Baron Dutton. A year later she made him a Knight of the Garter and, to his delight, appointed him ambassador to France. Had he carried out his plans and gone to Paris at once, the outcome might have been very different. As it was, he delayed his departure at the last moment, and on 13 November 1712 when he should already have been in Paris, he encountered Lord Mohun at the Chancery Temple. Mohun was drunk, and they quarrelled violently. Next day Mohun's friend General MacCartney called on the Duke with a challenge from Mohun. The result was that, at between seven and eight on the morning of November 15, the Duke of Hamilton left his St James's Square house for the last time. Accompanied by his illegitimate son Charles, he went to meet Mohun in Hyde Park. There they were to fight a duel. The Duke had fought many duels in the past, but he was now fifty-four, stout and out of condition. Mohun was a much younger man with an unsavoury reputation for violence. They fought fiercely, and the Duke managed to plunge his sword into his opponent, who died instantly. The Duke was ambidextrous, and he had been fighting with his sword in his left hand. This meant that his right arm was unprotected, and just before he killed Mohun, the latter slashed at this arm, severing an artery. The Duke staggered away, collapsed against a tree, and died there a few moments later.

His furious supporters now claimed that he had been murdered, declaring that Mohun's second MacCartney had struck the fatal blow. The matter was argued hotly at the time and MacCartney fled the country with a murder charge hanging over him. The accusation seems to have been groundless, but whoever was responsible, the fourth Duke of Hamilton was dead. His widow did not shed a single tear. She stormed and raged, inveighing against her dead husband as well as against Mohun and his friends. Excited pamphleteers elaborated on the murder theory,[16] and sightseers flocked to Hyde Park to carry away fragments of the tree at the scene of the duel as macabre souvenirs. In Hamilton Palace, the Duchess of Hamilton sat motionless in her room, stunned by the terrible news and by the whole tragedy of her son's wasted life. 'I am very much concerned', Lord Charles wrote to her two months later, 'to find by the account that Mrs Montgomery gives of Your Grace that you give so much way to melancholy and that you never stir out of your chair. I earnestly beg Your Grace will begin and do business as you used to do and when it is good weather be carried out to the garden in your chair ... nothing can be a greater trouble to me than the hearing of Your Grace's doing nothing to divert your melancholy thoughts at this time. I must again beg that Your Grace will go abroad [outside] some time and strive all you can against what is so prejudicial to your health on which so much depends.'

Much did indeed depend upon the Duchess. Once more she found herself paying the debts incurred by a male member of her family and once more she was bringing up the heir to the House of Hamilton. Perhaps, in the end, she found some consolation in the knowledge that, had James lived to inherit, much of her work would have been destroyed. Throughout her life she had used all

her energies for positive, creative ends. As far as she was concerned, she held her inheritance in trust for future generations
and her wholehearted devotion to the family in its widest sense
was entirely unselfish. If this almost mystical concept of the
family seems alien to modern ideas, its practical results were
undeniable. Her son's tragedy lay in the fact that he cared
nothing for the standards or for the conventions by which his
parents lived. Nor was his behaviour merely the rebellion of
youth. His disregard for the accepted way of life arose not from
any dislike of existing ways but simply from self-indulgence. He
would not live in Scotland because he enjoyed himself more at
Court. He would not marry unless he was forced to do so because
he wished to avoid all responsibility. He regarded the family
estates as a source of revenue, and he used the argument of 'the
good of the family' in a completely cynical way, caring nothing
for his mother's ideals but hoping to deceive her into giving him
what he wanted. Where the Duchess's activities were positive and
constructive, her son's outlook was negative and self-absorbed,
and it would be surprising if, in all their grief for the fourth Duke
of Hamilton, his family and friends did not experience a sense
of release.

The last years at Hamilton were peaceful. The Duchess did
recover from her son's death, and she did do business again. She
found pleasure in the company of the little fifth Duke. When he
was six, he was allowed to join the rest of the family for meals in
the dining room, and a year later he was given an exciting new
toy when 'the drum-maker of Gorbals' presented him with a real
drum. Thereafter the Duchess allowed him to beat his drum with
the town drummer,* 'for his diversion', and regular payments
were made for the repair of the drum. By the time he was nine he
was old enough to go to Hamilton School, where he remained
for five years, but in the summer of 1716 the Duchess decided to
send him to Eton. The world had changed greatly since the days
when her own children were young, and from 1707 onwards the
English influence on Scottish society was becoming more marked.
Until the Union, Scottish institutions and traditions had remained

---

* The seventeenth-century Hamilton town drum is preserved in Hamilton Burgh
Museum, itself a late seventeenth-century building.

Scottish, but now the situation was changing, and the Duchess's faithful housekeeper Mrs Montgomery explained to Lady Susan that the Duchess 'is now resolved to send My Lord Duke to London with his uncle My Lord Selkirk [Charles], that he may be settled at Eton School in her life, for if she were dead his mother would take it upon her to dispose of him as she thought fit. She has been often pressed to this, but could not condescend [agree] to it till now . . . I believe Her Grace looks upon herself as dying makes her the more ready to condescend to this. I doubt not but this will be a surprise to Your Ladyship as I am sure it was to me when I returned from Edinburgh, by My Lord Selkirk has said so much to her on this head and My Lord Orkney [George] wrote so much that his education will be lost and he will be fit for nothing and will never be able to speak [well in public] and that all the peers are breeding their sons at London, only Duke Hamilton must be bred at home, that others may outdo him and a great deal to this purpose which you know she is not able to bear.'

As always, the Duchess was ready to move with the times. She parted sorrowfully from the boy that autumn. She would never see him again, and she knew it, but for his own sake and for the sake of the House of Hamilton he had to go. She was still as busy as ever with estate business that September, but in mid-October she was not so well and on 17 October 1716, at six o'clock in the evening, she passed peacefully away in her own bedchamber. Her son Charles was with her at the end, and he saw to the funeral arrangements. As had been her own wish, she was laid in a simple coffin made of wood from her estates, and she was buried beside her husband in Hamilton Parish Church.

She had been Duchess of Hamilton for sixty-five years. Born at the Court of Charles I, she lived until the reign of George I, long enough to see her grandsons take part in the Jacobite Rebellion of 1715. She had outlived husband, sisters, seven of her children, daughters-in-law, grandchildren and friends. Yet in spite of the many sorrows she knew, hers was a vigorous, happy life. The House of Hamilton was indeed preserved in her, and her line continues to this day. By her own efforts she transformed her inheritance, not only restoring much of what had been destroyed in the Civil War, but creating a new Palace, new gardens, a new burgh and a new prosperity for her estates. Much of the world she knew has vanished now. Hamilton Palace has gone, demolished in the nineteen twenties. The deer park, the gardens and the fishponds have disappeared. The old Parish Church was taken down long since and the Duchess and her family now rest in Hamilton's Bent Cemetery. A few physical reminders of her life do remain. Her castles of Kinneil and Brodick are standing yet and her silver communion cups are used to this day in the seventeenth-century church at Dalserf. The most striking testimony of her fame, however, is that she is still remembered in the west of Scotland with affection and respect as 'Good Duchess Anne'. She would have been pleased and embarrassed by such a title, and she would probably have disclaimed it, but it is the most fitting epitaph for a woman whose life was a triumphant assertion of courage, of concern for others, and of faith in the future.

Appendix

Various inventories of Duchess Anne's furnishings have survived, and four of them are printed here, three for Hamilton Palace and one for Kinneil. They provide an intriguing record of interior decoration in the seventeenth century, and it is fascinating to trace the changes made with the passage of the years and try to work out from the Palace sequence the position of the various rooms. This is, however, no easy task, for not only was furniture frequently moved around and replaced, but the names given to the chambers vary, not least because each of the three inventories was made by a different person. The first is in a neat early seventeenth-century hand, the second is in the writing of the Duke's secretary, James Smith of Smithycroft, while the third was compiled by his successor David Crawford.

In transcribing the inventories I have modernised the spelling and included a short glossary. It should be noted that in writing Chapter 2 I also used information from financial accounts and memoranda. As a result some items, such as the tapestries of the world, are not specified in the inventories themselves. An analysis of the furnishings which includes an earlier inventory of 1607 is to be found in Rosalind K. Marshall, 'The Plenishings of Hamilton Palace in the Seventeenth Century', in *ROSC Review of Scottish Culture* (1987), 13–22. Also relevant is Rosalind K. Marshall, 'Scarce a Finer Seat in Scotland': Kinneil Castle and the 4th Duke of Hamilton' in *Scottish Country Houses 1600–1914*, (eds) Ian Gow and Alistair Rowan (1995, 1998).

Few of the Palace furnishings have survived. However, most of the family portraits are in the Hamilton Collection at Lennoxlove, Haddington, East Lothian, and two of the magnificent beds purchased in London by the 3rd Duke may be seen in the Palace of

Holyroodhouse, Edinburgh, where they were long known as 'Queen Mary's Bed' and 'Lord Darnley's Bed'. 'Queen Mary's Bed' is of crimson damask bordered with blue, pink and yellow silk fringes and tassels, and 'Lord Darnley's' is a yellow satin bed with a red and yellow velvet canopy. Their history is explained in Margaret Swain, 'The State Beds at Holyroodhouse', in *Furniture History*, xiv (1978), 58–60. Background information about seventeenth-century furnishings is provided in Peter Thornton, *Seventeenth-Century Interior Decoration in England, France and Holland* (1978) and Margaret Swain, *Historical Needlework: A Study of Influences in Scotland and Northern England* (1970).

INVENTORIES OF THE FURNISHINGS IN HAMILTON PALACE AND KINNEIL CASTLE

1. Inventory of the goods and plenishing within the Palace of Hamilton, drawn up on the 4 day of October 1647 years
[a few weeks after the death of Duchess Anne's grandmother, the 2nd Marchioness of Hamilton]

In the Wardrobe
First in a black trunk marked with the figure of 1, twenty four webs of linen and two webs of linen board clothing, item two webs of round linen gin hecklings, item nine webs and a piece of dornick board clothing, item thirteen webs of dornick serviettes, item a stick of black bonlace

In the Wardrobe
Item in another black trunk there marked with the figure of 2, two pieces of striped hangings, item two pieces of round cloth of holland for serviettes, item seven pieces of linen for the inside of a bed, item three pairs of holland sheets, 3 breadths viz. two pairs single sheets and the third whole, item a pair of holland sheets, 2 breadths and a half, item of holland sheets 2 breadths, three pairs, item of linen sheets, 3 breadths, seven pairs viz. a pair of them whole and the rest

single, item of linen sheets, 2 breadths and a half, six pairs viz. one pair of them single, item a single linen sheet, 2 breadths and a half, item of linen sheets, 2 breadths, four pairs, item of gin heckling sheets, 2 breadths, two pairs

In the Wardrobe
Item more in the said trunk marked with the figure of 2, two pair of holland head sheets, item of holland codwares four, whereof 2 meikle and 2 little, item of linen codwares twenty-three

In the Wardrobe
Item in another trunk marked with the figure of 3, eight damask board cloths, whereof one of them new, 5 of them long and 2 of them short, item two new damask dornick board cloths, item twelve old damask dornick board cloths, item seventeen dornick board cloths, item of coarse English linen board cloths five, item of old damask napkins a dozen and two, item three new damask towels, item four damask dornick towels and two holland towels, item two old damask towels and five linen towels, item six dornick towels and nineteen long serviettes of dornick, item another dornick towel, item six dozen and eight dornick serviettes, item an old dornick board cloth wherein all the rest is wrapped

In the Wardrobe
Item in a trunk marked with the figure of 4, two little green cloth carpets [for tables] with a green silk fringe about them, item a green counterpane of a bed, with three curtains for windows, of green and red Turkey damask, item two woven worsted waistcoats, item a pair of woven worsted trews, item the ticking of a bed, a bolster and a cod, item a green bed of four pieces with slips thereon, item a piece of green cloth and a little piece to cover stools

In the Wardrobe
Item in another trunk there, marked with the figure of 5, a new web of diaper of 25 ells of length for table cloths, item two long diaper board cloths and three short diaper board cloths, item two dozen and eleven diaper napkins, item eleven old diaper napkins, item eight little diaper new boardcloths unhemmed, item six damask

boardcloths and two dozen damask napkins, item three damask towels and four damask dornick covercloths, item two new dornick boardcloths and four dozen of damask dornick napkins, item six damask dornick boardcloths, item nine old damask dornick serviettes and four dornick boardcloths, item sixteen of long dornick towels and eighteen old dornick napkins, and a dornick cupboard cloth, item a linen cupboard cloth and two linen latter boardcloths [? for use in the Lattermeat Hall]

Note that this last trunk marked with the figure of 5 is in the custody of John Touche

In the Wardrobe

Item more there in John Robieson's custody, a blue cloth bed with blue and yellow laced roof and pand of that same, item four pieces of Turkey damask hangings, red and yellow colour, item two pieces of red flowered velvet for a partition, the one of them of a great length and the other about four ells, item a canopy of a bed of green serge, item a black cloth gown lined with fox skins, item four great velvet cushions for the church, whereof two of crimson, one incarnate and another green, item a dozen of new carpet cushions, item nine old carpet cushions, unlined, item six old sewed cushions, with a cushion of gilt leather, item five carpets whereof two are middle size, other two larger and another of them a very great one, item four feather beds, whereof three of Flanders ticking and one Scots, item five bolsters whereof two Flanders ticking, 2 of Scots ticking and one of fustian, item two quilts, one of holland and another of twill, item three cods, one of Scots ticking and two of fustian, item two lined, sewed coverings, a great rug and two pairs of waulked blankets, item a pair of blankets, 2 breadths and a half, item two pieces of green serge curtains for windows

In the Wardrobe

Item two pieces of arras hangings and a red cloth cloakbag, item an old sumpter cloth [for a pack horse or mule] and a piece of striped hangings, item in a white kist a number of broken trash and six folding stools whereof two covered and four uncovered, item eleven new carpet chairs with six little chairs uncovered, item seven chairs wanting the covering, item three folding stools uncovered and two other stools uncovered, item the timber of five beds, whereof three standing and two folding, item a pall and mortcloth of black velvet, item eight tin chandlers with the flowers, item four new close stools, item half a dozen new chamber pots with half a dozen iron snuffers, item two cabinets, one with strong waters and the other empty, item a press with vices, item two dozen and four of Irish work cushions unlined, that are new

In My Lady Crawford's Chamber [Duchess Anne's aunt]
Item seven pieces of gilt leather hangings and two window pieces, item a standing bed, with green and white taffeta curtains, roof and pand of the same, of the curtains there is five pieces with a quilted taffeta mat, item the four [bed] posts covered with taffeta and lace, item a Flanders feather bed and bolster, and a fustian cod with a holland quilt and a twill quilt, item two pairs of plaiding blankets, 3 breadths, item a pair of waulked blankets and a single English blanket, item in the by bed a Scots feather bed, a bolster and cod of the same, item two pairs of waulked blankets, a pair of plaiding blankets, 2 breadths and a chamber table, item a sewed, lined covering, item a blue damask chair with a folding stool of the same, item two folding carpet stools, a chamber carpet, an iron chimney and a pair of tongs, item a close stool and a chamber pot, with a looking glass, item in the outer room, seven old gilt leather chairs, item the timber of a standing bed, and an old coffer

In Clanbie's Chamber
Item four pieces of old brown cloth curtains with a sewed pand, item two Scots feather beds, two Scots bolsters and four cods, item three pairs of plaiding blankets, two breadths, and a pair 2 breadths and a half, with a pair of waulked blankets, item an iron chimney, a pair tongs, a water pot and a table

In the Great Hall without [outside] my Lord Lanark's Chamber [Duchess Anne's uncle]
Item six pieces of old arras hangings, with a table carpet, item a large long table of wainscot and three short fir tables, item two little wainscot forms, two leather chairs, item an old sewed chair and an iron chimney

In My Lord Lanark's Chamber
Item six pieces of arras hangings, item a bed of red damask, with double pand of velvet, laced, roof and head of the same, item five pieces of damask curtains and four stoups of the same with a damask covering lined with baize, item a Flanders bed [mattress] and bolster, with two fustian cods, a twill quilt and a pair of plaiding blankets, 3 breadths, item a pair of plaiding blankets, 2 breadths and a half, and a single English blanket, item a chamber table and a carpet with two chairs, and two stools covered with red buckram, item a pair of iron tongs, a close stool and a chamber pot

In the Cabinet within
Item a stand bed, with four pieces of red cloth curtains, a sewn pand and a feather bed, a bolster and a cod of Scots ticking, item a red rug, three pairs of waulked blankets and a pair of plaiding blankets, 2 breadths, item three leather backed chairs or stools, a table and a [table] carpet, item a close stool and a chamber pot

In the Chamber above
Item four pieces of landscape arras hangings with another piece of picture hangings, item a stand bed, with four pieces of blue curtains, pand, roof, head with white and blue lace, item a blue rug, two feather beds of Scots ticking, a Flanders bolster, a cod of Scots ticking, item two pairs of plaiding blankets, 2 breadths, and another pair two breadths and a half, item a table, and a [table] carpet, with three leather chairs and a carpet chair, item a close stool and a chamber pot

In the Doocot [Dovecote] Chamber
Item five pieces of striped hangings, item a stand bed with five pieces of brown cloth curtains, pand, roof and head of serge, the four stoups of cloth laced with brown silk lace of the same, item a cloth covering laced of the same, item two Scots feather beds, a bolster and cod of the same, item two pairs of plaiding blankets, 2 breadths and a half, and another pair of 3 breadths, item, in the by bed, a feather bed and bolster of Scots ticking, item two pairs of plaiding blankets, 2 breadths, item a sewed unlined covering, item a chamber board with a carpet, two leather backed chairs, item a carpet chair, a folding carpet stool, a close stool, item an iron chimney and a chamber pot

APPENDIX

In the Eastern Platform Chamber
Item four pieces of old arras hangings, item a green damask bed
laced with gold lace, with three pieces of damask curtains, pand, roof
and head of the same, and two stoups lined of the same, item a green
rug, a Flanders feather bed and bolster, a Scots ticking bed and cod,
a twill quilt, item two pair of plaiding blankets, 2 breadths and a half,
another pair 2 breadths, a single English blanket, item a by bed, a
bolster and cod of Scots ticking, and two pairs braided plaiding
blankets, item a sewed covering, a table and [table] carpet, two
carpet chairs, a close stool, a chamber pot and an iron chimney

In the Western Platform Chamber
Item four pieces of old arras hangings, item a standing bed, five
pieces of flowered taffeta curtains with a pand of the same, roof and
head of green taffeta and the stoups covered with the same, item of
Flanders ticking a feather bed, a bolster and a cod, item a yellow rug,
two pairs of plaiding blankets, two breadths and a half, and an
English blanket, item in the by bed of Scots ticking, a feather bed, a
bolster and two pairs of plaiding blankets, 2 breadths, item a sewed
covering unlined, a table, a [table] carpet, item two carpet chairs, a
close stool, a chamber pot, an iron chimney and a pair of tongs

In the Pantry Chamber
Item a stand bed with two pieces of red cloth curtains and a sewed
pand, item a feather bed and bolster of Scots ticking, and a fustian
cod and another of Scots ticking, item three pairs of plaiding
blankets, 2 breadths, and a sewed covering unlined, item two leather
chairs, a folding carpet stool and another carpet stool, item a table,
close stool and a chamber pot

In My Lord's Great Dining Room
Item eight pairs of rich Flanders hangings, item a Persian table
carpet, seven carpet chairs and nine carpet stools, with three folding
carpet stools, item two folding tables of wainscot and three fir tables,
item a screen and a pair of tongs with an old loose bible

In My Lord's Tile Hall or Withdrawing room
Item four pieces of rich Flanders hangings, item two great carpets, one of Persian and the other of Turkey, item four folding stools of red crimson velvet with a silver and gold fringe about them, item two red damask folding stools with a red silk fringe, item three folding stools of flowered velvet with silk fringe, item a great bible, two chess boards with their men, with a pair of indented tables, item four folding tables of wainscot with a long table of wainscot

In the Bedchamber of the Withdrawing room
Item three pieces of the same rich hangings with other two pieces of coarse arras hangings, item two pieces of red and yellow damask hangings, item a standing chapel bed of crimson velvet lined with yellow taffeta, with five pieces of curtains gold laced, the pand and top embroidered with gold and silver and the head also, item the counterpane thereof of the same velvet laid over with gold lace, gold and silk fringe, item the four stoups covered and laced with the same, item a feather bed and bolster of Flanders ticking, two fustian cods, a twill quilt, a holland quilt and a pair of fustian blankets, 5 breadths, two pairs of plaiding blankets, 4 breadths and a pair of English blankets, item two red damask chairs with silk fringe, two red damask folding stools with silk fringe about them, item two crimson velvet folding stools with gold fringe about them, item a velvet table cloth with gold lace, silk and gold fringe, item four little chamber carpets with a table, close stool and a silver chamber pot

In the Cabinet within
Item a standing bed with five pieces of yellow stamped curtains, pand of the same, item a feather bed and bolster of Flanders ticking and a cod thereof, item a feather bed of Scots ticking, a pair of waulked blankets, item a pair of plaiding blankets, 2 breadths and a half, item a sewed covering, lined, item a meikle green damask chair, with green silk fringe, two little carpet chairs, a table and carpet, close stool and chamber pot

In My Lord's Chamber
Item four pieces of landscape arras hangings, item a scarlet bed with red and yellow silk lace, fringes of the same colour, with double pand,

roof and head of the same and the stoups covered with the same, item five pieces of curtains lined with red taffeta, with four bongraces for the stoups, item a counterpane lined with the same and lined with red baize, item a Flanders bed and bolster, two fustian cods and a holland quilt, a twill quilt with a pair of fustian blankets of 5 breadths, item a pair of plaiding blankets, 3 breadths with three single English blankets, item a great chair and stool covered with red buckram, item a folding stool of red flowered velvet, item two striped window pieces, item a close stool, a silver chamber pot, an iron chimney and a pair of tongs, item a table and a carpet of Turkey with a leather cover, item in the by bed where John Taylor lies, a feather bed, bolster and cod of Scots ticking, two pairs of plaiding blankets, 2 breadths, a pair of waulked blankets, a lined sewed covering, item a table, a carpet, chamber pot

In the chamber next to My Lord's
Item seven pieces of red and yellow damask hangings, item a stand bed with six pieces of green curtains lined with green taffeta, the head of green serge, lined with taffeta, the cover buckram lined with taffeta, item a covering of French green taffeta lined with serge, item a feather bed and bolster of Flanders ticking, item another bed of Scots ticking, a twill quilt, a fustian cod and a pair of plaiding blankets 2 breadths and a half, item a pair of English blankets, two pairs small plaiding blankets, 2 breadths, item two incarnate velvet stools with silk fringe, two flowered velvet folding stools, a great carpet chair, a chamber table and carpet, item two striped window pieces, an iron chimney, a close stool and chamber pot with a pair of tongs

In the Outer Room
Item four pieces of landscape hangings, item two great leather chairs, two tables and a carpet and a little wainscot form, item an iron chimney and a sewed chair

In the Nurse's Chamber
Item a stand bed, two long settles, a table, a great leather chair and an iron chimney

In the Chamber above
Item two stand beds with four pieces of red sea bombazine curtains and a sewed pand, two feather beds of Scots ticking, a Flanders bolster and two bolsters of Scots ticking, item two cods, one of Flanders ticking and another Scots ticking, item a pair of plaiding blankets, 2 breadths and a half, item two pairs of plaiding blankets, 2 breadths and a pair of waulked blankets, item two sewed coverings unlined and a brown serge curtain, item a table and a carpet, two broken chairs, item an iron chimney and a pair of tongs

In Lady Anna Hamilton's Chamber [Duchess Anne]
Item three pieces of arras hangings, item a standing bed, with three pieces of crimson taffeta curtains, a pand of flowered velvet, red and white, with the head and roof of buckram lined with red taffeta, item a stitched quilt of taffeta, item a bed and bolster of Flanders ticking, two fustian cods, a twill quilt, a pair of fustian blankets, 3 breadths and a half, item an English blanket and a pair of plaiding blankets of three breadths, item a red damask chair, two folding stools of blue damask, two folding stools of green cloth, three green foot stools, a meikle chair with green cloth, item two folding stools, one wanting the covering and another having it in the closet, item a carpet chair, two tables, two carpets, an iron chimney and pair of tongs and a fire shovel, item a close stool and a chamber pot

In My Lady Anna Hamilton's Outer Room
Item four pieces of striped hangings, item a standing bed with four pieces of green cloth curtains, pand of the same with green silk fringe, with head and roof of green serge, item a green covering of cloth, a feather bed, a bolster and cod of Flanders ticking, with a fustian cod, a twill quilt, a pair of English blankets, a pair of waulked blankets

In the said Outer Room
Item in the by bed, a feather bed and bolster of Scots ticking, two pairs of plaiding blankets, 2 breadths, item another pair two breadths and a half, item a sewed covering lined with twill, item a carpet chair, a little chair covered with red damask, item a board and carpet, an iron chimney and chamber pot

In the Chamber next to the said Outer Room of Lady Anna Hamilton

Item four pieces of arras hangings, item a standing bed of red serge laid over with red and yellow silk lace, four pieces of curtains, double pand, head and roof all of the same, with four stoups covered with the same, item the covering of the same lined with yellow plaiding, item a feather bed and bolster of Flanders ticking, a fustian cod, a holland quilt, two pairs of plaiding blankets, 3 breadths, item another pair, 2 breadths, a pair of English blankets, item in the by bed, a feather bed, a bolster and cod of Scots ticking with a pair of waulked blankets, a pair of plaiding blankets, 2 breadths, item a sewed covering lined, two meikle chairs and a stool covered with red serge, a carpet stool, a chamber table and carpet, a close stool and chamber pot, item an iron chimney and tongs

In the Chamber next to the said Last Chamber in the end of the Gallery

Item five pieces of arras hangings, item a standing bed, with three pieces of green cloth curtains lined with green taffeta, and four stoups covered with the same, the head and roof of green serge, lined with green taffeta, item a stitched mat of green taffeta lined with green serge, item a great feather bed of Scots ticking, a bolster of Flanders ticking, a fustian cod, a twill quilt, a pair of plaiding blankets, 3 breadths, item another pair, 2 breadths, and another pair 2 breadths and a half, item in the by bed, a feather bed, a bolster and cod of Scots ticking, a pair of waulked blankets, a pair of plaiding blankets, 2 breadths and a half, a blue rug, two carpet chairs, a carpet stool, a leather chair, item a chamber table and carpet, a close stool and chamber pot, and an iron chimney

In the Stable Chamber

Item a stand bed with four pieces of green sea bombazine curtains, item a green and white figurata pand, head and roof of white twill stuff, a feather bed and bolster of Scots ticking, item a white rug, a pair of waulked blankets, a pair of plaiding blankets, 2 breadths and a half, item another pair, 2 breadths, two leather chairs, item a chamber board

In the Porter Lodge

Item two timber beds, a feather bed and two bolsters of Scots ticking, item two white rugs, four pairs of plaiding blankets, 2 breadths, item six silver chandlers, item seventeen brass chandlers, a tin chandler, two white iron chandlers, item five bowits, item a great lantern that hangs in the yett, item two iron chimneys standing in the coalhouse

In the Low Court Hall

Item two boards, three forms and an old cupboard

In the Kitchen

Item in James Bishop's custody there two great beef pots and four lesser of brass, item nine pans, little and meikle, and three skillet pans of brass, item fourteen spits, item two pairs of great racks and a pair of smaller, with a gallows that pertains to the said small rack, item a pestle, mortar, two branders, two ladles, a frying pan, item a great moyer [?mazer] and a skimmer and another skimmer that is old, item two axes, viz one for the kitchen and the other for the larder, item a fire shovel, a coal rake, a pair tongs, two brass pot boards, item a pair of clips and two baking pans of brass for the bakehouse, item a little baking pan of brass and three guis [?goose] pans, whereof one came out of Kinneil, item a chopping knife and a kettle and a brass strainer

William Thomson

Item in the custody of William Thomson two dozen of silver dishes of several sizes, item more in his custody, twenty pewter plates and other three which three are half melted all of several sizes, item more that he had from John Robieson, nineteen pewter plates also of several sizes, item more of old pewter dishes 14, item of sol plates for pasties 13

In the Larder

Item in the larder that John Leith has, six trees for beef and herring, item two candle kists, and a great press for cold meet, item four little vinegar barrels and two stands for butter, item a tub for steeping of beef, item two wine cellars, one of 20 glasses and the other of 9, item a meikle billiard board

In the Pantry

Silver work

Item in John Touch's custody there, four dozen of new silver plates or dishes whereof given in present service of the house to William Thomson 20, item more in John Thomson's custody ten old silver dishes of several sizes, whereof in service for the house to William Thomson 4, more in John Thomson's custody of new silver trenchers three dozen and eleven, item of old silver trenchers with the same arms, a dozen, item of old little narrow little lipped silver trenchers 17, item of new fruit silver dishes 18, item of broad shanked silver spoons 15 whereof lent to My Lord Lanark a dozen, rests 3, item of silver spoons that was bought marked with My Lord Lanark's arms 18 whereof lost at James Graham's time 3, item of old silver spoons 25, item a great saltfat of silver, item of silver trencher saltfats 7, item a great silver basin and a ewer, item a gilt silver basin and a ewer, item two little silver gilt cups, and a gilt nut cup broken, item a silver tankard, item a silver water cooler and ladle, item a silver voiding knife, item two pairs of silver candle snuffers with their plate, and chains and cases, item two silver pots whereof one in My Lord's Chamber (else noted), item of knives with silver hands 24, item a great sugar box and one lesser, with one spoon, item six silver saucers, item of plain silver candlesticks 4 and two wrought ones which are six in number and in the custody of John Robieson, item an old silver saltfat with My Lord's arms and a timber bottom in it

Pewter and other

Item in the custody of the said John Touch of pewter trenchers 12, item of pewter spoons 6, item a great pewter saltfat and 4 little ones, item a pewter tankard or flagon, item of timber trenchers 3 dozen, item of broad timber trenchers 21, item of lame trenchers 5, item of hart horned knives 12 and a fork, item of drinking glasses and ewers of all sorts 4 dozen, item some drinking wooden cups 12 and 4 beakers, item of bottles for wine 15

Brewing vessel in James Cook's custody

Item a lead and a vat, item of working vats 5, item of stands for bearing in of the ale and leading of the burn 2, item of cooling tubs 2, item of spouts 2 for burn and another for wort, item of legallons 3, item a tin moll, item three shearing trees, a tap tree and a thorn, item a coal rake and a shovel, item of barrows 2, item a pan and cover to the vat, item of hogsheads 7 and 14 barrels, item of tree stoups 12

A note of linens that John Robieson has in his charge
First of holland sheets 2 breadths and a half 4 pairs, item of holland sheets 2 breadths 2 pairs, item of linen sheets 2 breadths and a half 8 pairs, item of linen sheets 2 breadths 13 pairs, item of holland codwares 8, item of linen codwares 20

Linens in Lady Anna Hamilton's Chamber
Item of linen sheets 3 breadths 2 pair, item of linen sheets 2 breadths and a half 2 pairs, item of linen sheets 2 breadths 1 pair, item of linen codwares 8

Linens in Lady Margaret Hamilton's Chamber
Item of linen sheets 2 breadths 2 pairs, item of linen codwares 3, item a pair of harden sheets for the servant

For Margaret Maxwell and Elspeth Stewart's beds
Item of two breadth linen sheets 3 pairs, item of linen codwares 1

APPENDIX

2. An Inventory of Household Furniture in the Palace of Hamilton as it is in the several rooms July 9 1681

In the Low Tile Hall
Hung with horns, three tables, one long wainscot, the other two of fir, a form, 3 sconces and 2 in the entry to the halls, an iron grate and a porring iron in the Horn Hall

In the Low Dining Room
Hung with 5 pieces of arras figured hangings, 2 oval tables and a square one, 2 cupboards, 3 Turkey carpets, a dozen of gilded leather chairs and half a dozen of carpet ones, six maps, a clock and case, 2 window curtains, an iron grate, fire shovel and tongs and toasting iron, a screen, a picture

In the Drawing Room
Hung with 5 pieces of forest work hangings, 3 pictures, a fir table with a red damask cover and marble table, a pair of stands, a looking glass, a red taffeta curtain, a dozen of cane chairs, a chimney grate, fire shovel and tongs

In the Outer Room
Hung with 4 pieces of striped hangings, a fir table and tablecloth, a close stool, a wooden chair and a chamber pot

In Mr Porterfield's Room
A close bedstead with old striped curtains, a sewed pand, a feather bed and bolster, a pillow, 2 pairs of blankets and a single one, a blue rug, a table, a form and 4 chairs, another bedstead with feather bed and bolster, 2 pairs of blankets and a coverlet lined, an iron grate, shovel, tongs, a chamber pot

In the Great Stairs
Four sconces and six pictures

In the Great Hall
Hung with 5 piece of forest work hangings, 7 pictures, 6 sconces, 3

fir tables, 2 carpets and 2 dozen of carpet chairs, an iron grate, 2 andirons and a brass shovel

In the Drawing Room
Hung with 3 pieces of fine arras hangings, 4 sconces, a hanging candlestick, 5 pictures, a clock and case, 2 fir tables with 2 embroidered velvet tablecloths, 4 gilded stands, a dozen of cane chairs and a dozen of embroidered velvet cushions with slips, and a carpet for the floor, an iron grate and 2 brass andirons and 5 window curtains and a screen

In My Lady's Bedchamber
Hung with 4 pieces of arras hangings, 4 pictures, a great looking glass and 2 little ones, a bedstead with yellow mohair curtains with silk fringes, a stamped stuff tour de lit, two feather beds and a bolster, 3 pillows, a pair of English blankets, a yellow sarcenet quilt, a little resting bed and a quilt and a little bolster, a velvet cushion, a stitched counterpane lined with stamped calico, 2 big chairs and 6 little ones of yellow mohair with stamped stuff slips, a table and stands of outlandish wood, a cabinet, a screen, 2 great china pots with covers, a basin and a flower pot, 9 other flower pots, an iron chimney, 2 andirons, fire shovel and tongs, a fender all of brass, a door curtain of stamped stuff

In the Little Waiting Room
Hung with green stuff, a table and a green tablecloth, two wooden chairs. In the little closet lined with green stuff, a close stool

In My Lord's Room above stairs
Hung with 3 pieces of forest work hangings, 6 pictures, 2 window curtains, a bedstead, damask curtains and coverlet, a velvet pand and head, a quilt, a feather bed and bolster, 2 pillows and a pair of blankets, a little resting bed, a quilt, a bolster, 2 pairs of blankets, a red Indian satin quilt and a damask cushion, a fir table and stands with a red damask table cloth, 6 chairs, 5 of them little cloth ones with silver lace and slips and the other a big armed one, an iron grate

In the Drawing Room
Eleven pictures, a table with a carpet, 2 cane chairs and 4 little ones, and in the little closet above, a chair and a close stool at the stair foot

In My Lady Cassilis's Room [Duchess Anne's sister]
Hung with 4 pieces of arras hangings, 2 pictures and 2 window curtains, a great looking glass, a bedstead with red damask curtains and counterpane, 2 quilts, one feather bed, a bolster, 3 great pillows and 2 little ones, 2 pairs of blankets, a single Scots blanket and a single English one, a pair of dimity blankets, a little resting bed, a quilt and a damask bolster, a damask counterpane, a table and a damask tablecloth, 2 stands, 2 big damask chairs, 4 stools and another with arms, an iron grate, a shovel and tongs

In the little Drawing Room
Hung with arras hangings, a bedstead with green stuff curtains, a mat, a feather bed, a bolster, 2 pillows, 2 pairs of blankets and a single one, a green coverlet lined, a table with a green tablecloth and 3 wooden chairs, a looking glass, a close stool and 2 chamber pots, an iron grate and tongs

In the little Closet
Lined with green stuff, two hanging shelves, a green taffeta window curtain

In the Room next to My Lord's Closet
Hung with 4 pieces of forest work hangings, a bedstead with red cloth curtains lined with sarcenet, a quilt, a feather bed, a bolster, 2 pillows, 3 pairs of blankets, a single English one, a sarcenet quilt counterpane, a table, two stands, a looking glass, seven cloth chairs with silver lace and slips of baize, a red baize table cloth, an iron grate, brass shovel and tongs, a chamber pot

In the little Room next to it
A bedstead with green cloth curtains, a feather bed, a bolster, 2 pillows, 3 pairs of blankets and a green serge counterpane, a table with a carpet, 2 stands, 4 wooden chairs, a close stool and chamber pot, an iron grate

In My Lord Arran's Room [Duchess Anne's son]
Hung with 5 pieces of arras hangings, a bedstead, red cloth curtains and counterpane embroidered with black velvet, 2 feather beds, a bolster, 2 pillows, 3 pairs of blankets, a single English one, 4 wooden chairs and 4 velvet cushions, a table with a red tablecloth, 2 stands, an iron grate and tongs

In the Little Closet
A fixed bed with red curtains, a feather bed, a bolster, a pillow, 2 pairs of blankets and a single one, a red lined counterpane, a close stool and a chamber pot

In the Drawing Room
A table with a carpet and 3 leather chairs, an iron grate

In the Gentlemen's Chamber
Two beds with green curtains, one quilt, 2 feather beds and 2 bolsters, 4 pillows, 5 pairs of blankets and a single one, a rug and a lined coverlet, a table and a carpet, 3 carpet chairs, an iron grate and tongs, 2 chamber pots

In the Rubbed Room
Hung with 5 pieces of arras hangings, one picture, a bedstead with red stamped stuff curtains, a quilt, a feather bed, a bolster, 2 pillows, 3 pairs of blankets, a single English one and a red baize counterpane, a folding bed, a feather bed, a bolster, a pillow, 3 pairs of blankets, a coverlet and a red frieze cloth over the bed, a table with a carpet, 2 stands, 2 great chairs and 4 little ones, 6 damask cushions and a window curtain, an iron grate, 2 andirons and a pair of tongs, a close stool and a chamber pot

In the Drawing Room
Hung with 4 pieces of arras hangings, a bedstead, a feather bed and bolster, a pillow, 2 pairs of blankets, a single English one, red serge curtains and counterpane, a table and a red cloth, two chairs, an iron grate, a close stool and chamber pot, 2 pictures

In My Lord's Dressing Room
Hung with damask hangings, a bedstead, cloth curtains lined with red sarcenet and laced with silk lace, a quilt, a feather bed, a bolster, 2 pairs of blankets, a red counterpane laced with silk lace, a resting bed, a quilt, a velvet counterpane and cushion, a table with a damask cloth, a looking glass, 2 pictures, a little cedar wood table, a clock, a great hair stuff chair, a red chair, 2 little stands, 3 cane chairs and 3 cushions with silk lace, an iron grate and tongs and a brass shovel

In My Lady's Dressing Room
Hung with 6 pieces of arras hangings, 13 pictures, two window curtains, a cabinet and 2 stands, a chest of drawers and a dressing box, a table, a resting bed with two quilts, one pair of blankets, one pillow, a red counterpane, with silk lace a canopy, a red cushion with silk lace, a great looking glass and a little one, two hanging shelves, 5 flower pots, a Japanned box, 5 cane chairs, a red stool and a foot stool with silk lace, a cedar screen, an iron chimney, porring iron, shovel and tongs

In the Drawing Room
Hung with arras hangings, 12 pictures, a pair of virginals, a chest of drawers, a trunk, a resting chair, 4 wooden chairs and 6 carpet ones, eleven big cushions and 6 little ones, an iron grate

In the Little Closet
A little resting bed

In the Young Lords' Chamber [Duchess Anne's younger sons]
Hung with arras hangings, 2 bedsteads with blue curtains and silk lace, 2 feather beds, 2 bolsters, 4 pillows, 4 pairs of blankets and 2 half ones, a sewn coverlet and a green stuff one, in the little bed a feather bed, a bolster, a pillow, a pair of blankets, a single English one, a blue coverlet and silk lace, a table and a carpet, 2 chairs and 2 stools, a close stool and 2 chamber pots

In Mr David's Room [David Crawford, the Duke's secretary]
Two bedsteads, 2 feather beds, a mat and 2 bolsters, a pillow, 5 pairs of blankets and a single one, 2 coverlets, in the little bed a feather

bed, 2 bolsters and a pillow, 2 pairs of blankets and a single one, a table, 3 chairs and a cupboard, an iron grate and tongs, a close stool and 2 chamber pots

In the Gentlemen's Dining Hall
A square table, 5 forms, an iron grate

In Lady Katherine's Room [Duchess Anne's eldest daughter]
Hung with striped hangings and a green window curtain, a bedstead with white curtains and counterpane, a feather bed, a bolster, 2 pillows, a pair of blankets, two tables, a tablecloth, a great armed chair, 2 wooden chairs, a screen, an embroidered cabinet and an ebony cabinet, a chest, a great trunk and a little one, a looking glass, 3 boxes, an iron grate and a pair of tongs, a little standish, a chamber pot

In the Young Ladies' Room [Duchess Anne's younger daughters, Lady Susanna and Lady Margaret]
Hung with green hangings, a bedstead with white fustian curtains and counterpane, a straw quilt, a feather bed and bolster, 2 pillows, 3 pairs of blankets, in the folding bed a straw mat, feather bed and bolster, 2 pillows and a pair of blankets and a single one and a coverlet and a green cloth over the bed, a table with a green cloth, 4 stools, iron grate, tongs, shovel and a chamber pot

In the Little Stone Room
A bedstead, a feather bed, a bolster, 2 pairs of blankets and a single one, green curtains and counterpane, a table with a green cloth, a wooden chair, 2 stools and a chamber pot, an iron grate and a pair of tongs

In the Dressing Room
A bedstead, a feather bed, a bolster, a pair of blankets, 2 single ones and a coverlet, in the little bed a feather bed, a bolster, 2 pairs of blankets and a coverlet, 2 tables, a cupboard, an old carpet chair, a wooden stool, an iron grate, a shovel and a pair of tongs and a wooden box for linens and a little meal box and two brass pans and a water pig

In the Room within it
A bedstead, a feather bed, a bolster, a lined counterpane and green curtains, a table and stands, a trunk, a little table, 3 stills, an iron grate, fire shovel and tongs, a carpet and a chamber pot and two chairs

In the Porter's Lodge
2 beds, 2 feather beds, 2 pairs of blankets, 2 coverlets and an old one, a candle chest

In the Footmen's Room
3 bedsteads, 2 feather beds, 2 bolsters, 2 pillows, 4 pairs of blankets, 2 coverlets

In the Big Stable
2 folding beds, 2 bolsters, 4 pairs of blankets, 2 coverlets and a chaff bed

In the Little Stable
A folding bed, a feather bed, a bolster, 2 pairs of blankets and a coverlet

In the Dairy
Two tables, a cheese press, a cheese tub, two great pails and a little one, a churn and staff, seven trees and a cauldron, 2 shelves with feet, a cheese bridge, 3 splitters, 8 cheesefats, 4 sinkers, a skimming dish, a butter print, a milksie, 3 earthen pots, a great meal chest, a water pail, a syllabub pot

In the Wardrobe
23 trunks, a sweeting chair, a table, a cradle, 20 boxes, a silk winder, a pewter ring for sweetmeats, 2 warming pans and a little skillet, 2 feather beds, three bolsters, 20 pillows, great and little, a green rug, a coverlet, a chack reel, 7 maps, a little cannon, 29 great pewter dishes and 6 intermazers, 4 pewter stands and 2 saucers, a chafing dish, 6 cushions

In the Great Box, a trumpeter's coat, a page's coat, eleven pieces of red frieze, an old red pand and 2 curtains, 2 coach seats, 4 carpets, 8 pieces of hangings, 8 pairs of blankets

In another box, 15 pieces of old arras hangings, 2 barrels of soap, 2 close stools' pans and an old one, a broom and 5 little boxes

In the Closet next to it
A dozen and a half of jelly pots and 6 little ones, 2 lame cups, 6 great stone bottles, 3 dozen of glass ones, 4 wainscot boxes, a little wainscot cabinet, 6 fir boxes, 2 marble mortars and pestles, a ceringe, a chocolate pot and stick, a tea pot, 2 posset pots, a slikstone, a pound of weights and scales, a trunk, an apple roaster, a chair, a preserving pan and a cover

3. Inventory of Household Furniture in the Palace of Hamilton
9 December 1690
(Made by David Crawford, the 3rd Duke's secretary)

In the Low Dining Room
5 piece of arras hangings, 18 cane chairs, an oval table, two cupboards with carpets on them, 3 window curtains and rods, a pendulum clock, a little fire screen, a toasting fork for cheese, an iron grate, shovel and tongs, 3 pictures above the doors and chimney

In the Drawing Room
3 pieces of arras hangings, 12 cane chairs, 3 cushions, a stone table, a looking glass, an iron grate, shovel and tongs, 2 window curtains, a picture above the chimney

In the Horn Hall
4 tables, 4 forms, 5 maps of the world, a clock, My Lady's chair, an iron grate, a large fire fork, a bathing tub

In the Lattermeat Hall
A table and 3 forms

In Lord John's Chamber [Duchess Anne's son]
7 pieces of old arras hangings, 2 pieces of green stuff above the doors, a bedstead with red flowered stuff, a red quilted coverlet, a feather bed, bolster and pillow, a quilt and 3 pairs blankets, 6 armed cane chairs, a table and stands, a red tablecloth, an iron grate, a shovel and tongs, a close stool and chamber pot

In Lord Basil's Chamber [Duchess Anne's son]
5 pieces of old arras hangings, a green piece stuff above the chimney, a bedstead with green flowered curtains, a green flowered coverlet, a feather bed, bolster and pillow, a quilt and 3 pairs blankets, 5 chairs covered with green stuff, a table and green velvet cloth, a pair stands, an iron grate, a chamber pot

In the closet within it
A resting bed, a feather bed, bolster and quilt, 2 pairs blankets and an English one, a table and green cloth, a chair and a close stool

In William Murray and John Lamb's Chamber [servants]
Two bedsteads with blue curtains, 6 pairs blankets, 3 feather beds and 2 bolsters, 2 pillows and 4 chairs, a folding bed with a feather bed, a bolster, a pair blankets and a single one, an oven grate, a shovel and tongs, 2 chamber pots, 2 tables

In David Crawford's Chamber
Two bedsteads with red curtains, one feather bed, 2 bolsters, 3 pillows, 4 pairs blankets, 2 coverlets, a table and carpet, 3 old chairs, an iron grate, shovel and tongs, a chamber pot, an iron press of his Grace's Great Seal

In Rossière's Chamber [the 3rd Duke's valet]
A bedstead with green curtains, a green coverlet, a feather bed, bolster and pillow, 2 pairs blankets and a single one, 2 tables and a chest, three chairs, an iron grate and tongs, a close stool and chamber pot

In My Lord Duke's Chamber
A bedstead with red damask curtains, a red coverlet, a quilt, feather bed and bolster, 2 pillows and 4 pair blankets, 5 pieces flowered

hangings, a table, stands and looking glass, a little folding table, two armed chairs and cushions of those in the bedchamber, four cane chairs of those in My Lord's outer room, a little Holland chair, a black ebony cabinet, a standish for pen, ink and paper, an iron grate, a shovel and tongs, 2 window curtains, four pictures, a chamber pot

In His Grace's Outer Room
An escritoire, 2 chests of drawers, 2 little cabinets, a folding table and another table, 8 cane chairs of those in the chamber, 2 small trunks, an iron grate, a shovel and tongs, two window curtains, Duke James Hamilton's picture [Duchess Anne's father], 20 other pictures, a genealogy of the family of Stewart, a genealogy of the family of Hamilton, a genealogy of the family of Douglas, 9 new maps and 2 old ones, The Ten Commandments and The Royal Oak

In the High Dining Room
Two dozen carpet chairs, 4 tables and 3 carpets, a fire screen, 2 sconces, an iron grate, a shovel and tongs of brass, Duke James Hamilton and his Duchess's pictures, Marquis James's picture [Duchess Anne's grandfather], Duke William and the Duke of Lauderdale in one frame [Duchess Anne's uncle], The Duchess of Richmond, His Grace's pictures in his robes, The Earl of Denbigh's picture [Duchess Anne's grandfather] and other 6 pictures

Upon the Great Staircase
13 pictures, 2 brass sconces

In the Drawing Room next Her Grace's Bedchamber
3 pieces of arras hangings, 12 armed chairs with velvet cushions and covers whereof there are 2 in My Lord's Chamber so remains only 10, 2 tables and velvet cloths, 2 pair gilded stands, a fire screen, a large hanging candle flower, 5 window curtains and a foot carpet, King Charles I his picture, Gustavus Adolphus's, Duke James's [Duchess Anne's father] when he was young, His Duchess's when she was young, a chimney piece, 4 gilded sconces, a pendulum clock, an iron grate, a shovel and tongs

In Her Grace's Bedchamber
5 pieces of arras hangings, a mohair bed with a white satin counterpane and a tour de lit of stamped stuff. The curtains are lined with white satin. 4 quilts, a bolster and a pillow, 2 pairs blankets and a single one, an English blanket, one window curtain, one large green velvet armed chair, 4 armed chairs, and 4 without arms covered with the same mohair of the bed, one Dutch chair, a table and stands, a looking glass, a cabinet with a basin and ewer and 2 large jars of china on top of it, a little folding table, 2 little looking glasses, 6 chamie [? china] cups and 2 glass bottles on the chimney, a fire screen, an iron grate, a shovel and tongs and an iron fork, a pair brass andirons, a fender, a little clock, Their Graces' pictures, The Duchess of York's [Mary of Modena] and my Lady Cassilis's picture [Duchess Anne's sister], a chamber pot
In Her Grace's Closet

In the Little Green Room next Her Grace's Dressing Room
a suit of green stuff hangings, 3 chairs covered with green stuff, a chest of drawers, 3 black trunks, one red trunk on a frame, a sconce, a close stool

In Her Grace's Dressing Room
A red laced bed and coverlet, a quilt, a feather bed and bolster, two pillows and 3 pairs blankets, a suite of red flowered hangings and 2 red window curtains, a table covered with black velvet, a large looking glass and a lesser one, a chest of drawers, 2 little stands, a little armed chair, a little stool covered with green, 4 cane chairs and 4 cushions, 2 hanging shelves, a little resting bed with a red coverlet, a quilt and a feather bed, a pillow and 2 red velvet cushions, a fire screen and little hand screen, a stand with a candlestick on it, a frame for winding silk, 4 tea cups and 5 china flower pots on the chimney, an iron grate, a shovel and tongs, a picture above the chimney

In the Lady Baldoon's Chamber [Duchess Anne's daughter-in-law, Lady Mary Dunbar]
Six pieces of old arras hangings, a white dimity bed and coverlet, 2 feather beds, a quilt and a bolster, one pillow and 3 pairs blankets and a single one, a resting bed with a green coverlet, 2 quilts, a bolster and

a pillow, 3 pairs of blankets, a chamber pot, 5 chairs and 4 cushions, a little stool covered with green stuff, a table and green cloth, a looking glass and stands, a chest of drawers, a chimney picture, an iron grate, a shovel and tongs, a folding screen of green

In the Drawing Room next it
4 pieces of old arras hangings, 5 pieces of green cloth above the chimney and door and windows, a table and a carpet, 7 wooden chairs and 5 cushions, a red folding screen, an iron grate

In the Nursery
4 pieces arras hangings, a white bed and coverlet, a feather bed and a straw quilt, a bolster and pillow, 4 pair blankets and window curtain, a chamber pot, a folding bed with a quilt, a pillow, a table and a large armed chair and 3 little chairs and a stool, all covered with green, a chest of drawers, a cradle and a chair belonging to Lady Mary [Dunbar] and a basket, a candlestick

In Mrs Darlo's Chamber [servant in charge of the nursery]
2 pieces arras hangings and some green stuff hangings, a bedstead with green curtains, a coverlet, 2 pairs of blankets and two single blankets, a bolster, a pillow and 2 feather beds, a table and carpet, a chamber pot, a folding bed, a feather bed and bolster, a little English blanket, 3 leather chairs and a stool, a fir press, an iron grate, a shovel and tongs

In the Wardrobe next it
5 trunks, 5 pieces of old arras hangings, 2 bolsters and a little flowered one, 3 pairs blankets, 3 pieces of old green cloth curtains, a red laced counterpane

In the Wardrobe below in the new rooms, which are to be the kitchen
14 pieces of arras hangings, a suite of old gilded leather hangings, 2 carpets and 3 small pieces, 4 whole bedsteads and 3 ends of other, 2 beds, 2 resting beds, a hot stove tub, 3 tables, 2 wooden chairs, 3 close stools, 3 pairs brass andirons, 2 green doors, a pair of old virginals, 2 chimney boards, 6 pieces old matting, a cold still, 5 carpet chairs, 2

iron furnaces, 8 old trunks, an old meal chest, a back, breast and headpiece of armour, several old window casements and old boxes

In the [East] Platform Chamber above His Grace's Library
A bed with green curtains and coverings, a feather bed, bolster and 2 pillows, 2 pairs of blankets, 9 black wooden chairs, 2 black armed ones, an iron grate, a close stool

In the Drawing Room next His Grace's Library
3 trunks, a table and a carpet, 2 women's saddles, 7 old pictures, a close stool

In the Bedchamber next it
3 pieces arras hangings, a red cloth bed lined with silk, a coverlet of the same, quilted, a quilt, a feather bed and bolster, 2 pillows and 3 pairs blankets, 3 window curtains, 6 chairs covered with red serge, a table and a red cloth, a pair of stands, a large looking glass and a little one, an iron grate, shovel and tongs, two pictures,

In the closet within it
A cabinet, a bedstead with a feather bed, 2 quilts, 2 pairs blankets, a bolster and pillow, 2 little stools lined with silk, a coverlet on the little bed

In the Yellow Bedchamber and little closet
5 pieces of arras hangings, a yellow mohair bed with yellow lining, a coverlet of the same with the lining, a tour de lit of yellow stamped stuff, a quilt, a feather bed and bolster, 2 pillows, 2 pair blankets, 2 window curtains, 8 chairs covered with yellow, a looking glass table and stands, an iron grate, shovel and tongs

In the Closet
A resting bed, two quilts and a bolster, a pair of blankets and a single one, a table and a red coverlet, a close stool and chamber pot

In the Little Chamber next to the Yellow Chamber
A bedstead with green cloth curtains, a coverlet of green serge, a feather bed, bolster and pillow, 3 pairs blankets, a table and carpet, a pair of stands, 3 wooden chairs, a close stool, an iron grate and tongs

In the Drawing Room next the West Platform Chamber
4 pieces arras hangings, 6 chairs covered with green, a table and carpet, a picture, an iron grate

In the West Platform Chamber
3 pieces of arras hangings, a red damask bed and velvet pand, a coverlet of the same damask, 2 quilts, a feather bed and bolster, 2 pillows and 3 pairs blankets, 2 window curtains, 6 chairs covered with red serge, a table and red cloth, a looking glass and stands, an iron grate, a shovel and tongs, a chamber pot

In the Closet
A resting bed, a feather bed, a bolster, a pillow, 2 pairs blankets and a single one, a coverlet, a close stool and chamber pot

In the Chamber above that
A suite of striped hangings, a bed with green curtains and coverlet, a feather bed and a quilt, a bolster and 2 pillows, 2 pair blankets and a single one, 4 chairs lined with green, a table with green covering, a looking glass, an iron grate, shovel and tongs

In the closet
A bedstead with red curtains, a coverlet, a feather bed, a bolster, 2 pairs blankets and a single one, a wooden chair, a close stool and chamber pot

In the Woman House [for the female servants]
2 bedsteads with red curtains, 3 feather beds, 3 bolsters, 2 pillows, 7 pairs blankets, 3 coverlets, a warming pan, 3 tables, 3 wooden chairs, a napkin press, a chest, 6 irons and 2 stands for them, an iron grate, a shovel and tongs

In the Porter's lodge
2 bedsteads, 2 feather beds, 2 bolsters, 4 pairs blankets and a half, 4 coverlets

In the Footmen's Room
3 bedsteads, 3 feather beds, 3 bolsters, 5 pairs blankets, 3 coverings

In the Great Stable
3 feather beds, 3 bolsters, 6 pairs blankets, 3 coverlets, item a chaff bed and bolster and 2 pair blankets where Mitchell lies in Jenkin Street

4. Inventory of household furniture in Their Graces the Duke and Duchess of Hamilton's house at Kinneil 18 April 1688

In the Low Hall
A wainscot drawing table, 3 forms, 6 brass candlesticks, 4 white iron ones, 3 stair lanterns, 2 pairs of brass snuffers and 3 pairs of white iron, 2 hand brass candlesticks, an iron chimney shovel and tongs, 3 rullions for holding of guns, 3 cloak knaps, 2 rubbers, a mop, 2 besoms, a sponge for cobwebs, a lock, key, slot and sneck on the door and 3 coalboards

In the Pantry at the end of the said Hall
20 drinking glasses, 2 water stoups, a glass for vinegar and another for oil, a pewter stand and a quart stoup, 4 drinking cups for servants, a water tub, a pail with hands, 13 pewter trenchers, a quaich, 2 wand baskets, 2 crystal little bottles for water

In the Lobby on the other end of the Hall
A long fir table with 2 forms and a marble table without a frame

In the Dining Room
Fourteen red leather chairs, 2 square fir tables with 3 carpets, a round table with a carpet and leather cover, a chimney, a pair of tongs and a shovel with brass heads, 5 pieces of arras hangings, Marquis James and Duke James [Duchess Anne's grandfather and father] their pictures at length with other 3 pictures above the chimney and doors

In the Lobby next to the dining room
A square fir table with a carpet, a little oval wainscot table, 6 red leather chairs, a chimney, a pair of tongs, 2 pictures, 3 pieces of arras hangings

In the Drawing Room
4 pieces of arras hangings, 12 cane chairs, a square fir table with a carpet, a marble table with a walnut tree frame, 2 pictures, a large chimney with a porring iron, two stands

In the Bedchamber
3 pieces of the same arras hangings that are in the Drawing Room, a hair stuff bed lined with blue taffeta, a blue quilt, a tour de lit of printed stuff, a feather bed, 2 quilts, a pair of flannel blankets and 2 English ones, a bolster and 2 pillows, 2 armed chairs and six chairs of the same stuff with covers, a table with a drawer and 2 stands, a large looking glass, a chimney, a pair of tongs and a shovel, a pair of bellows, 2 window curtains with rods, 2 pictures, a little folding table with a footstool and a lame chamber pot and a red leather trunk

In My Lady Duchess's Dressing Room
A new piece of fine arras hangings [deleted, with a marginal note: a mistake, for there never was any hangings there], 4 carpet chairs and a table

In the Closet
A resting bed with a quilt, a bolster and red coverlet, 2 carpet chairs and a red stool and chamber pot and in the little closet within the same, a frame with a green velvet cushion

In the Backstairs Room
A green sewed bed and coverlet, a feather bed and bolster with 2 pillows, 3 pairs of blankets and a single one, a square fir table with a drawer and a sewed tablecloth, 3 stools covered with the said stuff, a carpet chair, a folding bed, feather bed and bolster, a chamber pot, a buffet stool, a chimney with shovel and tongs

In Mrs Mary Dunbar's Room next to My Lord Duke's Closet [the Duke and Duchess's ward]
4 pieces of green hangings, 2 Russia leather chairs, a bedstead with green curtains and a coverlet, a feather bed, bolster and 2 pillows, four pairs of blankets, a fir table with a drawer and green cover, a folding bed, a chimney, a pair of tongs and a lame chamber pot

In the Room above the Wardrobe where the women lie
A bed with blue curtains, a feather bed and bolster, a coverlet and 2
pairs of blankets, a folding bed, two stools and a chamber pot

In the Wardrobe
A marble mortar and pestle

In His Grace's Dressing Room above stairs
Six carpet chairs and an armed cane chair, a fir table, 2 stands, a
chimney, a pair of tongs, 4 pieces of cloth hangings, 2 pictures and a
close stool in the passage betwixt that and the back stairs

In the Closet next to the said Room
A bedstead with green curtains, a feather bed, bolster and 2 pairs
blankets, a lined green coverlet, a table, a leather chair and a chamber
pot

In the Lobby
A little fir table, 2 red leather chairs, a picture and brass sconce

In the Room next the Lobby called My Lord Murray's Room
Eight pieces of flowered hangings, a bed with plaid curtains, a
feather bed, bolster and 2 pillows, 3 pairs of blankets, a quilt and a
flowered covering, a table and tablecloth conform to the bed, 2 block
stands, 6 carpet chairs, a white window curtain and a rod, a chimney
with tongs and shovel and a lame chamber pot

In the Closet
A bed with red curtains and a coverlet, a feather bed, bolster and
pillow, 3 pairs of blankets, a table, a stool, a close stool and a chamber
pot

In the South Lobby
Three pieces of blue stamped hangings and a little piece above the
brace, a little table and tablecloth and 4 Russia chairs

In the Chamber off the said Lobby
Four pieces of new arras hangings with 2 pieces of red hangings above

the door, a curtain with an iron rod, a bed with scarlet curtains and a cover, a feather bed and bolster, a quilt, 2 pairs blankets and a half one, 3 stools with red covers, a table and red tablecloth, 3 carpet chairs, 2 stands, a chimney, shovel and tongs, a picture and a lame chamber pot

In the Closet
A bed with red curtains and coverlet, a feather bed, a bolster and pillow, 3 pair blankets, a timber chair, a close stool and chamber pot

In Lord John's Chamber [Duchess Anne's son]
Eight pieces of printed stuff hangings and bed with curtains of the same and coverlet conform, a feather bed, bolster and 2 pillows, 2 pairs blankets and a single one, 4 timber chairs with cushions of the said stuff, a table and tablecloth, two stands, a chimney and tongs and a lame chamber pot

In the Closet of Lord John's Chamber
A bed with stamped stuff hangings with a coverlet, bolster and pillow, a red leather chair, a close stool and a chamber pot, a feather bed and 3 pairs of blankets

In the Chamber off the 4th Lobby above My Lord Duke's Dressing Room
Two stand beds, a fir stool and an iron grate

In the South Lobby called the 4th
A fir table and two leather chairs

In the Chamber next to it
Five pieces of arras hangings, a bed with green cloth curtains and coverlet, a feather bed, bolster and 2 pillows and a quilt, two pairs of blankets, a single one, 6 carpet chairs, a chimney and tongs, a square table and 2 stands and a chamber pot

In the Closet thereof
A bedstead and cloth covering, a red leather chair, a close stool, a table and a chamber pot

264

In the Chamber at the top of the stair where the gentlemen lies
Two beds, in that next the fire, a feather bolster, 2 pairs of blankets
and a lined covering, and in the other the like, with two iron rods and
4 pieces of curtains, 2 stools, an iron grate

In the Outer Room
Two bedsteads, in that next the fire a feather bed, bolster and 3 pairs
of blankets and lined covering, in the other a feather bed, bolster, 2
pairs of blankets and a lined covering, 2 iron rods wanting curtains, 2
fir stools and a chimney

In the Kitchen
An iron grate, a pair of lying raxes, a pair of tongs and a brander, a
frying pan and an iron ladle, a fork, 2 iron dripping pans, 5 spits, 2
brass pots and one cover, 2 brass saucepans with covers, 4 other brass
pans, a brass grater, a pestle and mortar, a pair of pot bowls, 8 large
pewter dishes and 5 small ones, 1 pie plate, 3 fixed timber tables, 2
water tubs, a timber stool and salt box, a pewter saucer, a bell, a
colander, a little white iron ladle and a chopping knife, and in the
vault, 2 timber tables

In the Passage at the foot of the backstairs
Two bedsteads, in the one a chaff bed, bolster and 2 pairs of blankets
and a covering, and in the other the like

In the Larder
Two beef stands with covers, a salt tub and a powdering tub, two
little barrels, a little stool and a square table

In the Washing House
Two fir tables, two washing tubs and a lugged one, an armed chair
and a buffet stool, an old resting bed, an iron grate and a crook, a
handie and a pair of tongs

In the Bakehouse
Two fixed fir tables, a tub with two hands, a lead gallon, a boutting
tun, a little chest for bread, a rasp, a scraper, a souper for the table, a
fork and 2 pails

In the West Chamber above the Girnel House
Two bedsteads, in one of them a feather bed, a bolster and 2 pairs of blankets and a covering, and in the other a chaff bed, bolster, 2 pairs of blankets and a covering

In the Stables
A chaff bed and bolster and 2 pair of blankets and an old covering, a folding bed with a chaff bed and bolster and 2 pairs of blankets and a covering and a folding bed wanting clothes, 2 forks, a shovel and a wheelbarrow and 2 corn chests with locks and keys

Glossary

andirons   decorative metal hearth stands for supporting logs

baize   a woollen fabric

besom   broom

board clothing   tablecloths

bombazine   a twilled silk fabric

bonlace   a sixteenth-century name for lace possibly so called because the bobbins used to make it were of bone

boutting pan   ?sifting pan

bowits   lanterns?

brander   a gridiron

by bed   a small folding bed for a servant

ceringe   syringe?

chack reel   a reel with a check or catch for measuring thread

chandlers   candlesticks or chandeliers

cod   pillow

codware   pillowcase

crook   a pot hook

diaper   a woven, patterned fabric

dornick   linen

feather bed   feather mattress

fustian   cotton and flax or wool mixture

girnel house   storage chamber for grain

handie   a small wooden tub

harden   a very coarse cloth

holland   linen

incarnate   flesh-coloured or pink

kist   chest

knap   a rounded knob or tassel

lame   earthenware

legallon   lade-gallon, a wooden bucket for carrying liquids

lugged   with handles

meikle   large

milksie   a milk strainer

moll   ?mould

mortcloth   a pall used to cover a coffin on the way to the grave

pall   a cloth spread over a coffin at a funeral

pand   valance

plaiding   a twilled woollen cloth

porring iron   a poker

quaich   a drinking cup

raxes   a set of bars to support a roasting spit

round cloth   cloth made of thick thread

salt fat   a container for salt

sarcenet   a fine silk fabric

slikstone   ?a smoothing stone

slips   needlework motifs, embroidered on canvas and then cut out and applied to cloth

slot   a bar or bolt on a door

sneck   a latch of a door

stoups   bedposts

ticking   canvas to make it more compact, through shrinking, beating or pressure during manufacture

tour de lit   a protective cover round a bed

tree   a wooden barrel

will   a woven fabric

wand   willow

waulked blankets   blankets made of cloth which has been waulked or fulled

worsted   woollen

yett   a door made of interlacing iron bands

Note on Sources

This book is based on the Hamilton Archives, principally on the 12,000 letters in the extant seventeenth-century correspondence and on the large collection of household and estate accounts. The correspondence, formerly at Lennoxlove, is now the property of the National Archives of Scotland and has the number GD406, as do several other items, but most of the financial and legal papers remain at Lennoxlove. In order to eliminate a string of meaningless numbers, references to these Archives have been omitted from the notes but are given in detail in the author's PhD thesis, 'The House of Hamilton in its Anglo-Scottish Setting in the Seventeenth Century' (1970), which is available in Edinburgh University Library. The documents examined have been catalogued by the author in a series of calendars, copies of which are held by the National Archives of Scotland (formerly the Scottish Record Office), Edinburgh and by the National Register of Archives, London.

For purposes of comparison, collections of other family papers have been consulted and the most important of these are to be found in the notes. Many have been deposited in either the National Archives of Scotland or in the National Library of Scotland, on loan or as gifts. The abbreviations N.A.S. and N.L.S. in the notes do not imply ownership by the institution concerned, but serve merely as an indication of the location of the various documents. Spelling in all documents has been modernised.

(Except where otherwise stated, books are published in London.)

Aldis, Harry G., *A List of Books Printed in Scotland before 1700*, (Edinburgh 1904).

Baird, Alexander G. (ed.), *The Diary of Andrew Hay of Craignethan*, (Scottish History Society 1901).

Chambers, Robert, *Domestic Annals of Scotland from the Reformation to the Revolution*, (Edinburgh 1859).

Edgar, John, *A History of Early Scottish Education*, (Edinburgh 1893).

Ferguson, William, *Scotland: 1689 to the Present*, (Edinburgh 1968).

Finlay, Ian, *Scottish Crafts*, (*1948*): 'Treasures from Scottish Houses', Catalogue of Edinburgh Festival Exhibition, 1967.

Forbes, Mrs Atholl, *Curiosities of a Scots Charta Chest 1600–1800*, (Edinburgh 1897).

Fraser, Sir William, *The Annandale Family Book*, (1894); *The Book of Carlaverock*, (1873); *The Douglas Book*, (1885); *The Earls of Cromartie*, (1876); *History of the Carnegies, Earls of Southesk*, (1867); *The Lennox*, (1874); *The Lords Elphinstone of Elphinstone*, (1897); *The Melvilles, Earls of Melville and the Leslies, Earls of Leven*, (1890); *Memorials of the Earls of Haddington*, (1889); *Memorials of the Montgomeries*, (1859); *Memorials of the Family of Wemyss of Wemyss*, (1888); *The Red Book of Menteith*, (1880); *The Scotts of Buccleuch*, (1878); *The Sutherland Book*, (1892). (All published in Edinburgh.)

Gilles, William A., *In Famed Breadalbane*, (Perth 1938).

Grant, James, *A History of the Burgh and Parish Schools of Scotland*, (Glasgow 1876).

Hamilton, William, of Wishaw, *Descriptions of the sheriffdoms of Lanark and Renfrew compiled about MDCCX*, (Maitland Club 1831).

Hay, George, *Architecture of Scotland*, (Newcastle 1969).

Hume Brown, Peter, *Early Travellers in Scotland*, (Edinburgh 1891).

Kellas-Johnstone, J. F., *Notes on the Library of the Earl of Errol, Slaines Castle, Aberdeenshire*, (Aberdeen 1917).

Kinloch, George R., *The Diary of Mr John Lamont of Newton 1649–71*, (Maitland Club 1830).

Lindsay, Alexander W. C., *Lives of the Lindsays*, (1849).

MacDonald, R. H., *The Library of Drummond of Hawthornden*, (Edinburgh 1971).

MacGibbon, D. and Ross, T., *Castellated and Domestic Architecture of Scotland*, (Edinburgh 1887–92).

MacKenzie, W. C., *The Life and Times of John Maitland, Duke of Lauderdale*, (1923).

Matthew, David, *Scotland under Charles I*, (1955).

Miller, A. H. (ed.), *The Glamis Book of Record*, (Scottish History Society, 1890).

Monteith, R., *An Theater of Mortality*, (Edinburgh 1704).

Paul, Sir James Balfour (ed.), 'The Diary of Sir James Hope', in *Miscellany III of the Scottish History Society*, (1919).

Rogers, Charles, *Monuments and Monumental Inscriptions in Scotland*, (1871).

Smout, T. C., *Scottish Trade on the Eve of Union 1660–1707*, (1969); 'Scottish Landowners and Economic Growth 1650–1850' in *The Scottish Journal of Political Economy*, xi, (1964).

Warrack, John, *Domestic Life in Scotland 1488–1688*, (1920).

Notes

CHAPTER 1

The Duchess Anne

1. *Fourth Report of the Royal Commission on Historical Manuscripts, Appendix* (London 1874), Denbigh MSS., 258–9.
2. L. Gomme, P. Norman, W. Godfrey and others (ed.), *L.C.C. Survey of London* (1913–27), xvi, 48; E. B. Chancellor, *The Private Palaces of London, Past and Present* (1908), 161–5; Edgar Sheppard, *The Old Royal Palace of Whitehall* (1902), i, 176–9.
3. J. L. Chester (ed.), *The Marriage, Baptismal and Burial Registers of the Collegiate Church or Abbey of St Peter, Westminster* (Harleian Society 1876), 130; J. V. Kitto (ed.), *The Register of St Martin-in-the-Fields, London* (1936), 76.
4. Burnet, *op. cit.*, 407.
5. John Bruce and others (ed.), *Calendar of State Papers Domestic 1637–8* (1869), 431; Gervas Huxley, *Endymion Porter* (1959), 236.
6. Chester, *op. cit.*, 133. Edmund Waller's elegy on the Marchioness is printed in G. Thorn Drury (ed.), *The Poems of Edmund Waller* (1893), 40–2.
7. *Calendar of State Papers Domestic 1637–8*, 526–7.
8. *H.M.C. Report, Denbigh* (1911), v, 60.
9. Thomas Faulkner, *An Historical and Topographical Description of Chelsea* (1829), i, 325; Daniel Lysons, *The Environs of London* (1795), iv, 34; Richard Edmonds, *A Guide to Chelsea* (1947), 6; Wilberforce Jenkinson, *The Royal and Bishops' Palaces in Old London* (1921), 60; *Chelsea Official Guide* (1965), 22.
10. A ground plan of the house in 1706 exists in The Chelsea Library, London. Faulkner, *op. cit.*, reproduces a drawing of the exterior in the corner of the map which forms the frontispiece to his book.
11. Chester, *op. cit.*, 134.
12. Duchess Anne to Lady Katherine, 29 February 1696, Atholl MSS., 29 I (8) 95.
13. Burnet, *op. cit.*, 385.
14. *Register of the Privy Council of Scotland*, 3rd series, ii, 26–8.
15. Duchess Anne to Lady Anne Montgomerie, 6 November 1651, Seafield Papers, S.R.O., GD 248/556/1.
16. James Anderson, *The Ladies of the Covenant* (Glasgow 1851), 152.
17. Charles Rogers, *Social Life in Scotland from Early to Recent Times* (Grampian Club 1884), ii, 176.

18. This quotation comes from the 3rd Duke's own summary of the conditions of the entail.
19. Gilbert Burnet, *A History of His Own Time* (1837), 71n.
20. Burnet, *History*, 103.
21. D. Laing (ed.), *A Diary of Public Transactions . . . by John Nicoll* (Bannatyne Club 1836), 117.
22. Hamilton Old Parish Registers in the Registrar General's Office, Edinburgh.

CHAPTER 2

Hamilton Palace

1. See M. R. Apted, *The Painted Ceilings of Scotland 1550–1650* (Edinburgh 1966).
2. Captain Gawne to the Earl of Panmure, 10 September 1696, Dalhousie Muniments, S.R.O., GD 45/18/992.
3. See W. S. Sevensma, *Tapestries* (1965).
4. Dundas of Ochtertyre MSS., S.R.O., GD 35/6.
5. Dalhousie Muniments, GD 45/18/864.
6. The Marchioness of Douglas spent the last years of her life in Leith.
7. Hope, Todd and Kirk MSS., (Pringle of Whytbank and Yair), S.R.O., GD 246/26/5.
8. Breadalbane MSS., S.R.O., GD 112122/4.
9. Sir William Fraser (ed.), *The Scotts of Buccleuch* (Edinburgh 1878), ii, 289–92; Cosmo Innes (ed.), *The Black Book of Taymouth* (Edinburgh 1855), 346–51; Lauderdale MSS., 261131.
10. *C.f.* Margaret H. Swain, *Historical Needlework* (1970), 35–6.
11. *The Scotts of Buccleuch*, ii, 313–14; see also S. W. Wolsey and R. W. P. Luff, *Furniture in England* (1968), 45–6.
12. Francis Bamford, 'Some Edinburgh Furniture Makers' in *The Book of the Old Edinburgh Club*, xxxii (1966), 32–53.
13. Dalhousie Muniments, GD 45/18/997; Lauderdale MSS., 6/14.
14. Lauderdale MSS., 63/1; John Bonar's Account Book, S.R.O., RH 9/1/27.
15. Bo'ness Customs Books, S.R.O., E 72/5/2, E 72/2/24; Dalhousie Muniments, GD 45/18/982; *c.f.* Guthrie Papers, S.R.O., GD 188/19.
16. See Chapter 7.
17. Lauderdale MSS., 63/12.
18. See E. H. M. Cox, *A History of Gardening in Scotland* (1935).
19. Nicholas Culpeper, *Complete Herbal* (1923).
20. Henry Grey Graham, *The Social Life of Scotland in the Eighteenth Century* (1937), 10, 6–7.
21. Lauderdale MSS., 61/59, 26/14.
22. Donald Crawford (ed.), *Journals of Sir John Lauder, Lord Fountainhall 1665–76* (Scottish History Society 1900), 186.

23. Dalhousie Muniments, GD 45/18/746.
24. The Marchioness of Hamilton to Sir Colin Campbell of Glenorchy, [c. 1635], Breadalbane MSS., GD 112/560 *a* and *b*.
25. Breadalbane MSS., GD 112/560*b*.
26. Lauderdale MSS., 61/65; A. W. C. Hallen (ed.), *The Account Book of Sir John Foulis of Ravelston 1671–1707* (Scottish History Society 1894), 13; Dalhousie Muniments, GD 45/18/753.
27. *R.C.A.M. Inventory of Monuments and Constructions in the Counties of Midlothian and West Lothian* (Edinburgh 1929), 190–2; James S. Richardson, 'Sixteenth- and Seventeenth-Century Mural Decoration in the House of Kinneil' in *Proceedings of the Society of Antiquaries of Scotland*, lxxv (1940–1), 184–204.
28. *Register of the Privy Council of Scotland*, 3rd series, ii, 126–8.
29. *H.M.C. Report, Portland* (1891–1931), ii, 55.
30. *C.f.* Apted, *op. cit., passim.*

CHAPTER 3

The Servants

1. Tods Murray and Jamieson MSS., S.R.O., GD 237/204/4.
2. Helen Armet (ed.), *Register of the Burgesses of the Burgh of the Canongate* (Scottish Record Society 1951), 52.
3. Hamilton Old Parish Register, iv.
4. Armet, *op. cit.*, 18.
5. The marriage contract of David Crawford and Anne Auchterlony is in The Register of Deeds of the Commissary of Edinburgh, 21 April 1736. Their testaments are in The Register of Testaments of Edinburgh, 7 and 12 May 1736.
6. Hew Scott (ed.), *Fasti Ecclesiae Scoticanae* (Edinburgh 1920), iii, 247, 107.
7. Duchess Anne to Lady Katherine, 3 August 1686, Atholl MSS., 29 I (5) 14.
8. Yester Papers, S.R.O., GD 28/215/49; Bruce of Kinross Papers, S.R.O., GD 29/428.
9. George B. Burnet, *The Story of Quakerism in Scotland 1650–1850* (1952), 122–4, 135.
10. P. Hume Brown in his introduction to *Register of the Privy Council of Scotland*, 3rd series, xxiv–xxvii.
11. A. Strath Maxwell, 'Births, Deaths and Marriages of Quakers *c.* 1622– *c.* 1890', (xeroxed index); Burnet, *Quakers*, 122–4.
12. *Ibid.*
13. *Ibid.*
14. Nasmith Writs, S.R.O., GD 85129.
15. Grey Graham, *op. cit.*, 15.
16. Marguerite Wood (ed.), *Edinburgh Poll Tax Returns for 1694* (Scottish Record Society 1951), 11.

17. Yester Papers, GD 28/2205.
18. Robert Scott Moncrieff (ed.), *The Household Book of Lady Grisell Baillie 1692–1733* (Scottish History Society 1911); Dalhousie Muniments, GD 45/18/770; Buccleuch MSS., GD 224/418/1.
19. James R. Anderson (ed.), *The Burgesses and Guild Brethren of Glasgow 1573–1750* (Scottish Record Society 1925), 73, 108.
20. Dalhousie Muniments, GD 45/18/7380; *Edinburgh Poll Tax*, 11.
21. Elphinstone Muniments, S.R.O., GD 156/30; *Canongate Burgesses*, 22, 47.

CHAPTER 4

Clothing and Food

1. Gordon Donaldson, *Scotland: James V to James VII* (Edinburgh 1965), 323.
2. Anderson, *op. cit.*, 171.
3. Correspondence of the Dukes of Hamilton, NLS 1031.
4. Yester MSS., N.L.S. Accessions 4862183154; Morton Papers, S.R.O., GD 150/122; Lauderdale MSS., 63/2; Newhailes MSS., B 2/14; see Deborah Rutledge, *Natural Beauty Secrets* (1969), 128.
5. Stuart Maxwell and Robin Hutchison, *Scottish Costume 1550–1850* (1958), 36–63. For a fuller discussion of Duchess Anne's clothing, see Rosalind K. Marshall, 'Conscience and Costume in Seventeenth-Century Scotland' in *Costume*, vi, (1972), 32–5.
6. See frontispiece.
7. Cecil Saint-Laurent, *The History of Ladies' Underwear* (1968), 93–105.
8. Eunice Wilson, *A History of Shoe Fashions* (1969), 126–35.
9. Maxwell and Hutchison, *op. cit.*, 63.
10. *Ibid.*
11. *E.g.* the jewels of the Earl of Roxburgh. The list is in the Hamilton Archives.
12. James Laver (ed.), Mila Contini, *Fashion from Ancient Egypt to the Present Day* (1965), 164; Nora Waugh, *The Cut of Women's Clothing* (1968), 29; National Portrait Gallery Publication, *British Historical Portraits* (Cambridge 1957).
13. Newhailes MSS., Small Flat Box, 13.
14. Duchess Anne to Lady Katherine, 14 October 1702, Atholl MSS., 45 II 229; same to same, 22 September 1703, Atholl MSS., 45 III 94.
15. Lauderdale MSS., 61/58.
16. See also Customs Records, S.R.O., E 73/26.
17. These figures are based on accounts in the Hamilton Archives, but *c.f.* Scott-Moncrieff (ed.), *op. cit.*, 411.
18. *C.f.* Lauderdale MSS., 26/14; Morton Papers, GD 150/122; the Countess of Findlater's Testament, S.R.O., CC 8/10/16.
19. Lauderdale MSS., 26114.

20. Customs Records, S.R.O., E 72/15/39.
21. Sir John Lauder of Fountainhall, *Historical Observes of Memorable Occurrents in Church and State* (Edinburgh 1840), 121.

CHAPTER 5

Entertainment, Travel, Recreation and Celebrations

1. Lawrence Stone, *The Crisis of the Aristocracy 1558–1641* (Oxford 1965), 555–7.
2. Seafield Papers, GD 248/556/3.
3. *Register of the Privy Council of Scotland*, 3rd series, iv, 384, 567.
4. *Dictionary of National Biography*, vi, 49–50.
5. George Hamilton, *The House of Hamilton* (Edinburgh 1933), 701.
6. *Dictionary of National Biography*, xix, 1265–6.
7. *Fasti*, iii, 35, 240.
8. See Chapter 7.
9. *C.f.* Stella Margetson, *Journey by Stages* (1967), 1–34; Sir William Fraser (ed.), *The Annandale Family Book of the Johnstone Earls and Marquises of Annandale* (Edinburgh 1894), ii, 84–5.
10. Lady Katherine to Lord Murray, 5 March 1684, Atholl MSS., 29 I (4) 4, quoted in part in John, 7th Duke of Atholl, *Chronicles of the Atholl and Tullibardine Families* (Edinburgh 1908), i, 182–3.
11. Same to same, *Atholl Chronicles*, i, xlvi–xlvii.
12. Newhailes MSS., B 2/14.
13. *Account Book of Sir John Foulis*, 13.
14. J. Bray (ed.), *The Diary of John Evelyn* (1966), ii, 285.
15. Newhailes MSS., B 2114.
16. See Sir William Fraser (ed.), *Memorials of the Montgomeries* (Edinburgh 1859), ii, 339–40; Marjorie Plant, *The Domestic Life of Scotland in the 18th Century* (Edinburgh 1952), 234; Airlie Muniments, S.R.O., GD 16/58/47.
17. A photograph of the curtains is reproduced in Swain, *op. cit.*, Plate 16.
18. Lauderdale MSS., 6/59.
19. Lauderdale MSS., 63/1; see also Customs Records, S.R.O., E 72/5/3, 4.
20. Lauderdale MSS., 63/60.
21. The Marchioness of Atholl to Lord Murray, 1 December 1691, Atholl MSS., 29 I (6) 59; same to same, 30 December 1692, Atholl MSS., 29 I (6) 96.
22. S.R.O., RH 9/18/28/53.
23. Duchess Anne to Lady Katherine, 26 April 1703, Atholl MSS., 45 III (47).
24. D. Laing (ed.), *Correspondence of Sir Robert Kerr, 1st Earl of Ancrum and his son William 3rd Earl of Lothian* (Edinburgh 1875), ii, 443.
25. Yester MSS., S.R.O., GD 28/1947.
26. Ailsa MSS., S.R.O., GD 25/9/38.

CHAPTER 6

The Education of the Children

1. Atholl MSS., 29 I (3) 42; J. Balfour Paul (ed.), *The Scots Peerage* (1904), i, 263.
2. James Cleland, *The Rise and Progress of the City of Glasgow* (Glasgow 1829), 21; J. D. Mackie, *The University of Glasgow 1451–1951* (Glasgow 1954), 19, 45, 50; Cosmo Innes (ed.), *Munimenta Alme Universitatis Glasguensis* (Glasgow 1854), iii, 465.
3. J. W. Stoye, *English Travellers Abroad 1604–1667* (1952); Kathleen Lambley, *The Teaching and Cultivation of the French Language in England during Tudor and Stuart Times* (1920); G. E. Mingay, *English Landed Society in the Eighteenth Century* (1963), 138–9.
4. *H.M.C. Report, Mar and Kellie* (1930), ii, 70–99; Duncan Thomson, 'A Virtuous and Noble Education', Catalogue for the Scottish National Portrait Gallery Exhibition, 1971; Margaret F. Moore, 'The Education of a Scottish Nobleman's Sons in the Seventeenth Century' in *The Scottish Historical Review*, xxxi, (1952), 1 *et seq.*
5. *Mar and Kellie*, 89–93; Lord Lindores to the Earl of Menteith, Cunninghame-Graham of Ardoch MSS., S.R.O., GD 22/3/595.
6. See Plate 9.
7. Stone, *op. cit.*, 701–2. Lennox was English in everything but title.
8. Hew H. Dalrymple (ed.), *Memoirs of My Lord Drumlangrig's and his brother Lord William's Travels Abroad* (Edinburgh 1931), 17.
9. Lady Katherine to Lord Murray, 1 August 1693, Atholl MSS., 19 I (7) 15.
10. Dalhousie Muniments, GD 45/26/99.
11. John Stuart in his preface to *Registrum de Panmure, compiled by the Honourable Harry Maule of Kelly* (Edinburgh 1874), i, lxviii.

CHAPTER 7

The English Influence

1. Sir David Hume of Crossrig, *A Diary of the Proceedings in the Parliament and Privy Council of Scotland, 21 May 1700 – 7 March 1707* (Bannatyne Club 1828), 23.
2. O. Airy, *The Lauderdale Papers* (Camden Society 1884–5), iii, 69.
3. *Register of the Privy Council of Scotland*, 3rd series, xii, xix.
4. F. J. Fisher, 'The Development of London as a Centre of Conspicuous Consumption in the Sixteenth and Seventeenth Centuries' in *Transactions of the Royal Historical Society*, 4th series (1948), xxx, 37–50.
5. *Oxford English Dictionary*, ii, 638–9.

6. J. Douglas Stewart, *Sir Godfrey Kneller* (1971), Catalogue of the Kneller Exhibition at the National Portrait Gallery, London, 77.
7. C. H. Collins-Baker, *Lely and Kneller* (1922); Lord Killalin, *Sir Godfrey Kneller and his Times 1646–1723* (1948).

CHAPTER 8

The Marriage of the Heir

1. Stone, *op. cit.*, 599.
2. J. P. Kenyon, *Robert Spencer, Earl of Sunderland 1641–1702* (1958), 175–6.
3. Bray, *op. cit.*, 273.
4. Copy invitation to Lady Anne's funeral, Society of Antiquaries Papers, S.R.O., GD 103/4/35.

CHAPTER 9

The Great Design

1. Kerry Downes, *English Baroque Architecture* (1966), 57–88; John Summerson, *Architecture in Britain* (1953), 156–60.
2. Laing, *op. cit.*, i, cviii, 534.
3. D. Knoop and G. P. Jones, *The Scottish Mason and the Mason Word* (1939), 39.
4. John G. Dunbar, *The Historic Architecture of Scotland* (1966), 101–4.
5. *Ancient Monuments of West Lothian*, 190–2; *Proceedings of the Society of Antiquaries of Scotland*, lxxv, 184–204; Thomas J. Salmon, *Borrowstounness and District* (Edinburgh 1913), 46.
6. Buccleuch MSS., GD 224/171.
7. B. Sprague Allen, *Tides in English Taste 1619–1800* (Harvard 1937), 41–7.
8. Grey Graham, *op. cit.*, 7; *c.f.* Lauderdale MSS., 63/11.
9. See Plate 17.
10. John, 1st Marquis of Hamilton, Duchess Anne's great-grandfather.
11. Daniel Defoe, *A Tour Through the Whole Island of Great Britain* (1962), ii, 339; D. W. Kemp (ed.), *Richard Pococke, Bishop of Meath: Tours in Scotland 1747, 1750, 1760* (Scottish History Society 1887), 47–8; Thomas Pennant, *A Tour in Scotland* (1790), i, 139; James Muir, *Brown's Hamilton Directory for 1855–6* (Hamilton 1855), 55.
12. See Plate 11.
13. Lauderdale MSS., 63/26.
14. *Ibid.*

15. See Plates 13, 14, 15.
16. David Walker and John G. Dunbar, 'Brechin Castle, Angus, I. The House of the Earl and Countess of Dalhousie', in *Country Life*, 1971.

CHAPTER 10

The Fatal Flaw

1. Duchess Anne to Lady Katherine, 29 February 1696, Atholl MSS., 29 I (8) 95.
2. Same to same, 27 March 1697 and 24 April 1696, Atholl MSS., 29 I (9) 164, 29 III (8) 166.
3. Defoe, *op. cit.*, 340.
4. Duchess Anne to Lady Katherine, 26 August 1698, Atholl MSS., 29 I (10) 199.
5. Same to same, 4 April 1700, Atholl MSS., 45 I 99.
6. Same to same, 14 October 1702, Atholl MSS., 45 II 227.
7. Same to same, 10 September 1705, Atholl MSS., 45 V 120.
8. J. Hill Burton, *The Darien Papers* (Bannatyne Club 1849), 371–417.
9. Duchess Anne to Lady Katherine, 26 February 1700, Atholl MSS., 45 I 75.
10. Same to same, 7 September 1705, Atholl MSS., 45 V 119.
11. Same to same, 20 September 1705, Atholl MSS., 45 V 122.
12. Same to same, 29 February 1696, Atholl MSS., 29 I (8) 95.
13. Same to same, 19 June 1701, Atholl MSS., 45 I 204.
14. *Atholl Chronicles*, i, 489.
15. Duchess Anne to Lady Katherine, 19 June 1701, Atholl MSS., 45 I 204.
16. *A True and Impartial Account of the Murder of His Grace the Duke of Hamilton and Brandon by Mr Mackartney* (Edinburgh 1712); *The Examiner's Account of the Duel fought by the Duke of Hamilton and my Lord Mohun* (1712); *A Letter from a Gentleman in London to his Friend in Edinburgh* (n.p., 1712); *Lord Mohun's Vindication* (1712); *A Huy and Cry after George McArtney who killed His Grace the Duke of Hamilton in Hide Park* (n.d., n.p.); Daniel Defoe, *A Strict Enquiry into the Circumstances of the Late Duel* (1713); *A True and Impartial Account of the Animosity, Quarrel and Duel between the late Duke of Hamilton and the Lord Mohun* (1712); *An Elegy on the Death of His Grace James, Duke of Hamilton and Brandon* (n.p., 1712).

Index

Abercorn, Claud, 4th Earl of 33
Abercorn, James, 2nd Earl of 27, 30–1, 197
Abercrombie, James, illeg. son of the 4th Duke of Hamilton 175
Aberdeen 65
'Aberdeen', a racehorse 116
Admiralty House 14
Airlie, David, 3rd Earl of 131
Airlie, James, 2nd Earl of 134
Airybog 99
Ale 49, 69, 77–8, 100, 245
Allanton 64
Alnwick 20, 111
Althorp 185
Alvared, Colonel 26
America 90
Amsterdam 134
Anderson, Henry, gardener 59
Anderson, William, Provost of Glasgow 100, 107
Angers 135–7
Annandale, James, 3rd Earl of 73, 106, 131
Annandale, William, 1st Marquis of 32, 73
Anne, Queen 218, 221–2, 228
Antelope 59
Antonine Wall 58
Archery 115
Argyll, Archibald, 1st Marquis of 21, 24, 80

Argyll, Elizabeth, 1st Duchess of 81
Arran, Anne, Countess of See Lady Anne Spencer
Arran, Earls of See Hamilton
Arran, Island of 13 22, 26–7, 30, 57, 98, 114, 213, 215, 226–7
Atholl, Amelia, 1st Marchioness of 120
Atholl, Duchess of See Lady Katherine Hamilton
Atholl, John, 1st Marquis of 60, 85, 114, 131, 147
Atholl, John, 1st Duke of; formerly Lord Murray and Earl of Tullibardine 63, 80, 103, 110, 120, 122, 146–8, 163–4, 195–6, 225, 263–4
Auchterlony, Anne, wife of David Crawford 64
Aven Bridge 56
Avendale 22, 118, 213, 226
Avendale Castle 27, 57
Ayr 27, 70, 105, 111
Ayrshire 21, 63, 111, 148

Baillie, Lady Grisel 74
Baillie, Mary 227
Balcarres, Colin, 3rd Earl of 151
Baldoon 200
Balfour, Charles, valet 68, 78–9
Balgonie, Alexander, Lord; heir of the Earl of Leven 134

Ballinbreich 54

Banks, Matthew, carpenter 193–4

Bannantyne, Mr John, governor 66, 131–3, 135–7

Bannerman, Mr George, advocate 107

Baptisms 14, 78, 121

Bargany, Jean, 1st Lady 29

Bargany, John, 1st Lord 29

Bargany, John, 2nd Lord 106, 183

Barillon, Paul de, French ambassador 177

Barncluith [Barncluth], The Laird of 121

Barnton, The Laird of 121

Bath 113, 153, 161–2, 164

Bath, John, 1st Earl of 138, 142

Bauchop, Tobias, mason 193

Bauchop, The family of 207

Beaufort House 16

Beauvoir, Richard, jeweller 159–60

Bedfordshire 112

Beldam, Valentine, groom 62, 69–71

Belford 110, 113

Belhaven, John, 2nd Lord 80

Belhaven, Lady See Margaret Hamilton

Bellshill 114

Berwick-upon-Tweed 108, 111

Biel, The 113, 196

Billiards 116, 244

Birkenshaw 192

Birthdays 120–2

Bishop, James 244

Blackwood, Robert 46

Blois 137–8, 144

Boghead 99

Bologna 141

Bolton, Charles, 1st Duke of 153

Bonar, John, merchant 46

Bo'ness 46, 55, 57, 100, 155, 165, 203, 226

Bonhart, Monsieur, mathematics teacher 137

Books 44, 116–18, 139–40, 162–3, 239–40

Bothwell 202

Bothwell Brig, Battle of 84–5

Bothwellmuir 26

Bourges 139

Boutchart, James, skipper 155, 165

Bowling 115, 119

Bowling green 51, 115

Boyd, Archibald, overseer of Hamilton Spinning School 227

Brandon, Dukedom of 228

Breadalbane, John, 2nd Earl of 212

Bridges, Captain 165

Brodick Castle 29n., 57, 73, 232

Brodie, Mr David, chaplain 65

Brown, James, shoemaker 88, 91

Bruce, Lord Charles 138–9

Bruce, Sir William, architect 69, 114, 189, 193, 207

Buccleuch and Monmouth, Anna, Duchess of 44, 63, 74, 155, 175

Buccleuch, Francis, 2nd Earl of 42

Buckingham, George, 1st Duke of 13–14

Buckingham, Katherine, 1st Duchess of 14, 16

Bugden Inn 195

Burnet, Gilbert, Bishop of Salisbury 30, 32, 116, 132–3

Burnside, Andrew, skipper 165

Cadzow Castle 37

Caen 139

Calder, Lady 118

Callander, Alexander, 2nd Earl of 55

Cambridgeshire 71

Cambuslang 22, 26, 99

Cambusnethan 108

Campbell of Glenorchy, Sir Colin 34, 42, 55–6

Canongate, The 48–9, 64
Canterbury, John Tillotson, Archbishop of 153
Card games 116, 118–19, 173
Carmichael, Sir Daniel 107
Carmichael, John, 2nd Lord 107
Carnegie of Pitarrow, Sir Alexander 134
Carpets 41, 233–66 *passim*
Carriden 57
Caskieberrie 205
Cassie, Margaret, Mrs William Miller 72–3
Cassilis 105, 111, 113, 225
Cassilis, Countess of See Lady Susanna Hamilton
Cassilis, John, 7th Earl of 60, 122, 150, 158
Catherine of Braganza, Queen 92
Cavendish, Lady Arabella, daughter of the 2nd Duke of Newcastle 175, 209
Centurion, The a ship 165
Chaigneau, Monsieur, hatter 159
Charenton 138
Charles I 14–15, 17–18, 21, 23–5, 31, 44–5, 60, 107, 150, 231, 256
Charles II 25–6, 28, 31, 42, 84–5, 105, 113, 116–17, 129, 150, 156, 160, 162, 168–72, 175, 178, 188–9
Chelsea 16–17, 20, 22, 95, 129, 153, 168, 216
Chimery, Mademoiselle 136
Chocolate 100, 155, 157–9, 254
Christian and Mary, The a ship 203
Christmas 120–1
Civil War 17, 23, 26, 39, 45, 47, 57 107, 123, 129, 232
Clanbie, 237
Clancarty, Elizabeth, 4th Countess of 188
Clephan, James 54
Clinsh, Richard 151

Clocks 17, 46, 152, 160, 167, 233–66 *passim*
Clothing 15, 20–1, 30, 34, 49, 59, 67, 70, 76, 83–96, 112, 122, 138, 146, 147, 149, 154, 159, 163, 165–7, 182–3, 199, 227, 233–66 *passim*
Clyde, River 13, 20, 37, 53, 57, 68, 79, 114, 226
Coaches 20, 34, 108–11, 142, 155–6, 166–7, 196
Cochrane, Sir John 103
Cochrane, Lady 103
Cochrane, Lord See John, 2nd Earl of Dundonald
Cochrane, William, Master of 115
Cockburnspath 196
Cockfighting 115–16, 131
Cole, Andrew, servant 92, 151
Colquhoun, Bailie 54
Conway, Lady 175
Cook, James 245
Cooper, Nathaniel, merchant 87
Coplestone, Sir John 173
Cornhills 99
Cornwall of Bonhard, Walter 163
Correggio 45
Corstorphine Church 30 and n.
Cotterell, Lady, wife of Sir Clement Cotterell 17
Covenanters 18, 21, 23, 71, 84–5, 106, 118
Coventry, George, 3rd Baron 171–2
Craighall 54
Crawford 199
Crawford, Countess of See Lady Margaret Hamilton
Crawford, John, 17th Earl of 22, 56–7
Crawford, William, 18th Earl of 54, 59, 74, 81
Crawford, Archibald 64
Crawford, David, secretary 43, 63–5, 74, 77–8, 93, 112, 119, 121, 124,

162–3, 165, 185, 195–7, 205, 214–15, 220, 225, 233, 251, 254, 255
Crawford of Knockshinnoch, Duncan 63
Crawford, William 163
Crewe, Thomas, 2nd Baron 210–11
Cromwell, Oliver 24–7, 30–1, 117
Cromwell, Richard, 31
Culross Palace 39
Cunison, Alexander, merchant 99
Cunningham, Lady Anna See Anna, 2nd Marchioness of Hamilton
Cunningham of Enterkin, William 106
Cunningham of Robertland, Sir David 105
Cupar 54, 116
Curling 115
Curtains 41, 125, 157, 167, 233–66 *passim*

Dalmahoy, John 66
Dalmahoy, Thomas, gentleman 67
Dalrymple, Sir David, lord advocate 112, 117
Dalserf 20, 65, 227, 232
Darien, Isthmus of 220
Darlo, Mary, servant 69, 163, 258
Darlo, Robert, overseer 73
Darnley, Henry, Lord 234
Darnton 196
Davidson, William, writing master 22
Deer 55–6, 73, 163, 232
Defoe, Daniel 205, 216
De Gloxin, Elizabeth 151
Denbigh House 20
Denbigh, Basil, 2nd Earl of See Lord Basil Feilding
Denbigh, Dorothy, Countess of, widow of Lord Basil Feilding 124, 210

Denbigh, Susan, 1st Countess of 15, 20
Denbigh, William, 1st Earl of 15, 45 and n., 256
De Roussi, Comte 170
De Roussi, Mademoiselle 170
De Tang, French servant 225
De Vallé, Monsieur 138
De Vilar, Marquis 140
Devonshire, William, 1st Duke of 153, 209
Dishes 43, 47, 59, 71, 77, 102, 154–5, 158, 167, 233–66 *passim*
Dobie, Janet, washerwoman 81–2
Doctors 15, 19, 67, 161–2, 186–7, 196
Dolls 120
Donaldson, James, merchant 159
Doncaster 20, 187
Douglas, Lord George See George, 1st Earl of Dumbarton
Douglas, Lord James, brother of the 3rd Duke of Hamilton 32, 106, 143–4
Douglas, Janet, illeg. daughter of the 3rd Duke of Hamilton 30
Douglas, Lady Mary, sister of the 3rd Duke of Hamilton 32
Douglas, Mary, 1st Marchioness of 28, 41
Douglas, Lord William See William, 3rd Duke of Hamilton
Douglas, William, 1st Marquis of 28–9
Douglas, Margaret, washerwoman 49
Douglas, William, tailor 86
Drumlanrig Castle 72
Drumlanrig, Lord See James, 2nd Duke of Queensberry
Drummond, Major-General William 107
Duelling 143, 228–9

INDEX

Dumbarton, George, 1st Earl of; formerly Lord George Douglas 138, 140–2, 170, 182
Dunbar, Mary See Lady Mary Hamilton
Dundee 131
Dundonald 108
Dundonald, Countess of See Lady Susan Hamilton
Dundonald, John, 2nd Earl of 148, 163
Dundonald, William, 1st Earl of 148
Dunkeld 91, 120
Durham 111–12
Durie 54
Dysart, William, 1st Earl of 149

Earlshall 39
Earnock, The Laird of 121
East Indies, The 90, 117
East Lothian 51, 55
Edinburgh 21–3, 29, 39, 45–6, 48–50, 52, 60–1, 63–4, 68, 72–3, 79, 81, 86–90, 95–6, 99–102, 108, 110–13, 115, 117–18 120–3, 142, 144, 149, 154, 159, 161–2, 165–6, 180, 183, 187, 191–2, 196, 199, 203, 217, 219–23, 227, 231
Edmiston, Mrs 46
Education 22, 65–6, 78, 129–48, 227, 231
Edward, Mr Alexander, minister and architect 207
Elephant 120
Elphinstone, Alexander, 6th Lord 81
Embroidery 119
England 14, 21, 24, 26, 33, 46, 55, 69, 98, 101, 104, 109, 117, 119, 121, 134, 145, 149, 174, 189, 193–4, 196, 203, 212–13, 219
Etinger, Conrad, Jeweller 95

Eton 230–1
Evan, Mr, coachmaker 156
Evelyn, John, diarist 116, 157, 183

Fall, Mr James, governor to the Earl of Drumlanrig 144
Far East, The 90, 157
Faubert, Monsieur 138, 142
Feilding, Lord Basil; later 2nd Earl of Denbigh 40, 44–5, 124
Feilding, Lady Mary See Mary, 3rd Marchioness of Hamilton
Fencing 137–8, 143
Fenton, Mr, governor to Lord Charles Hamilton 144
Ferguson, Harry, Seedsman 52, 59
Fife 21, 24, 38, 51, 54, 114, 120
Findlater, Countess of See Lady Mary Hamilton
Findlater, James, 1st Earl of 80
Findlater, James, 3rd Earl of 106
Fireworks 139
Fitzroy, Lady Barbara, illeg. daughter of Charles II 188
Flamsteed, John, Astronomer Royal 146
Florence 140
Fontainebleau 139
Food 47–9, 51–2, 59, 68, 73, 75, 77, 83, 96–103, 115, 121–3, 152, 155, 157, 159, 164, 217–18, 230, 233–66 passim
Football 115
Forbes, Mr James, governor to the Earl of Arran 136–42, 170
Forfar, Archibald, 1st Earl of 76
Forrester, James, skipper 165–6
Forth, Patrick, 1st Earl of 41
Forth, River 57–8
Foulis of Ravelston, Sir John 46, 57, 115
Fountainhall, Sir John Lauder, Lord 53, 55, 103

Founteine, Mr Edward, dancing
    master 147
France 54, 105, 134–6 141–2, 144,
    148, 159, 168, 170–1, 175, 218,
    228
Frizel, Alexander, footman 76
Fruit trees 53–5, 59, 158–9, 163, 165
Funerals 25, 78, 82, 98, 101, 122,
    125, 144, 188, 198–9, 231
Furniture 25, 30, 41–7, 58, 60, 64,
    70–1, 77, 125, 149, 154–7, 163,
    167, 186, 233–66

Galloway 225
Gardens 50–5, 59, 71–2, 83, 99,
    130, 137, 158, 166, 207–8, 232
Gazeau, Daniel, confectioner 164
George I 231
Gerard, Digby, 5th Baron 212
Gerard, Lady Elizabeth, widow of
    Digby, 5th Baron Gerard 213, 228
Gerard, Lady Elizabeth See
    Elizabeth, 4th Duchess of
    Hamilton
Germany 14
Gibson, Sir Alexander 163
Gilly, Mr Simon, chaplain 65
Gilmour, Robin, groom 165
Glamis 189
Glasgow 13, 18, 37, 54, 63, 65–6,
    70, 80, 90, 99–101, 107, 114, 116,
    139, 143, 159, 161, 191–2, 194,
    203
Glasgow Grammar School 132, 143
Glasgow High Church 90
Glasgow University 63, 80, 132–3,
    144–6, 200
Glen, Henry, fowler 76
Glencairn, James, 6th Earl of 21
Goddard, William, glazier 203
Godolphin, Sidney, 1st Earl of 182
Golf 115
Gorbals 107, 230

Graham, James 245
Grand Tour, The 67, 133–48, 149,
    168, 191
Grange 59
Gravesend 142
Gray, John, musician 73
Gray, Mary, servant 67
Greene, John, merchant 158
Greenland 142
Greenlees, James, master cook 68,
    74, 76, 79
Greenlees, James, undercook 68, 79
Greenwich 113
Greyhounds 114
Grudeh, Monsieur, French teacher
    139
Gustavus Adolphus 14, 256

Haddington 131, 206
Hague, The 25
Hale, Sir Matthew 163
Halifax, George, 1st Viscount 138,
    142
Hamilton, Barony of 22, 26, 99
Hamilton, Bent Cemetery 232
Hamilton, Burgh of 20, 37, 45, 49,
    56–7, 64–5, 72, 76, 80–1, 88, 90,
    99–100, 123, 131, 161, 192, 221,
    226–7, 230n., 232
Hamilton Burgh School 78, 131,
    226–7, 230
Hamilton Hospital 78, 199, 227
Hamilton, Jenkin Street 261
Hamilton, Nethertoun of 20, 70–1,
    192
Hamilton, The Orchard 37
Hamilton, Palace of 13, 20–2, 257,
    30–2, 37–83, 85, 88–90, 97–102
    104–8, 114–15, 117, 119, 121,
    123, 130–1, 144, 152, 154, 156,
    160–1, 166–7, 170, 189–208,
    213–14, 223–5, 229–30, 232,
    233–66

Hamilton Palace Parks 37, 49, 73, 75, 98

Hamilton Parish Church 25, 37, 121, 123–4, 188, 199, 201, 231–2

Hamilton Spinning School 227

Hamilton Woollen Manufactory 227

Hamilton, Lady Anna Cunningham, 2nd Marchioness of 14, 16, 18–23, 28, 38, 48, 55–8, 73, 81, 85, 99–100, 103, 124, 234

Hamilton, Lady Anna, Countess of Southesk, daughter of the 2nd Duke 25–6, 105

Hamilton, Lady Anna (1), daughter of Duchess Anne 31

Hamilton, Lady Anna (2), daughter of Duchess Anne 31

Hamilton, Anne, 3rd Duchess of; birth, 13, 121; childhood, 14–21; youth, 22–5; inherits titles, 26; temperament, 27; marriage, 28–9; appearance, 29; birth of children, 31; household, 32, 37–61, 97–103; servants, 62–82; religious opinions, 73, 85; clothing, 89–94; jewellery, 94–5; friends, 104–7, 113; travel, 109–11; recreations, 118–19; relationship with children, 129–48, 168–71, 174, 175–6, 180–1, 211–29; visits to London, 153; rebuilds Hamilton Palace, 189–206; grief on death of husband, 197–8, 200–2; politics, 220–1; charity, 226–8; death, 231; inventories, 233–66

Hamilton, Lady Anne, daughter of the Earl of Arran 185–6

Hamilton, Lord Anne, son of the 4th Duke 218

Hamilton, Lord Archibald 31, 145–6, 148, 150, 161, 199–200

Hamilton, Lord Basil 31, 33, 113, 121, 145, 148, 150, 159, 161, 197, 200, 204, 206, 212, 215–16, 220, 223–5, 255

Hamilton, Charles, Earl of Arran, son of the 1st Duke 14, 19

Hamilton, Lord Charles, Earl of Selkirk, son of Duchess Anne 31, 87, 144–5, 148, 150, 161, 175–6, 199, 209, 224–5, 229, 231

Hamilton, Charles, illeg. son of the 4th Duke 188, 208, 228

Hamilton, Lady Charlotte, daughter of the 4th Duke 218

Hamilton, Lady Diana, daughter of the 2nd Duke 25

Hamilton, Elizabeth, 2nd Duchess of 34, 149

Hamilton, Elizabeth, Lady Kilmaurs, later Lady Cunningham of Robertland, daughter of the 2nd Duke 25–6, 105–6, 130

Hamilton, Elizabeth, 4th Duchess of 100, 212–19, 221, 224, 228–9

Hamilton, Lady Elizabeth, daughter of the 4th Duke 218

Hamilton, Elizabeth, 6th Duchess of 227

Hamilton, Lord George, Earl of Orkney 31, 145, 148, 161, 176, 200, 231

Hamilton, Lady Henrietta, daughter of the 4th Duke 218

Hamilton, Lady Henrietta Maria, daughter of the 1st Duke 13

Hamilton, James, 1st Lord 13, 132

Hamilton, James, 2nd Earl of Arran and Duke of Châtelherault 13, 57, 190

Hamilton, James, 2nd Marquis of 13, 18, 20–1, 44–5, 108, 115, 122–3, 150, 174, 227, 256, 262

Hamilton, James, 3rd Marquis and 1st Duke of 13–14, 15 and n., 16–

27, 29, 34, 39–40, 42–5, 54, 56, 62–3, 70, 89, 92, 94, 116, 124, 129, 132, 168–9, 233–46, 256, 262

Hamilton, Lord James, son of the 1st Duke 14, 17

Hamilton, Lord James, son of the 2nd Duke 25

Hamilton, James, Earl of Arran and 4th Duke of 31, 45, 64, 66, 75, 79, 91, 95–6, 112, 114, 120, 122, 124, 130–45, 147–50, 152, 156, 160–1, 168–91, 194, 198–9, 201–4, 206, 209–23, 228–9, 250

Hamilton, James, Marquis of Clydesdale and 5th Duke of 122, 218, 230, 231

Hamilton, John, 1st Marquis of 37, 108, 115, 201

Hamilton, Lord John, Earl of Ruglen 31, 59, 64, 112, 145, 148, 150, 161, 176, 180, 184, 186, 193, 195–6, 200, 207, 209, 225, 255, 264

Hamilton, Lady Katherine, Lady Murray, later Countess of Tullibardine and 1st Duchess of Atholl 31, 68, 79, 89, 91, 96, 109–10 113, 120, 122, 146–8, 159, 161 and n., 195–6, 198, 211, 214, 216, 218, 223–6, 252

Hamilton, Lady Katherine, daughter of the 4th Duke 218

Hamilton, Katherine, daughter of Lord Basil 225

Hamilton, Lady Margaret, Countess of Crawford, daughter of the 2nd Marquis 21–2, 24, 237, 246

Hamilton, Margaret, Lady Belhaven, illeg. daughter of the 2nd Marquis 22, 113, 196

Hamilton, Lady Margaret, Mrs William Blair, daughter of the 2nd Duke 25–6, 106, 130

Hamilton, Lady Margaret, Countess of Panmure 31, 96, 119, 121, 146–8, 161, 183, 207, 252

Hamilton, Mary, 3rd Marchioness of 13–14, 15 and n., 16, 19–20, 23, 45, 94–5, 256–7

Hamilton, Mary, Mrs Hay of Park, illeg. daughter of the 1st Duke (Mistress Mary) 26, 105, 119

Hamilton, Lady Mary, Countess of Callendar, later Mrs Livingstone of Westquarter, later Countess of Findlater, daughter of the 2nd Duke 25–6, 105–6, 130

Hamilton, Lady Mary, wife of Lord Basil Hamilton; formerly Mary Dunbar of Baldoon ('Miss') 93, 101, 121, 160, 225, 258, 263

Hamilton, Lady Mary, daughter of Duchess Anne 31

Hamilton, Lady Mary, daughter of the 4th Duke 187–8, 199, 209, 214–15

Hamilton, Lady Susan, Lady Cochrane, later Lady Yester, later Marchioness of Tweeddale 31, 96, 110, 113, 121, 146–8, 161, 204, 231, 252

Hamilton, Lady Susan, daughter of the 4th Duke 218

Hamilton, Lady Susanna, Countess of Cassilis, daughter of the 1st Duke 14, 15 and n., 19–20, 23–4, 26, 32, 43, 105, 111, 123, 130, 197, 249

Hamilton, William, Earl of Lanark and 2nd Duke of 15, 19, 24–6, 31, 34, 39, 42, 62, 66–7, 89, 105, 115, 132, 149, 168–9, 217, 237–8, 245, 256–7

Hamilton, Lord William, son of the 1st Duke 14, 17, 123

Hamilton, Lord William Douglas, Earl of Selkirk and 3rd Duke of;

parentage, 28; marriage, 28–9, appearance and temperament, 29–30; becomes Duke, 31; children, 31; household, 32, 37–61, 97–103; servants, 62–82; political career, 83–5; clothing, 86–9; visits to London, 92–4, 101, 149–68; companions, 107–8, 114; travel, 108, 113; recreation, 114–18; relationship with children, 129–48, 168–88; rebuilds Hamilton Palace, 189–95; illness and death, 195–7; funeral, 198–9; furnishings, 248, 249, 251, 255–6, 257, 259, 263
Hamilton, Lord William, son of Duchess Anne 143–5, 197
Hamilton, Lord William, son of the 4th Duke 218
Hamilton, William, son of Lord Basil 121
Hamilton, Daniel, chamberlain of Kinneil 59, 72
Hamilton, Elizabeth, shopkeeper 78
Hamilton, Gilbert merchant 91
Hamilton, James, in Middleraw 228
Hamilton, Sir John 24
Hamilton, John, Master Household 122
Hamilton, Katherine, daughter of Lord Bargany 106
Hamilton, Margaret, servant 66, 69
Hamilton, Mr William, advocate 107
Hamilton of Preston, Sir William 107
Hamilton, William, page 135–7
Hampton Court 16–17, 123, 193
Hangings See Wall hangings
Hare coursing 114
Harper, Henry, merchant 48, 96
Hatfield 191
Hatton See Richard, 4th Earl of Lauderdale
Hawking 114–15, 118–19

Hay of Park, Mary See Mary Hamilton ('Mistress Mary')
Henry VIII 16–17
Herbs 51–2
Heriot, James, goldsmith 159
Higgins, Mr, posture master 120
Highwayman 112
Hinchingbrooke 191
Holland 25, 39, 46–7, 55, 59, 62, 100, 138, 157–8, 201
Holy Land, The 155
Holyroodhouse, Palace of 38, 52, 60–1, 66, 72–3, 90, 101–4, 108, 114, 119, 121, 162, 183–4, 187, 189, 197, 199, 226, 234
Holywell, Abraham, warrender 73, 79, 164
Home, James, 5th Earl of 114
Hope Family 189
Hopetoun House 189
Horse-racing 116
Howard, Cardinal Philip Thomas 140
Hunting 57, 114–15, 140
Huntingdon 20, 191
Hutchison, The Rev. John 108
Hyde Park 228–9

Illnesses 15–17, 19, 23, 26, 51, 78, 110, 118, 140–1, 143–4, 161–2, 175, 187, 195–7, 215, 221–2, 225, 231
Inglis, Mrs Dorothy, servant 96
Ingoldsby, Colonel 26, 62
Italy 117, 134, 139–40, 142, 148, 206

James VI and I 13, 105, 121, 149
James VII and II 43, 105, 161, 169, 178, 180, 184, 186, 209–10
Jenkin, Valentine, painter 38–9, 58
Jewellery 21, 23, 25, 64, 85, 94, 125, 154, 159–60, 163, 177, 182, 228
Jugglers 119

Kelso 72
Kennedy, Mr Gilbert, chaplain 65
Kennedy, Lady Margaret, wife of
    Gilbert Burnet 32, 130
Kennedy, Robert, gentleman 66–7,
    74
Kennedy of Culzean, Sir John 134
Kilmarnock 65
Kilwinning 54
Kimbold, Rebecca, servant 20, 66
King, Sir Edmund 162
Kinneil, Barony of 22, 26, 30
Kinneil Castle 13, 38–9, 41, 49, 57–
    60, 72, 108–9, 113, 115, 117,
    140, 144, 166, 168, 171, 187–8,
    190–2, 213, 216–17, 226, 233,
    244, 261–6
Kinross House 193, 207
Kitchen utensils 48–9, 70, 81–2,
    233–66 passim
Kneller, Sir Godfrey 29n., 91, 95,
    160–1
Knibb, Joseph, clockmaker 46, 152

Laborde, Monsieur, wigmaker 159
Lace making 119, 227
Lamb, John, caterer 78, 152, 163,
    255
Lamlash 226
Lanark 116
Lanark, Earl of See William, 2nd
    Duke of Hamilton
Lanarkshire 20, 107, 205
Lancashire 212, 219, 224
Lang, John, shoemaker 77, 192
La Rochelle 135
Lauderdale, Elizabeth, Duchess of
    47
Lauderdale, John, 1st Duke of 30,
    32, 42, 47, 52, 57, 83–4, 86, 103,
    107, 119, 149, 189, 194, 205–6,
    256
Lauderdale, John, 5th Earl of 100

Lauderdale, Richard, 4th Earl of;
    formerly known as Hatton 206
Laundry 49
Law, James, skipper 165
Leclerc, Louis, shoemaker 159
Le Havre 117
Leith 41, 113, 115–16, 165, 203
Leith Glassworks 102
Leith, Gilbert, falconer 79
Leith, John 244
Lely, Sir Peter, artist 160
Lennox, James, 4th Duke of 141
Lennoxlove 206, 233
Leslie 114
Lesmahagow 26
Lethington 47, 194, 206
Levant, The 157
Lilburne, Colonel 26
Lindores Abbey 54
Lindores, Patrick, 2nd Lord 134, 139
Lindsay, Lady Anna, cousin of
    Duchess Anne 22
Linlithgow 59
Linlithgow, James, 5th Earl of 60
Lisburne, Adam, 1st Viscount 209
Livingstone, The Laird of 64
Livingstone of Westquarter, Sir
    James 106
Lochleven Castle 105
Lochore, John, mason 192
Lochranza 226
Loftus, Lucia, daughter of Viscount
Lisburne 209
Loire, River 135, 190
London 15–18, 20, 23–4, 46, 55–6,
    63, 67, 78, 84, 86–8, 90–2, 94,
    104–5, 108–9, 111–14, 118–21,
    142, 145–6, 149–68, 172, 175,
    179, 183–6, 188, 191, 193–5, 198,
    203, 206, 209, 211, 224, 228, 231,
    233
Lord Clerk Register See Sir George
    MacKenzie

Lothian, Anne, Countess of 123, 189
Lothian, Robert, 2nd Earl of 189
Loudoun, Hugh, 3rd Earl of 63
Louis XIV 135, 139, 161, 175
Low Countries 143, 157
Luxembourg 145
Lyons 140

MacCartney, General George 228–9
McFlahertie, Jago, harper 73
MacKenzie, Sir George, Lord Clerk Register 60, 116–17
McLellan, James, wright 45–6, 193–4, 199
Mabillon, Jean, palaeographer 117 and n.
Macclesfield, Charles, 2nd Earl of 228
Machanshire 22
Maleverer, Colonel 26
Mangle 49–50
Maps 43, 117–18, 133, 155, 233–66 *passim*
Mar, John, 7th Earl of 134, 139
'Margaret' of Grangepans, a ship 46
Marshall, James, tailor 87–8
Mary of Modena, Queen, wife of James VII and II 43, 161, 180, 185, 210, 257
Mary, Queen of Scots 13, 60, 105, 115–16, 234
Mary, The a yacht 113
Maxwell, Margaret 246
Maxwell, Sir William 121
Medicine 15–16, 51–2, 78, 118, 145, 157, 186–7, 227
Meinner, Heinrich, joiner 47
Melfort, John, 1st Earl of 178, 180–1, 184
Melville House 189
Merlin, The a yacht 142
Middleraw 228

Middleton, Charles, 2nd Earl of 182
Miller, James, coppersmith 48, 72
Miller, William, gardener and Quaker ('The Patriarch') 72–3
Millington, Sir Thomas 162
Minnoch, River 225
Minstrels 119
Mitchell, Servant 261
Mohun, Charles, 4th Baron 228–9
Monck, General George 26, 30, 58
Monmouth, Duchess of See Anna, Duchess of Buccleuch and Monmouth
Monmouth, James, 1st Duke of 85, 160, 171–2
Montgomerie, Alexander, Lord 121
Montgomerie, Lady Eleanor 118
Montgomery, Mrs Anne (née Hay), housekeeper 229, 231
Moray, Sir Robert 131–2
More, Sir Thomas 16
Morgan, William, carver 206–7
Morton, William, 6th Earl of 123, 134
Muirhead, John, tailor 90–2, 96, 120
Murray, Lord See John, 1st Duke of Atholl
Murray, Anthony, butler 75
Murray of Blackbarony, Sir Archibald 151
Murray, William 255
Musical instruments 46, 73, 136, 147, 251, 259
Musselburgh 114
Mylne, John, mason 189
Mytens, Daniel, artist 15n., 45

Napery 49, 77, 102, 154, 158, 234–66 *passim*
Naples 139–40
Nasmith, Anna 65
Nasmith, Arthur, carpenter 45, 78

Nasmith, Arthur, lawyer 65, 163, 223
Nasmith, John, wright 49
Nasmith, Michael 77
Nasmith, Mrs 64
Nasmith, Robert, mason 192
Nasmith, Robert, servant 62
Nepho, Mrs 151
Newark 72, 111–12
Newbattle 189
Newcastle 165
Newcastle, Henry, 2nd Duke of 175, 209
Newspapers 118, 158
New Year 121
Nicoll, John, diarist 30
Nisbet, James 163
Norfolk, Cardinal See Cardinal Howard

Ochiltree 103
Orkney, Earl of See Lord George Hamilton
Orleans 138–9
Ormiston, The Laird of 55
Osborne, The Rev. John 108
Over Crewkburn 228
Oxford 132

Padua 139
Paintings 17, 25, 42–4, 45 and n., 143, 233–66 passim
Palmer, Richard, steward at Chelsea Place 17
Panmure, Countess of See Lady Margaret Hamilton
Panmure, James, 4th Earl of 39, 46, 74, 121, 148, 189
Panmure House 57, 81, 147, 189, 207
Paris 117, 134–6, 138–9, 141–2, 144, 175, 228
Parrots 21, 119

Paterson, Anne 81
Paterson, James, servant 81–2
Paterson, Margaret 82
Paterson, William 220
Paudevin, Jean, cabinetmaker 156–7
Paulet, Lord 156
Paulett, Francis 172–3, 175
Paulett, Mrs Francis 172–5
Paulett, Nellie 172–4
Peacock, John, butler 75, 79
Peden, Mr George, chaplain 65
Pendennis Castle 21, 23–4, 26
Pepys, Samuel, diarist 157
Perth Academy 131
Perth, James, 7th Earl and 1st Duke of 40, 106
Perthshire 120
Pets 64, 119–20, 217
Pitt, Moses 118
Planting 56–7
Plate See Silver plate
Plymouth, Charles, 1st Earl of, illeg. son of Charles II 138
Poitiers 144–5
Poland 117
Pollock, The Laird of 56
Polmont 26–7, 30, 57
Polwarth, Patrick, 1st Lord 151
Porterfield, Anna 67
Porterfield, Bethia 67
Porterfield, James 67
Porterfield, John, elder, page 67, 74, 76, 247
Porterfield, John, younger, page 67, 220–1
Portland, Hans, 1st Earl of 153, 209
Portraits 15 and n., 23, 29 and n., 43, 44, 45 and n., 90–1, 95, 141, 160 and n., 161 and n., 233–66 passim
Preston 24–5
Puppets 120, 131

Quakers 71–3
Quarter 50
Queensberry, James, 2nd Duke of; formerly Lord Drumlanrig 144, 221
Queensberry, William, 3rd Earl, 1st Marquis and 1st Duke of 72, 81, 124, 189–90

Raphael 45
Rawlinson, Ralph, carver 51
Reay, George, 3rd Lord 115
Resolution, The a ship 146
Riccarton 200
Richelieu 137
Richmond 185
Richmond, Mary, Duchess of 45 and n., 256
Robertson, Finlay [Phinla], footman 76
Robieson, John 56, 236, 244–5, 246
Rochester, Laurence, 4th Earl of 174, 178, 211–12
Rochester, Thomas Sprat, Bishop of 183
Rokeby, Colonel 26
Rome 40, 134, 139–41
Rose, The a ship 155, 165
Ross, William, 12th Lord 80
Rossière, Mark 255
Rothes, Anne, Countess and later Duchess of, cousin of Duchess Anne 49–50
Rothes, John 7th Earl and 1st Duke of 115, 124–5
Rotterdam 103
Rouen 117
Roumieu, Paul, clockmaker 46
Roxburgh, William, Master of 134
Royston 71, 111
Rubens 45
Ruglen, Earl of See Lord John Hamilton

Rugley, Mrs 151
Rullion Green, Battle of 84
Russia 107
Ruthven, Katherine, illeg. daughter of the 4th Duke of Hamilton 175
Ruthven, Mary, illeg. daughter of the 4th Duke of Hamilton 175

Salisbury, James, 3rd Earl of 191
Salisbury, William, 2nd Earl of 141
Sandwich, Edward, 3rd Earl of 191
Saumur 135, 138
Savoy 140
Savoy, Charles Emanuel, 2nd Duke of 140
Savoy, Marie Jeanne Baptiste, 2nd Duchess of 140
Scone 25
Scott, William, cabinetmaker 46
Scougall, David, portrait painter 29n., 90
Seafield, James, 1st Earl of 63
Sedan chairs 113, 156
Selkirk, Earls of See William, 3rd Duke of Hamilton and Lord Charles Hamilton
Seton 115
Sharp, James 99
Shoes 76, 86, 88, 91–2, 155, 159
Sidney, Harry; later Henry, 1st Earl of Romney 182
Silver plate 25, 47, 102, 159, 165, 186, 233–66 passim
Simpson, George, falconer 79, 114
Sinclair, Henry, 10th Lord 63
Smith of Smithycroft, James, secretary 63, 233
Smith, Mr James, architect 64, 189, 191, 193–5, 201–4, 207
Smith, James, younger, architect 193, 201–4
Soap 49, 155, 254
Southesk, Countess of See Lady

Anna Hamilton
Southesk, David, 1st Earl of 134
Southesk, Robert, 3rd Earl of 105
Southwark 24
Spain 100
Spencer, Lady Anne, Countess of
    Arran 161, 177–88, 190, 210, 215
Spens, John, servant 79, 163
Spring Gardens See Whitehall
St Andrews University 145
St Bride's Church, Bothwell 202
Staffordshire 212
Stair, James, 1st Viscount 98
Steven, Thomas, tenant 99
Stewart, Elspeth 246
Stirling 38
Stonehill 72
Strathallan, William, 2nd Viscount 80
Strathaven 57, 227
Strathaven Church 226
Strathmore, Patrick, 1st Earl of 189
Struthers 24, 55, 113
Sunderland, Robert, 3rd Earl of
    177–84, 187, 228
Sutherland, George, 14th Earl of
    196
Sweden 117

Tapestry See also Wall hangings
Tay, River 54
Taylor, John 241
Tea 100, 155, 157
Tennis 115, 136–7, 140
Thames, River 17, 165, 203
Thirlestane Castle 57, 189, 205–6
Thomas of Wenvoe and Ruperra,
    Anne 210–11
Thomson, John 244
Thomson, Matthew 227
Thomson, William 244
Thurman, Mr Archibald,
    confectioner 103
Tilting 116

Timothy, John, The Black 80
Tofts, Andrew, master household 80
Tollemache, William, son of
    Elizabeth Duchess of Lauderdale
    120
Touche, John 236, 245
Toys 120, 166
Traquair House 189
Travel 76, 104, 108–13, 186–7
Trent, River 112
Tullibardine 115
Tullibardine, Earl of See John, 1st
    Duke of Atholl
Tunbridge Wells 101, 153, 161
Turenne, Henri, Vicomte de 170
Turin 140
Turnbull, James, shoemaker 86
Turner, Sir James 107
Tweeddale, John, 2nd Earl and 1st
    Marquis of 60, 69, 74, 81, 151
Tweeddale, John, 2nd Marquis of;
    formerly Lord Yester 74, 151
Tweeddale, Marchioness of See
    Lady Susan Hamilton
Tweedie, James, master household
    68
Tyninghame 113, 115

Union of the Parliaments 33, 149,
    216, 220–4, 230
Uttoxeter 24

Van Dyck 15 and n., 45, 95
Vegetables 52–3, 59, 97, 102
Venice 44, 139–40
Versailles 134, 138, 190
Vilant, The Rev. William 108
Villiers, Henrietta 212
Voet, Jacob Ferdinand, portrait
    painter 141

Wall hangings 25, 38–9, 40 and n.,
    41, 44, 58, 125, 233–66 *passim*

Wall paintings 38–9, 58
Wallingford House 14, 16
Warming pans 43, 155, 253, 260
Warrender, Thomas, house painter 203, 205
Watkins, Mary 71
Watkins, Sara, servant 20, 70–1
Watson, Mr, language master 140
Weddings 78, 101, 106, 122, 183
Weir, William, burgh treasurer of Hamilton 221
Wells 172, 175
Wemyss Chapel 54
West Indies 146
Westminster Abbey 16–17, 19, 123
Wharton, Philip, 4th Baron 210
Whitehall, Palace of 13–14, 85, 116, 150–51, 153, 184–5
Whitehall, Spring Gardens at 14
Wickliffe, Harry, servant 164
Wigs 67, 154, 159, 161
Wigtown, John, 2nd Earl of 80, 123
Wilbraham, Rachel 66–7
William of Orange 22, 86, 148, 150, 153, 162, 186

Winchester, John, 5th Marquis of 172
Windsor Castle 24, 179, 194
Wine 49, 69, 78, 100–1, 103,107, 159, 166, 244
Woburn 112
Wood, Alexander, gardener 72, 75, 205
Wood, Hew, gardener 71–2, 166, 192, 205
Wood, James, gardener 72
Worcester 25, 66–7
Wren, Sir Christopher, architect 194

Yachts 113, 142
Yester House 189
Yester, Lady See Lady Susan Hamilton
Yester, Lord See John, 2nd Marquis of Tweeddale
York 113
York, Duke of See James VII and II
York House 14
Young, Patrick, postilion 75

4117